culture and insight, Mockett takes us on a compelling and illuminating journey of the heart and soul."

—Gail Tsukiyama, author of *A Hundred Flowers*

"Depicts a Japan both secular and spiritual, and a people whose apparent stoicism can be a bulwark against chaos."

—Roland Kelts, *Christian Science Monitor*

"This affecting memoir . . . effectively evokes the beauty of Japanese culture and the sorrow that swept the country in the tsunami's wake."

—Georgia Rowe, *San Jose Mercury News*

"An illuminating journey into grief and Japanese culture, a place that few would dare to venture." —Kris Kosaka, *Japan Times*

"There are some extraordinarily beautiful passages grounded by Mockett's intensely introspective authorial voice . . . every moment seems to have a poetic gravitas that can be breathtaking."

—Stephen Hongsohn, *Asian American Literature Fans*

Praise for

WHERE THE DEAD PAUSE, AND THE JAPANESE SAY GOODBYE

"[Mockett] has the ability, fully available only to those on the margins, 'to see through more than one set of eyes, if one learns to pay attention to one's environment.' It is this gift of double-sightedness, of bringing to bear both the 'dry' rationality of the West and the 'sticky' sensibilities professed by the Japanese, that makes this the most interesting book so far to have come out of the disaster."
—Richard Lloyd Parry, *New York Times Book Review*

"Mockett's travels in Japan affirm the lost art of pilgrimage, a participatory form of mourning that relies on collective experience as a powerful consolation for loss. If grief really is a two-way street, to reach the dead sometimes we have to start walking. Chances are good we will meet others on the same road, lit with lanterns, littered with blossoms."
—Jodie Noel Vinson, *Los Angeles Review of Books*

"Mockett is the perfect translator for the ways East and West frequently miss each other, and these observations are one of the book's many pleasures . . . a fascinating, wide-reaching exploration of the religious and cultural elements of this island nation."
—Zoe FitzGerald Carter, *San Francisco Chronicle*

"Mockett skillfully knits together a portrait of loss and recovery, pulling together many individuals' experience of grief into a collective search for peace."
—Meganne Fabrega, *Minneapolis Star Tribune*

"This book speaks to my heart. Grief is part of what it means to be human, and Marie Mutsuki Mockett's book models an approach to grief, an attitude of courage, curiosity, and inquiry that is our birth-

right, as humans, wherever we happen to be born. Read it. You will be uplifted."　　　　　　　　　—Ruth Ozeki, Zen priest, author of
A Tale for the Time Being

"What a remarkable and moving book about traveling from one land to another, and learning different ways of coming to terms with death amid life. Engrossing and powerful, it speaks volumes about the many ways people grieve and live."
　　　—Will Schwalbe, author of the *New York Times* bestseller
The End of Your Life Book Club

"Marie Mockett has taken the most spectacular catastrophe of our era and used it to teach us astonishing things about faith, perseverance, and the mysteries of the soul. Her journey through personal grief and the devastation of Japan after the 2011 tsunami and nuclear disaster brings us into a sacred space. With this book, Marie Mockett brought me into the high drama of the tsunami, through her most personal landscape, and into the awe of the eternal."
　　　—Luis Alberto Urrea, Pulitzer Prize finalist for
The Devil's Highway

"A beautiful tale that is part evocative travelogue and part lyrical meditation on grief, this soulful and haunting book made me cry in a way I like to cry when reading a good book. *Where the Dead Pause, and the Japanese Say Goodbye* will resonate with anyone who has lost a loved one, a homeland, or a home and hoped for healing on the other side."　　—Heidi W. Durrow, *New York Times* best-selling author of
The Girl Who Fell from the Sky

"*Where the Dead Pause, and the Japanese Say Goodbye: A Journey* is a fascinating look into the complexities of Japanese spiritual traditions, while also telling an intimate and poignant story of author Marie Mutsuki Mockett's own grief just after the devastating March 11, 2011, earthquake and tsunami. . . . Richly layered in

Where the Dead Pause, and the Japanese Say Goodbye

ALSO BY MARIE MUTSUKI MOCKETT

Picking Bones from Ash: A Novel

WHERE THE DEAD PAUSE, AND THE JAPANESE SAY GOODBYE

A JOURNEY

Marie Mutsuki Mockett

W. W. NORTON & COMPANY
Independent Publishers Since 1923
New York • London

For information about permission to reproduce selections from this book,
write to Permissions, W. W. Norton & Company, Inc.,
500 Fifth Avenue, New York, NY 10110

For information about special discounts for bulk purchases, please contact
W. W. Norton Special Sales at specialsales@wwnorton.com or
800-233-4830

Manufacturing by Courier Westford
Book design by Ellen Cipriano
Production managers: Devon Zahn and Ruth Toda

Library of Congress Cataloging-in-Publication Data

Mockett, Marie Mutsuki.
Where the dead pause, and the Japanese say goodbye : a journey /
Marie Mutsuki Mockett. — First edition.
pages cm
ISBN 978-0-393-06301-1 (hardcover)
1. Mockett, Marie Mutsuki—Travel—Japan—Iwaki-shi. 2. Iwaki-shi
(Japan) —Description and travel. 3. Iwaki-shi (Japan)—Religious life and
customs. 4. Mockett, Marie Mutsuki—Family. 5. Grandfathers—Japan—
Death. 6. Grief—Japan. 7. Buddhist temples—Japan—Iwaki-shi. 8. Funeral
rites and ceremonies—Japan—Iwaki-shi. 9. Fukushima Nuclear Disaster,
Japan, 2011—Social aspects. 10. Japanese Americans—California—
Biography. I. Title.
DS897.I88M63 2015
952'.117—dc23
2014032438

ISBN 978-0-393-35229-0 pbk.

W. W. Norton & Company, Inc.
500 Fifth Avenue, New York, N.Y. 10110
www.wwnorton.com

W. W. Norton & Company Ltd.
Castle House, 75/76 Wells Street, London W1T 3QT

1 2 3 4 5 6 7 8 9 0

FOR MY MOTHER

Contents

Prologue

Once upon a time there was a monster made of water who slept deep in the ocean under a mass of rock. There were people living in homes on top of the rock, delicate creatures whose bodies were made mostly of water, with a little bit of bone and cartilage thrown in. The people liked to eat fish from the ocean, but this didn't bother the monster. For the most part, it got along fine with the people.

The water monster had an enemy in the giant catfish named Ōnamazu, who supported everything—the heavy rock, the monster, and the people and their homes—on his back. Like all catfish, Ōnamazu had an urgent and continuous desire to twitch, and when he stirred, the rock on his back moved too. Alarmed by the shuddering, the people fled their homes and rushed to the safety of the highest points on the rocks. Then the water monster woke up.

The monster took a while to suck in its breath—one long, slow inhalation. It sucked the water into its lungs, filling itself until it was so large, it rolled out from its comfortable resting place and veered deep out into the ocean. Now the monster was fully awake and very angry to have been so disturbed. It hurled itself back toward the catfish and the blanket of rock on Ōnamazu's back. The monster devoured some of the people on the rocks, and thrashed others against the sand and stone, before its own body shattered from the impact. The people's bodies, once broken, could not recover from such fury. But the monster could recongeal.

As night fell, the wily monster lulled the remaining people on the land into the false conviction that all was safe. It was cold and dark, and everyone wanted to go home. They were fairly confident that the monster had gone back under the water, and they went home to make sure that no one had stolen their most valuable possessions. Only then did the monster return—three, four, seven times. More people died, and the houses that had not been destroyed by the previous waves were washed away. Then the people learned that their most valuable possessions had never been the things in their homes.

Because the monster was and is immortal, it knew the cruel pleasure of waiting through the generations. It often struck just as the oldest people who'd last seen it were dying out, and the new people were too young to think it was anything but a legend. But one thing remained consistent. Once it was sighted, the people, old or new, always knew who the monster was. They called it *tsunami*.

Where the
Dead Pause,
and the
Japanese
Say Goodbye

ONE

THE DISASTER

O N MARCH 11, 2011, I woke to a text from a friend alerting me that Japan had been jolted by an earthquake.

At first I dismissed the news; Japan often has earthquakes. I'm originally from California, and it, too, often has earthquakes. But the urgency of the message intrigued me, and I eventually got out of bed and inspected the news on my computer.

This was no routine earthquake. I checked the epicenter. It was 8.9 or 9.0 on the Richter scale and 130 miles off the coast of Sendai. Reports streamed in that the earthquake had triggered a tsunami, and a graphic of Japan showed an increasingly wide area of impact. The coast of Tōhoku, the northeast region on Japan's main island, had been eviscerated. Even though it was morning, my husband poured me a glass of wine from a bottle we'd half drunk the night before, and I sat and watched the Internet, with the radio on in the background.

For thirty-six hours after the earthquake and tsunami, I was unable to get any word from my mother's family, who own and run a Zen Buddhist temple in Iwaki, a city about eighty-five miles from Sendai on the Tōhoku coastline. Thirty-six hours does not seem like a very long time given the distance (around seven thousand miles) from Japan to New York, where I lived, and the time difference (thirteen to fourteen hours, depending on the time of year). But this waiting period felt akin to a week. Friends phoned and sent emails and texts. The attention made me self-conscious. I was not in danger. I called my mother in California and told her not to go to the beach.

Japanese temples, especially older Zen temples like my family's, are often safely located high up on a hill. This is because a temple is supposed to bring you closer to Buddha and to the gods, who almost always live up in the sky, out of mortal reach. Tsunamis usually impact coastlines, but this particular event was so powerful, the water infiltrated rivers, scaling heights previously considered secure. I watched the images as they were updated, looking for any indication of my family's fate. A photo came in from Onahama harbor, the seaside port in Iwaki. I picked up the phone again. Nothing.

Before the tsunami, the great tragedy that everyone skirted in conversation in my Japanese family was World War II. On August 9, 1945, my great-uncle was out fishing in the Pacific, far enough away from Nagasaki, Japan, where he lived, that he missed the immediate impact of the atomic bomb dropped by the Americans that day. My great-aunt was in their new house outside Nagasaki; the entire family had fled the city only a few days earlier because my great-uncle feared a repeat of the bombing of Hiroshima.

I heard this story many times during my childhood. Back then it made me feel that my great-uncle was a clever man. As an adult, I realized he was also very lucky, because cleverness alone cannot keep you safe.

I wondered if my family in Iwaki would also be lucky and smart.

I wanted to know, and I did not want to know. I kept dipping into the world of the Internet, with its videos of water raging over the farmland and crushed ferries, and then quickly backed out. Not looking at the videos kept reality at bay, because the images of the coastline did not match the Japan that I knew and loved from childhood.

In the Japan that I knew, I boarded the Jōban Line train from Ueno station in Tōkyō and traveled up the northeast coast to Iwaki. If it was spring, the *bentō* stalls in Ueno station sold cherry blossom–themed meals to eat on the train: pink cakes made of *mochi* rice paste cut into flower shapes. The train would stop at Kairakuen, a park in the city of Mito that is famous for its plum blossoms.

Not long after leaving Kairakuen, the train curved along the tracks and began to hug the coast. Then I knew that I had entered Tōhoku, the northern region of Japan where the goddesses and demons of legend seem alive and seafood is sweet. My Japanese grandfather was particularly fond of *mehikari*, or "flashing eyes," a succulent fish that is an Iwaki specialty.

Often on this journey, I would switch to a local train to get off at Nakoso, a town famous for its inns and hot springs, and formerly a way station on the footpath connecting Tōhoku to Edo, the old name for Tōkyō. My favorite spa, Sekinoyu, is just yards off the beach, a vegetation-thick cliff at its back. The waves of the North Pacific crash right outside the windows.

I did not see how the spa could have survived the tsunami. Its Web site was eerily still online, with numerous photos of ocean views through the windows of the bathing room and the dining rooms; no status update was posted on its main page.

Now the Jōban train was not running any farther than Mito; past this, the tsunami had battered train tracks and highways, making passage nearly impossible. A section of one train was found on its side just north of Iwaki, the cars abandoned.

As a child traveling through Japan with my mother, I kept an illustrated journal of our adventures. In one entry, I was swimming in the waters off the beach at Ōarai, a town located on the Tōhoku coast whose name means "big washing," which sounded romantic before the tsunami. Now Ōarai was covered with sludge. In another illustration, I was standing under the gigantic, chandelier-like ornaments of Sendai's famed Tanabata star festival. But Sendai had been pummeled, and its airport closed. In yet another diary entry, my mother was knee high in dark blue water and holding an umbrella while I clung to her back. I remember laughing as my mother carried me to the safety of an elevated train platform, but we were also afraid. What if the flooding did not stop?

All these towns had a beach. Whenever we visited the beach, my mother would ask, "What do you do if the water suddenly disappears?"

"Run," I would answer.

"Why?" she would fire back.

As I got older, this questioning became annoying. Born in Japan, my mother had trained to be an opera singer in Europe, where she met my father, an American. Both had a tendency to behave as though they were on a stage. Sometimes I got to be on stage with them. Sometimes I was the audience. It made it tricky to know what to take seriously.

"Come on. Why?" she'd press.

"Because it means tsunami is coming," I'd sigh.

Whatever that was.

AFTER THIRTY-SIX HOURS, my mother got through to the "temple"—this is how we refer to our relatives. "Marie, I spoke to the temple. Ryōko answered the phone." The temple comprises a family of five. Sempō, the head priest, is my mother's cousin. He is married to Ryōko, and together they have three boys, whom I will call Daisuke, Takahagi, and Masa. Daisuke is the oldest and Masa the youngest.

Ryōko, a tiny and attractive woman with a round mouth and large eyes, is an efficient person, accustomed to making sure the four men in her family make all their appointments on time, wear clean clothing, and eat the excellent meals she cooks. Ryōko is vintage Tōhoku in that beneath her practical exterior are glittering flashes of good humor, like bubbles in a glass of champagne. She cuts an elegantly trim figure in the kimonos she wears to the numerous funeral services conducted at the temple, which are the main source of her family's income. She is equally, or perhaps even more, at home in a *sunakku*, or pub, trading jokes with locals, her slim hand holding a beer aloft.

Ryōko explained that the earthquake had not caused any major damage to the temple's structure or, more importantly, to any of the tombstones. Everyone was unharmed. My mother hung up.

Not long after, we learned that a new monster was now awake in Tōhoku: radiation. The Fukushima Daiichi Nuclear Power Plant was just thirty miles from Iwaki. Over the next thirty-six hours, news coverage shifted to the unfolding disaster: one reactor had been damaged by the waves and was on fire, the wind scattering invisible, destructive particles. In some parts of Tōhoku it was snowing, and I imagined the radiation camouflaging itself with snowflakes, so beautiful, but so deadly.

Nearby towns had been evacuated, but not Iwaki because it was on the outer edge of what the government deemed to be safe territory. We managed again to get through to the temple on the phone. This time I spoke to Sempō myself.

Sempō's voice is rich and musical. In general, his style of conversation is not the modern, quickly discursive, or frank kind favored in cities. He pauses, he thinks, he builds up to his point, and then, as though dissatisfied that he hasn't sufficiently expressed the truth, he begins to dig around some more.

It can take a long time to talk to Sempō.

He listened to me on the phone as I went on hysterically about the dangers of radiation and reminded him of other family members who had survived the bombing in Nagasaki. Their ordeal had given them *hibakusha* status, which not only afforded them lifetime free medical care from the Red Cross but also marked them as official radiation victims, which isn't always a good thing in a culture where people scrutinize family health records and possible weaknesses in DNA before agreeing to marriage. I suggested that the Japanese government was concealing the true extent of the nuclear reactor's problems. I thought that perhaps the American media was more truthful. He and his family should leave the area.

Sempō responded with vague phrases like "That is true." And "Yes. I see what you mean." These answers didn't commit to any sense of urgency and only made me more frantic. Instinctively, I began to talk more, to try to clarify what must surely be a misunderstanding. Couldn't he urge his children to leave? Sempō was in his sixties, but the boys were in their twenties and thirties.

"Yes," Sempō said. "Of course. If we come to that kind of a situation, I will of course send the children away."

"Hasn't the time come now?"

"The truth is . . ." Sempō hesitated. "We are out of gas."

"I thought you had one car with gas," I said. "Can't you at least get over the mountains and away from the radiation and then buy more gas?"

"The roads are clogged," he said. "Everyone else is trying to escape."

Summer blockbuster movies had taught me the rules of escape: you fled with whatever tools you had, making up your plans as obstacles emerged. That's the narrative. "Go as far as you can," I said. "And then walk." I was sure that this was what I would do, were I in his shoes.

"My back hurts."

"Then send your children."

After a long pause, Sempō said, "The truth is, I'm not going to leave. The truth is, I'm not afraid to die."

"Your children . . ."

"We would all like to stay together."

In the news coverage of Japan immediately after the nuclear power plant accident, Western reporters praised the Japanese for their stoicism and their selflessness and marveled at the Japanese for being so meticulous in their clean-up efforts. This was true admiration. But I knew it also meant something else.

I knew that the reporters were also asking, "How can they do this?" How could fifty volunteers go into the Fukushima Daiichi Nuclear Power Plant to do cleanup? It was the Western reporters who anointed the many engineers and workers at the nuclear power plant with the collective name "the Fukushima Fifty." The name conjured up the image of other selfless, self-sacrificing figures from Japanese history: the inscrutable samurai who committed ritual suicide, to say nothing of the kamikaze pilots in World War II.

I knew what the Western news reporters were thinking but not saying. They were thinking, "You are not quite human and that is why you are not afraid. I admire you, but I could not be you." I knew this to be true because a part of me was also thinking these things. Another part of me was horrified by the stereotypes now emerging in the media. But then here was Sempō saying he wasn't afraid of death.

What can you say to someone who has declared that he isn't afraid to die? On the phone to Sempō, I said, "I want you to be okay."

"Right now we are okay. And I . . ." Here, his voice caught. He said something that sounds awkward in English, no matter how many times I try to translate it. "I am deeply honored that you care so much. And I am so sorry to make you worry to this extent."

I sensed something unspoken in this exchange, something that made me think I had approached this situation incorrectly. The feeling that you have put your foot in your mouth is a common experience in Japan, even to a relative insider. I remember, for example, visiting Aizu Wakamatsu castle in Fukushima Prefecture when I was a teenager. The castle is famous for an episode in 1868 when fifteen young samurai, aged sixteen or seventeen, committed suicide after mistakenly believing the castle under their protection had been taken by the enemy. I was overcome with rage that boys my age would kill themselves, and that we would now celebrate these deaths as beautiful.

An older man who was also visiting Aizu watched me as I carried on to my mother. He gave me a tolerant and compassionate smile. "I'm so sorry you are upset," he said. "But you don't understand. You aren't Japanese."

I WAS FORTY when the tsunami struck, and death and grief were very much on my mind. My American father, to whom I had been extremely close, had died less than three years before, and I was still struggling to cope with his loss. My Japanese grandmother was dead, and my Japanese grandfather had died at the end of January in 2011. Now my Japanese grandfather's house was for sale. I had an eighteen-month-old son, and I wanted to give him the same kind of cultural foundation my parents and grandparents had given me. It was my paternal grandmother, an American, who had paid for my airfare to go to Japan every year since I was four, an opportunity she would love to have had; she died in 1993. I, too, wanted my son to feel like he was a citizen of the world. I wanted to rejoice in the future, but I was struggling.

After three years of grieving for my father, I was supposed to be feeling better. Instead, I knew I had what modern Western psychology calls "complicated grief." A few friends had kindly suggested to me that I might be experiencing postpartum depression. One suggested I get my thyroid checked. I laughed all this off. For me, the continuum of grief had been going on for so long, I couldn't see where one form of depression started and another began. By the time the tsunami struck Japan, I was feeling hopeless about ever managing the voyage from grief to any semblance of "normalcy" or "healing," the terms most often associated with where you are supposed to go after you have been very sad.

I can see now that the death of so many people so close together had shaken me deeply. The foundation of my life was eroding—particularly my roots in Japan. I had taken for granted a certain kind of security, nurtured since childhood, that I was a small part of something much larger, and that this much larger thing would always be there, shining its light on me. Now I felt thrust into the cold place of the shadow. I did not have any confidence that I could give my son the same rich cultural history that I'd been so fortunate to receive. The tsunami and the nuclear disaster made me fear that one day I would have nothing to pass on at all.

THREE WEEKS AFTER the tsunami, I went to Japan with my mother and my son. This was supposed to be the trip during which we buried my grandfather at the temple in Iwaki. Trains from Tōkyō still did not travel north, and the roads were closed to everyone except rescue personnel and recovery teams. Burying my grandfather's bones was a low priority in the middle of such a disaster. We had considered postponing our trip but decided to go anyway, partly as a show of solidarity. There was also quite a bit for us to do at my grandfather's home; we needed to remove the items we wanted before the old house, whose foundation was infested with termites, was bulldozed and the empty lot put up for sale. I was intent on finding as many letters and photographs as I could. If any of my grandmother's kimonos could be saved, I was hoping to take these back to America as well.

The nearly empty plane circled a wide berth around Japan's east coast, still shuddering with aftershocks, and its shore a massive wound. The flight attendant alerted us to the damaged nuclear reactor, visible far in the distance, and the seven of us on the plane all rubbernecked to take a look. In the airport, everyone was dressed in black and moved with solemn, apologetic dignity. Already the Japanese energy commission had created a mascot for a new advertising campaign: a little lightbulb with two eyes closed shut. It seemed to be either sleeping or sad or both, and it reminded us to use as little energy as possible. From the airport, to the train, to the city of Tōkyō, all was dark. Japan, an island nation, had lost its power. But as we wended our way west, away from the disaster, Japan was flowering with spring. Here, the Japan I remembered from childhood was still resplendent. The cherry trees were blooming, and for a moment we were able to forget our sorrow.

TWO

THE TEMPLE

MY FAMILY'S ASSOCIATION WITH the temple in Iwaki began in the late nineteenth century, when my great-grandfather Sennō—my grandfather's father—took over a temple known as Empukuji, which means "Circle of Good Fortune." I like to think of the circle as being the mouth of a bag, and that the name implies the possibility of catching good luck in a sack and carrying it around with you. Empukuji, which was founded about five hundred years ago, belongs to the Sōtō sect of Buddhism, which Americans know of as Zen. My grandfather, or "Ojiisan" in Japanese, was once slated to inherit Empukuji, but he rebelled, leaving the future of the temple in the hands of his younger brothers, all of whom died during the war years.

There are around eighty-six thousand Buddhist temples in Japan, but the number is falling as Japanese turn away from the traditions that support historical institutions. Most temples are run by families, with the ideal succession transferring from father to son. This creates the potential for a War of the Roses–like drama to be played out with each generational handoff. There are also the lures of Western-influenced modernity. Who wants to meditate or go through the punishing regimen required to become a priest when a city like Tōkyō, with its ever-morphing neighborhoods, undulates with excitement just beyond the horizon?

When I traveled to Japan as a girl, my mother and I often began our trips at the temple in Iwaki because it was closer to the airport in Tōkyō than my grandparents' house farther west. In those days, the temple was run by Great-Aunt Shizuko, my grandfather's younger sister.

I have a letter from Sennō to Ojiisan dated around 1950, in which my great-grandfather expresses his worries about Empuku-ji's fate. "I have not been feeling well for the past twelve months, and am writing this letter from my futon. I want to talk about the future of the temple. I am worried about your sister Shizuko. I can't die and leave the temple to her, because she is not healthy." My mother remembers Sennō coming for a visit around this time, bringing a sack of sweet, dried persimmons for the children to eat. On this visit, Sennō asked his recalcitrant son, my Ojiisan, if one of my mother's brothers might take over Empukuji—or if a marriage could be arranged between my mother and a priest. But Ojiisan refused. Sennō died in 1968, leaving his daughter, Shizuko, alone to take care of Empukuji—and to search for an heir.

My mother and I visited Aunt Shizuko as often as we visited my grandparents, and I have vivid memories of arriving in the town of Iwaki, then called Taira, at dusk, after a several-hour train ride from the airport in Tōkyō. From Taira, we always hired a taxi to get to the temple. I loved taking taxis in Japan because they were a luxury in which we otherwise rarely indulged. Taxis in Tōhoku were as they were everywhere in Japan: a model of Western-inspired modernity and comfort, with air-conditioning, white lace-covered seats, and a driver wearing white gloves and a hat. The lace on the seat was usually covered by a tightly fitted plastic sheet that stuck to the back of my sweaty legs.

"Do you know the temple Empukuji?" my mother would ask the

driver once he had stopped complaining about the amount of lug-gage we had to put in the trunk; Taira had few international visitors in those days.

When the driver answered, his dialect and accent were so heavy, my mother winced. Here the façade of the uber-modern taxi driver fell away. We were in Tōhoku, the wild northeast, where not every-one had learned to speak in the standard dialect. "That place up in the hills run by that woman who is all alone with no heirs?"

"That woman is my aunt."

"All her brothers died in the war. What's she gonna do living up there all alone? Remarkable woman, they say. Reading sutras every morning and ringing the bells and everything after her dad died. Myself—I'd get depressed."

Primly: "Could you take us there, please?"

"I guess it'll be cooler up there than it is down here. That's for sure. Hey—where did you say you were from?"

The taxi pulled out from the station parking lot, and the driver openly stared at my foreign face in his rearview mirror. I turned my head away and looked out the window, craning my neck to be the first to catch sight of Empukuji perched on a hillside in the narrow and verdant valley. Aunt Shizuko would be outside, high up on the hill, wearing an apron and welcoming us with wide, enthusiastic waves.

The car turned and began to navigate a narrow road through a stretch of rice paddies flanked by fat-leafed clover patches. In the morning, my mother and I would sit here and make a crown of flowers. The road forked, and the right side led up to a landing next to a house, where Aunt Shizuko was waiting. The left side of the fork led to a car park. From here, a set of steep stairs threaded through a series of gates, which in turn were flanked by cherry trees that capped the walk with pink froth in the spring. At the top of the stairs was the temple, the slope of its eaves flexed like hands pressed together in prayer. To the left was another building set up for pilgrims, meetings, and meals. Higher above was a cemetery, which nestled against the edge of a bamboo forest, home to tangled vegetation, badgers, and bears.

In those days, the valley was nearly empty, except for the rice-growing farmers who made up most of Empukuji's congregation. The size of a Buddhist temple is determined by the number of households, or *danka*, it oversees. In those days, our family temple oversaw only fifty households, which is a very small number; to survive, most temples must have an average of two to three hundred. It is common to hear temple families literally say, "If you do not have at least two hundred *danka*, you cannot eat."

At Empukuji, all the buildings—house, temple, meeting rooms—were connected by ramps, making it possible to travel from the house to the altar without first going outside; this was a handy shortcut for a priest who needed to meet waiting guests, or more importantly, for the wife who needed to bring in some tea or treats when acting as a hostess. But here there was no priest and no wife. There was only Aunt Shizuko, stoically protecting her family's legacy and providing for her fifty households.

Up here on the hill, one had the feeling of calm. Aunt Shizuko spoke the language of nature and the garden. If I had too many mosquito bites, she knew how to make a salve to ease the itching. In the spring, she collected bamboo shoots and other wild vegetables to eat for dinner. Like my grandfather, she knew the names of birds just by their voices, and she knew when the season was changing because the *hototogisu*, known to us in English as the lesser cuckoo, would start to sing in the trees outside after managing the flight from Taiwan. Before he died, my grandfather taught me to listen for the *hototogisu*. He said that when I heard it singing at the temple, it would mean that he was with me, that he had ridden the bird's back from Taiwan to Japan when it migrated in May.

In the one air-conditioned room, with the black-and-gold family altar behind us, we sat and ate chilled slices of watermelon while the hot sun passed overhead. At dusk, if the season was right, *jangara*—musicians who play flat, metal chimes and *taiko* drums—would gather around the temple to rehearse for a midsummer festival when the spirits of the dead would return to visit their families. Aunt Shizuko brought out some *katori senko*, spiral-shaped incense that was particularly potent against mosquitoes. While the smoke unfurled, I sat on the tatami-mat floor, my feet dangling over the edge of the opened wood-and-rice-paper sliding door, while the men kicked up dust outside. At night we slept in a fine mesh net to hide away from mosquitoes. In the morning, my mother might take me to nearby Sōma for the horse *matsuri*, or festival, or to Ōarai beach to cool down.

When I was ten years old, my mother and I arrived to the temple to find that Aunt Shizuko had company. She had adopted a young man named Sempō and designated him as her heir. Now, when we took the taxi from Taira station, there were two figures waiting for us on the hill. Now, when I woke up early in the morning to the sound of the temple drum, it was Sempō's deep, baritone voice singing the sutra while the quiet audience of the temple sculptures watched and listened.

IT TOOK ME until July in 2011, when travel restrictions had eased, and a portion of the Jōban Line had been restored, to make it to the temple for the first time after the disaster. As soon as I stepped out of the taxi onto the temple grounds, the *hototogisu* began to sing in the cherry trees overlooking the temple. I imagined the spirit of my grandfather on the back of his favorite bird. But the moment was bittersweet. The temple grounds had been transformed. The flower garden in front of the main house was gone, and in its place, large, eerie sunflowers turned up their shaggy-maned yellow faces to the sun, in unblinking poses.

A Buddhist priest had given the seeds to Sempō and was urging people across Tōhoku to plant sunflowers; it is believed that sunflowers have the ability to remove radiation from topsoil. The sunflower project was part of a wider effort across much of Tōhoku to make the ground safe again for children to play.

Behind the house, the large new *hondō*, or main temple hall, stood unfinished, its metal ribs open to the elements. A blue tarp covered the roof. The new temple was supposed to have been completed by the end of the year, but after the earthquake and tsunami, construction had been halted. Every able-bodied carpenter was focused on repair and reconstruction.

Sempō greeted us as we got out of the taxi. He then immediately started in on his plans for taking care of my grandfather's bones. The speed with which he directed the conversation was disconcerting. Usually when we arrived at the temple, there was time for pleasantries, for tea, talk, and old-fashioned manners. Instead, Sempō barreled on in a business-like fashion, and his wife Ryōko did not come out to say hello. She spent nearly our entire visit in the kitchen doing *kumihimo*, a Japanese craft in which single strands of thread are wound together tightly to create straps or belts. As a sometimes obsessive knitter, I understood. Knitting took me through the aftermath of 9/11 when I lived in New York.

Sempō said, "We should bury these bones before Obon. This August will be his Niibon." Obon is the Buddhist celebration of ancestors when the souls of the dead are able to return home to visit family, and Niibon means "the first Obon after someone's death." In other words, this coming August would be my grandfather's first visit home since dying. We needed to give his soul a new and permanent home. Yes, even if, as he promised, his spirit had ridden the back of the *hototogisu* to see us in May. This is a good time for me to point out that Japan is, among other things, the land of exceptions and acceptable contradictions.

While my mother and Sempō tucked themselves into a corner of the house to talk about my grandfather's bones, the middle son, Takahagi, and I retired to the elevated walkway connecting the main house to the temple. Takahagi was thirty years old and the temple relative to whom I am closest. When he was younger, he was an eccentric fashionista, driving his secondhand American hearse down to Harajuku boutiques to buy his clothes. Whenever I arrived in the past, our eyes darted over each other, furtively, looking to see who was wearing what, before we launched into conversations about his girlfriend and my boyfriend. Even now, a married man, Takahagi had a penchant for hats, drapey sleeves, and dramatic jewelry. But on this visit he did not have the youthful look of one hungrily searching for a happy diversion.

As the second son in the family, Takahagi has always been the Prince Harry to his older brother's Prince William. Takahagi spent two years at Komazawa University, a prestigious Buddhist college founded in 1592 in Tōkyō. He simultaneously went to the Eiheiji Betsuin, the Tōkyō branch of the great Zen monastery Eiheiji. After two years in Tōkyō, Takahagi received an associate's degree from Komazawa University and Buddhist priest certification from the Eiheiji Betsuin. Then he returned home.

Because Takahagi had only been at the Eiheiji Betsuin part-time—most students study full-time and are unable to leave the confines of the temple until graduation—he had taken it upon himself to buy chocolate, magazines, and other treats from the secular world not allowed on the monastery grounds. Takahagi had done this to raise the morale of his fellow priests-in-training, but he had constantly gotten caught and been punished accordingly. Mostly he'd been made to sit in silence for six hours at a time, something he learned not to mind too much because he became adept at napping while sitting up. Takahagi said that even at the Betsuin, which was not nearly as remote as the main monastery of Eiheiji, the training was very hard, and half a dozen boys were unable to take the pressure and escaped. One by one the boys who ran away from the Betsuin went straight to the police—monks-in-training have no cell phones and no money—where they phoned their parents. A day or so later, the parents would arrive sheepishly and pick up their sons' belongings. "I hear there are easier places to train," Takahagi told me, "though I don't really know anything about places like that."

Takahagi now lived in an apartment with his wife and commuted most days to the temple to help with overflow work. He also picked up freelance jobs from other temples in the surrounding area when they needed an extra hand. Even though young people are increasingly not interested in taking over family temples—indeed many temples are closing down due to either a lack of support from young people or a fading local population, or both—there are temples that have an overflow of parishioners but not enough staff. Over the years, Takahagi had received several offers from temples who wanted him to marry their daughter and take over their temple. He had always rejected this arrangement. The only temple he ever wanted to run was his own.

In his twenties, Takahagi had chafed under his role as spare to the heir. He knew the names of all the *dankasan*, how to flirt with the women, and how to make the men laugh, while his older brother, Daisuke, hid inside the family house. But Takahagi, as the second son, was not the designated heir.

Daisuke had gone full-time to Komazawa University, where he had received a bachelor's degree. After school, Daisuke went on to spend a year at Sōjiji, which along with Eiheiji is the head of all the Sōtō Zen Buddhist temples in Japan. Daisuke's education, for a Buddhist priest, is akin to a physician going to Harvard for an undergraduate degree and Stanford for medical school.

But Daisuke did not have Takahagi's social ease, his flair for mixing black clothing with silver jewelry, or his success with women. Daisuke could tell you the origin of every Buddhist deity and the proper sutra for every education. But he also liked to stay home and play with his PlayStation, unlocking game achievements while keeping an eye out for future game releases. He was particularly fond of RPGs, or role-playing games, which empower a player to act as the lead character in a fantastic story. An occasional gamer myself, I once tried to engage him in a conversation about what he was playing. He waved me away. He knew more about the video game Zelda than I could ever hope to. My grandfather, before he died, thought that Takahagi ought to inherit the temple, and he unabashedly said so to anyone who listened. His brutal honesty made for uncomfortable visits.

Takahagi had been at Nakoso enjoying the spa waters the day of the big quake. He was already on his way home when the tsunami started. What should have been a twenty-minute drive took nearly four hours.

Not too long after, the funerals started. Empukuji did not lose any *danka*, or parishioners, as a direct result of the disaster, but nearby temples did, and Takahagi had been asked to help with the overflow of work.

"Did you go to the evacuation centers?" I asked.

He lit a cigarette. "What I most remember is the smell. It was terrible." He exhaled. "I've put on four kilos [about nine pounds]. We don't go outside."

Did any priests run away? Takahagi laughed and told me about a priest who fled Iwaki for a hotel in the south, though he later claimed that he had only done so to work out a deal with the hotel owner so his *dankasan* could stay there too.

"After the tsunami, people kept coming by here," Takahagi explained. "Especially older people. It was like—they wondered if we were here." He took another puff. "They would joke about how they were eighty years old and not afraid of getting cancer. We couldn't leave. Everyone was watching."

"Did you want to leave?"

He smiled shyly, apologetically. "Marie, we needed water. You can't do much without water."

Most of my Western friends have the impression of Japan as being a technological wonder of a country, with people at once so anally efficient as to be repressed. They report, confidently, of the news stories about panties being available in vending machines and robots that do everything from museum curatorial work to the duties of stand-in girlfriends. But the Japan I remember from childhood is practically pre-technological. Well into the 1990s, there were still plenty of people in Tōhoku, particularly farmers, who lived the old-fashioned way, heating their baths and drawing water from a well.

After the March 2011 quake, the water supply in Iwaki and other parts of Tōhoku had been cut off for nearly a month, but some people retained their access to water because they had never converted from a private well system to modern piping. Once a day, Ryōko went over to the neighbor's and dredged up water from a well. She filled up tanks and transported them back to the temple for basic cooking. There was no water to spare for bathing.

"I was obsessed with water," Takahagi said to me. "I didn't have time to think about radiation."

All at once, we heard Ryōko's high-pitched voice cry out: "Okay, so Oniichan [older brother] is going home now. Bye bye! Everyone say bye bye!" I leaned against the railing to say goodbye. From within the house, I heard my mother moving to the doorway. Japanese houses are like this—light and airy so you hear movements from far away.

Daisuke gave a perfunctory wave, his mouth in a half smile,

as though embarrassed and annoyed by the attention. He climbed onto his bicycle and rode off to the apartment where he now lived; Daisuke had been urged to move out of the temple home by his parents, who hoped their oldest son might learn some independence.

"How was he?" I asked Takahagi. "During the . . ."

"Exactly the same," Takahagi shook his head. "You know he hates to bathe anyway. He just rode his bike around. Came here every day."

"Didn't he worry about the radiation?"

"But you know. You can't see it." Then he added matter-of-factly, "It's good you didn't bring your son here. Who knows how much radiation is out there? I've stopped listening to the reports. My brother reads the reports every day. He can tell you what the numbers are in every location and how they are changing and where the wind is blowing." He paused. "I'd like to have a child. But it wouldn't be right to bring a baby into this world now, would it?"

SEMPŌ OFFERED TO drive us to the water's edge where we could see some of the damage from the tsunami. We went out to the coast and down a little hill to a small harbor by the shore. There were no boats. The concrete seawall had cracked, and in places the landing had been lifted up. "I haven't been here until now," Sempō said, almost shyly, a look of wonder on his face. "We try not to go out because of the radiation."

The harbor was very peaceful. All I heard were birds chirping and the lapping of water. There were no other people. I turned around and saw a house partway up the hill. Half of its face had been sliced off. Inside I could see a poster for Sapporo beer hanging on the wall. It occurred to me that fishermen must have gone there for drinks after a day of work. The headlands were not supposed to be so empty. Before the tsunami, there had been other houses here.

"Do you feel better, seeing that we are still alive?" Sempō asked.

"Oh, yes," I said automatically. Actually, I didn't feel better. I felt deeply disturbed. But as much as he didn't want me to worry, I didn't want him to worry. There is a lot of this kind of mutual warding off of worry in Japan. It's the kind of behavior that causes Westerners to accuse the Japanese of "vagueness" or "dishonesty."

As we walked along the shore, Sempō told me that he had decided we would not bury my grandfather until the following year. He didn't want to ask my mother's uncles to travel here now, while the situation was still so unstable. And he didn't want to touch the ground with his hands. "First they told us there was no meltdown, then it turned out there was a meltdown," he said ruefully. "Now there is a melt-through. Who knows what will happen. You should not be in a hurry to come back."

"Sempō," I said, "why didn't you leave?" I meant this as a kindness, but he was gruff with his response.

"That would not have been an easy thing to do, for many reasons." He closed his eyes, like a cat, and gathered his thoughts. "First of all, temples in Japan have tax-free status because we are supposed to be here for people precisely in the case of an emergency. And further . . ." A storm was gathering in him. "It is difficult for you to understand as a Westerner. Buddhism is very different from Christianity, as far as I can tell."

He went on. "Buddhism saved this country from itself. Think about the last war we fought. 'Die for your country. The emperor is a god.' Those kamikaze pilots. Stupid. Do you know what your Aunt Shizuko used to say? She said, Even the emperor must bow at a temple. The point of Buddhism is that everyone is equal. There should be no war. We should take care of each other. You make Buddhism complicated because you are a foreigner. That's the main reason you don't understand."

·   ·   ·

IF YOU ARE a Westerner and you spend enough time in Japan—
and you speak Japanese—you will eventually be told that you cannot truly understand the Japanese. Only the Japanese can understand
themselves.

There is a word for people who are not Japanese, composed of
the Chinese characters for "outside" and "country." There are those
in the country—the Japanese—and those who are "outside of the
country"—or *gaijin*. The term is a legacy of Japan's long period
of isolation in the years between 1600 and 1868, when there was
almost no contact between the island nation and the outside world.
Any Japanese who dared to venture out was not allowed back in.
History has preserved a few extraordinary accounts of adventuring
Japanese fishermen who explored the landmasses beyond their own,
but they were never permitted back home after their disobedience
was uncovered. With very few exceptions, no Westerners were ever
allowed to live in Japan.

Even after more than one hundred years of contact with the
Western world, some of this isolationist attitude lingers. When I
visited Japan as a child, it was very common for other children to
point and stare at me because I was the very first *gaijin* they had
ever seen. I could hear kids asking their parents with the singular
guilelessness of the very young, "Mom, is *that* a *gaijin*?" as though
to ask if I, the strange creature, was in fact the long-rumored foreigner they had seen in their picture books.

There is also an element within the Japanese culture that persists
in telling itself and others that it is special and unlike any place else
in the world. The Japanese, in fact, are so special that only they can
understand their culture. A *gaijin* cannot be expected to "get it."

To many scholars—Western and Japanese—the notion that
Japan is "special" is uncomfortable and potentially dangerous.
It prevents the Japanese from asking for help when they need it.
Believing that the Japanese people were special was part of what

sparked Japanese aggression in World War II. Being special does not align with modern Western ideals of multiculturalism, equality of the sexes, and rationality's power to understand all things. At the same time, there is a persistent Japanese anxiety, often reflected in the media and in books, that Japan is still somehow different—must be different—even if the Japanese cannot articulate exactly how.

There are many good reasons for the Japanese to feel apprehensive about being misunderstood. The cultural bases from which Japan and the West draw are unrelated; the same cannot be said of the United States and Great Britain, for example, who have significant cultural differences but share deep roots. And yet, because Japan looks modern on the surface, Westerners feel like it ought to be "just like us," and are surprised when it is not. Under such conditions, it is easy for misunderstandings to arise.

Fledgling scientific research, such as the work of Richard E. Nisbett in *The Geography of Thought*, suggests that East Asians and Westerners literally perceive the world differently, to the point of picking out different objects in the landscape. His research also indicates that how one sees the world can be somewhat fluid. First- and certainly second-generation children of an East Asian immigrant in the United States will see the world the way their fellow Westerners do. Asians who grow up in regions with a strong Western influence, like Hong Kong, will behave somewhere in between these two extremes. Perhaps it is possible, then, to see through more than one set of eyes, if one learns to pay attention to one's environment in a slightly different manner than one is accustomed to from birth.

I have always believed that in a great many ways Japan is indeed unique, and the Japanese are justified in being proud of their cultural sensitivities and unique accomplishments. I had always thought that I was able to appreciate these things. But after my conversation with

Sempō, I wondered if I needed to try a little bit harder to see things through his eyes.

I HAD SEMPŌ's words on my mind when, in April of 2013, I was asked to participate in a Japanese documentary series called *Tomorrow Japan*, which focuses on life in Tōhoku after the disaster. The film's producer, Endo Shigeru, had been interested in my connection to Iwaki, and my focus on exploring the spiritual traditions to which the Japanese were turning in the aftermath of the tsunami. When we first met in a suburb of Tōkyō, Endo brought some research and reading material for me to peruse, and I became particularly intrigued by a short folktale in a collection of stories called *The Legends of Tōno*.

Often referred to as Japan's *Grimm's Fairy Tales*, *The Legends of Tōno*, compiled in 1912 by the amateur folklorist Yanagita Kunio, is a strange and eerie collection of folk stories. Most of the tales are set in and around the town of Tōno, which is located about 277 miles northeast of Tōkyō and twenty miles from the coastal city of Kamaishi. Endo wanted me to read tale number 79, which takes place on the Tōhoku coast and is the only tale to reference a tsunami.

In the story, a man is living in temporary housing with his child after his wife and his other child perished in a tsunami. One summer night, the man goes out to the bathroom—the toilet was in a separate location from the main house. As he walks along a path, he sees a figure out by the water and realizes it is his wife. Then he sees that his wife is walking with another man.

Before the tsunami, his wife had been rumored to be in love with this other man, though she did not marry him. "What's the matter with you?" the man cries out to his wife. "Don't you miss your children?" At this, the wife cries too, and begins to slowly walk away. The man follows her for a while, until she disappears into the mist with her ghostly partner. After this, the man becomes sick for a long time. The story ends here, somewhat inconclusively to Western tastes, as is the case with many of the legends of Tōno.

Endo told me that when he first read this story, he thought that it was about regret, and how people leave many things undone and unsaid when they die, and that the burden of such grief—for the living and the dead—is quite possibly the greatest torture any person will ever undergo. But then, as we discussed the story, we decided that it was really about how the man had let go and come to accept that the wife was gone, though the process had made him ill for a while. The distance between losing someone and accepting that they are gone is of course the very essence of grieving, and in this simple ghost story, we both saw a blueprint for how grief in Japan might work itself out.

Traditional Japanese believe that the soul has a path to take, though the journey may be full of pitfalls and dangers. In many instances, this journey includes physical places one can visit in Japan, as is the case with Mount Osore, whose name means "Mount Fear" or "Mount Doom. Mount Osore is an extinguished volcano far in the north, where the dead are said to pause before leaving the world completely. But the Japanese don't believe this journey is a clear-cut, one-way street. The souls of the dead come home during the Buddhist festival Obon, and then it is important to prepare their graves and to honor them before helping them find their way back to the other world. Sometimes the dead can't move on because we won't let them, and this stymied progress brings madness to the living.

Across Japan, the tsunami has unleashed a whole flock of fledgling monsters as thousands of people are reported to be suffering from post-traumatic stress, severe depression, and other related mental-health issues. There are numerous reports of ghosts. Some of these apparitions are welcome, as survivors rejoice in seeing their loved ones again, and some are not welcome, because, like the man in the folktale from Tōno, citizens of Tōhoku have become ill.

It may seem odd to a Westerner to learn that Tōhoku is awash with ghosts; we associate ghosts with superstition, and Japan has the image of being a highly modernized country. But the soul of Japan is still very much connected to her twelve-hundred-year-old history, and within that belief system, ghosts are a powerful and meaningful presence. The Japanese Buddhist priest Kaneta Taiō once said to me that it should not be a surprise that the tsunami has released so many ghosts in Japan. "So many people died at one time. It is natural that people are still in shock."

Japan is often criticized for her failure to adopt Western-style mental-health care. But I'm wary that everything modern is always the best medicine for an individual if it isn't also connected to a person's culture. In my travels to Japan since the March 11, 2011, disaster, I have been moved by how many of Japan's spiritual workers are adapting the Japan of the old for the Japan of today. I have also been greatly inspired by the many people I have met who are tracing the old spiritual paths in Japan laid down by ancient pilgrims, in an effort to heal their personal hurts. To me, these actions reveal a part of what it is that is "special" about Japan, and signal that within this terrible disaster is a chance for the Japanese to rediscover what makes their culture unique. Perhaps all of us can benefit from such wisdom.

THREE

THE GREAT PARTING

SEVERAL TIMES A WEEK, the Zen Buddhist priest Kaneta Taiō heads out in his pickup truck with a small group of helpers to visit one of the dozens of temporary housing shelters on the Tōhoku coast. Kaneta calls himself "Café de Monk." The term is a pun; the Japanese love puns. Kaneta is a priest, which he says is a kind of monk. The word "monk" also sounds like *monku*, which means to complain, and one of Kaneta's jobs since the tsunami is to try to listen to people's complaints. But the word "monk" is also a reference to the jazz artist Thelonious Monk, whose music Kaneta plays whenever he sets up his cafés.

"Monk," he says, "has a groove, which keeps things lighthearted. But there is tremendous sadness in his music. Monk is the perfect soundtrack for what we are experiencing today."

Kaneta is from the town of Kurihara, where he runs a four-hundred-year-old temple called Tsūdaiji, or "Temple of the Great Way." Kaneta's temple is located inland, which meant that after the devastating earthquake, he found himself on his feet for hours and hours, day after day, reciting sutras for the dead, as bodies were recovered and cremated in his local crematorium. He did not know most of the people whose cremations he conducted, but he saw his job as necessary and important because it is at the cremation that people must experience something which the Japanese call *owakare*, or "the great parting."

In Japanese, *wakare* (wa-KA-ray) means "parting," and the word can be used in many contexts. When I take a guided tour of, say, a formal Japanese garden in Kyōtō, I am usually told at the end of the tour, "And here is our *wakare*." Here is our parting. This is a signal that I will now be on my own. When you add the prefix "O" in Japanese, you automatically elevate a word so it takes on a sense of honor. *Tōsan* is "father," but *otōsan* is "honored father," as in your own father and not the general concept of father. The word *daiji* is used to ask someone to "take care," but *"odaiji"* is "take care greatly." So it is with parting. There are many partings in life, but the great and most honored parting, the *owakare*, is the most significant of all, because it is permanent. Ushering the body of the dead into the crematorium is the *owakare*, and it requires the presence of family and a priest for it to be handled with dignity.

ONCE THE CREMATIONS finally came to an end, Kaneta was moved to do something else to help all the survivors. He started by taking some udon noodles to the survivors of the tsunami in the town of Togura, who belonged to the Buddhist temple Kaizōji, which is run by his second cousin, and where fifty *danka*, or parishioners, had died in the great waves. But the noodles didn't feel special enough. The next time, Kaneta brought a selection of cakes from a bakery in his hometown and served them with some strong coffee. He intended mostly to provide a little cheering up, but was surprised by a tremendous outpouring of grief and emotion. The mostly female participants drank their coffee and ate their cake and cried as they told and retold their stories of survival. One round of coffee and cake was not enough.

The stories of terror continued well after the tsunami passed.

Survivors had nightmares. They saw ghosts. Some of them wanted to see ghosts, as the ghosts were comforting. Some of them were possessed by ghosts and needed help relieving themselves of the ghosts. One afternoon when I visited Kaneta in his home, he told me about a female medium who phoned him in the middle of the night because she was suicidal. So many spirits of the dead inhabited her body that she had lost the will to live. Kaneta asked the medium to come to his home straightaway and met her in the evening. For the next three hours, he spoke with twenty-five different "entities," almost all of whom were lost and confused. "You are dead," Kaneta informed each entity. "There was a tsunami and many people died. You are one of the dead. And now you must leave the earth and go toward the light."

Kaneta began to visit survivors regularly, always arriving with cake, coffee, and Thelonious Monk. First he visited people in shelters, but after temporary housing communities were established, he began to make rounds there. One by one, the temporary communities reached out and asked for him to come and visit. For over two years now, Kaneta has been going out several times a week to meet with survivors and to listen to their stories. He is accompanied by a faithful group of volunteers and is often joined by new priests, who come and go as time permits. The day I met Kaneta, it was in the company of a group of priests who were undergoing grief-counseling training at Tōhoku University.

Kaneta trained at Eiheiji, the top monastery for Sōtō Buddhist priests; only Sōjiji, where my cousin Daisuke went, may be considered equal in prestige. Though Kaneta is proficient in sutras, funerals, and memorial services, he did not receive any sort of training for exorcisms or grief counseling. This is not what modern priests learn to do. And yet, once upon a time they did, as, for example, indicated in the classic Noh plays, whose high period was from 1336 to 1573, and coincided with the medieval Muromachi era.

These dramas frequently depict the sad fate of beautiful women who turn out to be spirits roaming the earth, unable to rid themselves of an attachment to a passionate love affair gone awry when they were alive. Invariably, it is a Buddhist priest who recognizes what ails these tragic women and who is able to release them from their torment. The fact that Kaneta and others are now performing this role speaks to the fact that such traditions, which might otherwise seem to have died with Japan's modernization, are in fact merely slumbering until needed.

ISHINOMAKI IS A small fishing town about twenty-three miles northeast of Sendai. On March 11, 2011, it was struck by numerous waves, with some estimated to reach the height of thirty-three feet. Over three thousand people from Ishinomaki, including hundreds of schoolchildren, lost their lives. Twenty-nine thousand people out of a population of just over 160,000 lost their homes. A temporary housing community built for the citizens of Ishinomaki is where I first met Kaneta and watched him work.

The temporary houses had been built fairly quickly and were of a uniform size. Rooms in Japan are measured by the number of tatami mats required to cover the floor. A modest room in a nice hotel, for example, is often made up of eight tatami mats, which converts roughly to 142 square feet. The temporary housing units at Ishinomaki had two rooms, each with six tatami mats, as well as a kitchenette and a bathroom with bathtub and shower. The back of each house had a laundry rack. Japanese rarely use dryers, even at coin-operated laundromats. On a sunny day, driving through Tōkyō, you will see futons pinned to balconies, baking in the sun, while laundry dries on racks. Even in a temporary housing unit, one hangs one's laundry to dry. Altogether, the space was smaller than your average Best Western hotel room, and I cannot imagine most

Western families managing to live in such a unit for a few weeks—sleeping on the floor—let alone for an indefinite period of time. The Japanese government still does not know how long many evacuees will have to wait for a new home or to go home, though some of the Fukushima evacuees have been told they will never be allowed to return home at all.

The houses were clustered together, and each shared a wall, except for those lucky few who were on the ends of a row. Each house had a number on it and, in some instances, a name. It was easy to spot the homes that had children; it was May, and there were little *koinobori*, or carp-shaped flags, in the window or hanging out with the laundry rack. *Koinobori* are hung up in conjunction with Children's Day, which is celebrated on May 5 in Japan, though the decorations often stay up for the entire month. Here and there a hand pulled aside a curtain, and an elderly face—almost always a woman—peered out to see who was there.

All of a sudden Kaneta pulled up in his truck outside the community hall, and instantly the mood in the community changed. It was as though Santa Claus had arrived on his sleigh. Kaneta, about sixty years old, was quite tall—particularly for a Japanese of his generation. He was bespectled and had shaved his head bald, as most Japanese Buddhist priests do. He had a slightly toothy smile and bright eyes that darted around, searching for information and for any problems that need to be addressed. He told me later that he had been to so many temporary housing shelters across Japan that he could determine the story of the people inside just by looking at the parking lot. He knew how much money they had by their cars, if the shelters were mostly full of elderly, if there were children, if the men had been fishermen before the tsunami, or if the people were from Fukushima.

With the magical proficiency of Mary Poppins, Kaneta and his staff unloaded tables, chairs, boxes of cake, coffee, tea, clay and origami materials from the back of the truck. I couldn't help but wonder how they fit so much stuff in the truck in the first place. Seemingly within minutes appeared two picnic tables with canopies, chairs, a hand-painted sign that read "Café de Monk," and trays of cake. More tables were set up inside the community hall, which sparkled with the sound of jazz and the smell of burnt sugar and hot coffee. One by one, or two by two, the residents began to enter the building.

Around me, in the community hall, women had seated themselves in chairs or on pillows on the floor. A few men sat quietly together. The volunteer priests went to work, serving cake and coffee. And then, after just a few minutes, in a corner, Kaneta was with two women who were crying.

They were a mother and a daughter and they had lost everything. The girl's name was Nami, which means "wave."

"You lost everything," Kaneta said bluntly.

"Yes," they cried.

"Are you fighting a lot?" he asked.

"Yes," they wailed louder.

"You can't fight," he grinned. "You have to stop that." Then he laughed, as if the situation of a mother and daughter who had been displaced from their home by a tsunami were humorous. As if the entire situation were so absurd, one could only laugh at it. "Have you ever wondered about the difference between life and death? They can be separated by such a small thing as a second. You are here for a reason, and you must find it."

The daughter sulked, and the mother looked around, a little embarrassed. They wiped tears from their eyes. Then Kaneta leaned forward. "Okay, guys. Why are you fighting? Huh?" Then he laughed.

Earlier that week, in the grief-counseling training run by Tōhoku University, I met a motley crew of priests hailing from various religious sects: Buddhists of various sects, Christians priests, and New Agers. One was a highly impressive-looking Tendai Buddhist nun whose shaved head and bright saffron robes gave her a distinguished, androgynous appearance; Tendai Buddhism, brought to Japan in the ninth century, is among the oldest sects that still exist in Japan, and it stresses that all living things are capable of attaining enlightenment. I became particularly friendly with a young Pure Land priest named Tokita who hailed from Fukushima. Before the disaster, Tokita had been uncertain about his future; he was the third son in his family and would not be inheriting his family's temple. But once the tsunami struck, he felt galvanized to turn his priestly training to use and to help those in need. His family owned and ran a very old Pure Land Buddhist temple; Pure Land Buddhism originated in the twelfth century and sought to provide the common people with a simpler way to achieve enlightenment. Unlike Zen, the sect to which Kaneta belonged, which emphasizes meditation, Pure Land Buddha stressed that an individual only needed to recite a simple prayer in order to be reborn in the Buddha's Western Paradise, a place that is always described as a golden palace.

Overseeing all these trainees was a fascinating young man named Morita. He was a priest of the Yuzu Nembutsu sect, and he told me he had eschewed his own family's temple in lieu of working for a hospice at a hospital in Nagano; this is unusual, as Japan does not have the kind of chaplain/hospice program that is the norm in the West. Morita's main goal as a teacher was to help train more priests to do hospice work, but he now also helped train priests on how to work with tsunami survivors. A slight man with a patient, smiling, and sorrowful expression, Morita moved with the purposefulness of someone so engaged in the painful art of healing that he almost seemed to be undergoing a kind of penance.

Late in the morning, the participants of the group gathered

in a circle and offered up their stories, one by one, as to why they had decided to come for grief-counseling training. A young man, dandily dressed in a tweed jacket with a striped scarf looped at his throat, explained that his job was to call people to give them the results of their radiation tests. Most of the time, he said, the test results were negative, but on one occasion, he had to call a mother and tell her that her two children were sick. She began to cry on the phone to him—a stranger—and he did not know what to do. He found himself repeating phrases from the training manual. "Don't worry! There's always hope! Don't worry!" Then he added, "It's not your fault." He immediately regretted this last sentence. By introducing the concept of "fault" into the phone call, he was concerned that he was implying that it *was* her fault, and he hated himself for his offense; Japanese manners are full of such subtleties, which may seem odd to a Westerner, but they are essential to the graceful way so many Japanese interact with each other on their small island nation. The man did not want to go back to work. He never wanted to pick up the telephone again.

Morita listened compassionately to this story and then leaned forward. Gently he said, "What exactly is it that you are afraid of?" Morita wondered why it was that people became afraid of talking to the dying and the grieving. He suspected it was because when the living had to speak to someone who was sick or dying, they also had to face the fact that all life will one day come to an end. But there was no use running away from such information, Morita said. It could be helpful to know that death was the thing we most feared. If we understood that, it would make it easier to listen to other people.

Now in Ishinomaki, at Café de Monk, I was surrounded by priests who had been through Morita's training and were doing their very best to be empathetic listeners. Morita himself was folded compactly on a small pillow, smiling gently and listening to a group of women talk about life in the temporary housing unit. The androgynous Tendai nun was holding an elderly lady's hand, while Tokita sat ensconced in a corner, deep in conversation with another woman.

Then there was Kaneta, whose style was the complete opposite of Morita's. The general feeling that Kaneta conveyed was one of strength and health. There was something almost martial about him, a pure Zen quality; Zen Buddhism was the favored sect of Buddhism for many samurai in Japan's medieval period. He had a constant half smile on his face, as though even in the face of ghosts, or insanity, or a tsunami, he would be able to stand, unafraid and wholly rational, and even be amused. But even as he spoke to some of the women with a blunt, almost badgering tone, he was empathetic. He might laugh if you told him you were fighting with a relative, but you knew he would not laugh if you told him about a ghost. Though your story of suffering was one of many, you knew he would listen and tend to it.

For those who did not want to immediately launch into a story about the tsunami, Kaneta had devised other activities, each with a therapeutic purpose, and each quintessentially Japanese. At one table, a young priest was helping women to make rosary bracelets on an elastic band. He had a jeweler's box of plastic beads, each color symbolizing something different: hope, life, happiness, and so on. In another box he had actual rosary beads from discarded or retired priests' rosaries. The women used beads from both boxes to make their own personalized bracelets. At another table, a young priest was enthusiastically showing women how to fold origami lotus flowers (the lotus being a key symbol in Buddhism). Most had never folded a lotus before, though all were immensely skilled with their hands. Some bragged how good their flowers were on the first try. The flowers were made out of thin plastic, which meant they could float in a glass of water. "Take these home," said the priest with enthusiasm. "And you can put in a floating candle. It'll make a great decoration!"

In another corner, tucked away from the foot traffic to the cake and the coffee, there was a table with a few *ihai*. These are funerary tablets. Typically, when someone dies in Japan, they are given a new name, as death is a kind of "rebirth," and just as the newly born are christened, so must the dead receive a new name as they cycle through the great karmic process of being reborn into Buddha's paradise, or as some other living entity.

In some forms of Buddhism, priests can't give an *ihai*—or perform a funeral service—if there is no body. Such is the case with Zen. Takahagi, Sempō's middle son, told me that he had been to many memorial services after the tsunami, but that often these families could not have a true funeral service without any remains. And so the living went on with the cruel uncertainty of wondering what happened to the body, and thus what would happen to the soul of their loved one.

Kaneta dispensed with this torture. If someone was dead, he made an *ihai* and performed the funerary sutra. The *ihai* could then be placed on the family altar in the home, giving survivors a focal point for their grief. Kaneta also went into people's homes and recited additional sutras if they so desired.

Then there was the marquee therapeutic activity: the making of a Jizō. The Jizō is a particularly compassionate character in the Buddhist pantheon that is greatly loved by the Japanese. While he has the ability to transcend reality and become enlightened like the Buddha, the Jizō stays behind to help humans who are suffering. He is often depicted with slightly childlike features and a warm smile; the Jizō is a figure of serenity and warmth in an otherwise frightening world. About two hours after he arrived, Kaneta pulled out a tub of clay and passed out handfuls of it and molding instruments to a group of women seated on the floor around a rectangular

table. In the world of Jizō making, he remarked, it was now fashion-
able to make sure that each statue had long ears. This was because
a large-eared Jizō was able to catch more coins in the ears than a
statue with small ears, and since everyone staying at a temporary
housing unit needed more money, the women were to make the ears
as large as possible. The ears, of course, were simply metaphoric in
function—they were not literally expected to catch any money.

Next, Kaneta said, if anyone had lost someone in a tsunami,
they were to write the name of the person on the back of the clay
Jizō. He would then make sure to give that person a special bless-
ing when he returned the next time, after the Jizō had been fired
and glazed in the kiln he had at home. I sat and helped the woman
next to me attach the ears and the "third eye," a bump between the
eyes that most Buddhas and bodhisattvas have, and that is often a
symbol of wisdom. As they made the Jizōs, the women laughed and
gossiped.

People came and went. Cups were refilled with coffee or tea and
redistributed. We ran out of cups. Children came home from school
and playfully tackled the priests. Late in the day, Kaneta motioned
to me and to the young Pure Land priest, Tokita, to follow him
to visit a woman, whom I will call Maruyama. She had spent the
better part of two hours speaking to Tokita, and she now wanted
Kaneta's help too.

We followed Maruyama out of the community building to the
door of her home. She was a plump lady with a full, fleshy face and
short hair. Her voice was soft and high. One hand was in a cast. She
had asked for Kaneta's help because she saw her deceased mother
night after night and was tormented by nightmares.

Maruyama's home was less of a home and more of an enlarged
closet into which she had desperately stuffed mementos from a former life. Mashed into the space were a bicycle, an actual Western-
style metal bedframe (most people use futon mattresses, which can

be folded up during the day and put away to create more space), a portrait of her mother dressed as a beauty queen, numerous cardboard boxes, a shrine to her mother, photographs, cards, medication, jewelry, and other small items Maruyama had managed to rescue from the ruins of her home.

There was something almost adolescent about Maruyama, and I was shocked to learn that she was fifty-six years old. In a childlike voice, she helplessly gave herself over to the story of the tsunami. She had lived with her mother in Ishinomaki, where the two of them ran a restaurant. Both had been home during the earthquake. Then the tsunami alarm had sounded.

As Maruyama spoke, I found myself struggling to follow her narrative. At first I thought this was because of my imperfect Japanese. Later, others told me that they had also struggled to follow her story in a linear fashion. One moment she was remembering the earthquake, and in the next she said that her mother promised to evacuate the home after she went to the bathroom. They agreed to meet each other at the local funeral parlor. Maruyama watched the bathroom door close, and then she left the house, got into her car, and drove off.

From here, the story leapt to Maruyama stuck in traffic. She said she looked around and saw that everyone else driving a car was frantically circling their arms. "Like this," she said, turning her arm around and around, as one does when manually opening a car window. Or, perhaps, to signal to someone else that they must hurry. From here the story leapt forward in time again. Maruyama said that she was in the water, and that she was drowning. A boat came by, and people screamed at her as they lowered a pole—the kind used to hang laundry—and told her to grab it. "Whatever you do, don't let go," they yelled. "We will never let go. Your job is to hang on." So she hung on to the pole, on the side of the boat.

The water rushed in all around. It was filthy and dark and cold, and at points only her face and hands were out of the water; the rest of her body struggled against the current. She thought to herself that she could not hang on, even as the people on the boat continued to scream at her not to let go. She was certain she would die. All of a sudden, she said, the specter of her mother came rushing at her with the water. It came straight toward her and then passed through her, and she knew that her mother had died.

She wasn't sure how long she held on, or even how she ultimately recovered from the water. At some point, though, she found herself in a temporary shelter, searching for the remains of her mother. She went back to her home and found that it was only partially damaged. She wanted to remove a silk kimono from one of the closets so she would be able to bury her mother in the finest outfit they had owned, but thieves had ransacked the house and taken anything of value.

I gasped at this. The stories we were told in the West were only of how unselfish and cooperative the Japanese had been.

Here Maruyama broke from the earnest, trance-like persona she had adopted to say to me, in a slightly lower and more adult voice, "Yes. Really. This is Japan today. This is how we now are." Around me, everyone, including Kaneta, nodded. Then, like a medium, Maruyama resumed her story in her girlish, childlike voice. Workers had not found her mother's body right away; it had taken ten days or more. When Maruyama saw the body in a makeshift hospital, it was completely naked.

She had then tried to get her mother's remains cremated, but the local crematorium was inundated with bodies. There was a wait of two weeks. The body was beginning to decompose. There was not enough electricity or dry ice to keep all the bodies preserved. In desperation, she arranged to have the remains driven to Kurihara.

"You came to Kurihara?" Kaneta brightened.

"Yes. That's where we were finally able to cremate her."

"Oh, well. Then I was at your mother's funeral," he beamed. "I thought you looked familiar. I did almost all the cremations there. Night and day," he said. Then he shook his head and put his hand to his forehead. "Oh. That was such an awful time. *Taihen deshita.* Wasn't that just awful!" he exclaimed and laughed again, in his patented way of mocking absurdity. He shook his head and tut-tutted.

Maruyama continued. Now her mother came to see her at night. Here the narrative became fractured again. Maruyama thought she should have saved her mother, but her mother had wanted to use the toilet. At night, Maruyama had nightmares. She saw people waving their arms in circles. "Look," she said, "I hurt myself in the middle of the night." She pulled out her cell phone and showed us pictures of her arm before it had been put in a cast. "Look how swollen my arm is," she said with wonder. But there were nice things. She received emails, for example, from someone in Canada. This was a nice thing. But there were so many bad things. There were levels of disparity in the temporary housing. Anyone with any money or any family had left. One by one, people were leaving. And then there were people like her who were left behind. She wanted the world to know that there were still hundreds of people like her who were left behind.

While Maruyama was speaking, I found myself trying to do my very best imitation of Morita. I was listening with all the empathy that I could. And yet the story did not stop. I was not able to get more than a word in edgewise. I thought to myself that this was how madness must be. A whirlpool. How would any of us ever manage to get out of the house? Then—how selfish was I for wanting to escape?

"Do you know," Maruyama pressed, "what you hear when a tsunami comes? You hear car horns. I still hear the car horns. I thought that it was car horns because people were honking at me to get out of their way, and I was so irritated because I couldn't get my car to move. But they weren't honking. The cars were flooded. That is the last sound you hear when a car is flooded with water. The pressure of the water hits the horn, and it honks and honks until finally the car is so damaged it cannot make a sound."

"All right!" Kaneta said abruptly. Very quickly he put his priest's over-apron on and pulled a rosary out of his pocket. The effect was of Moses parting the Red Sea, of a wizard holding up his hands to stop the mischievous machinations of a growing swarm of unruly spirits. Just like that, Maruyama stopped speaking.

Kaneta strode over to the shrine and, peering over the top of his glasses, inspected the portrait of Maruyama's mother. "Yes, I think I remember her." He shook his head. "It was a very hard time for me too, you know. What a total pain this tsunami has been." He nodded at Tokita, the young priest who was with us, and asked him which sutras he knew. Tokita, who had also been cast under Maruyama's spell, shook his head and snapped to attention. They entered the safe haven of priest-speak, settled on a sutra, and began to chant aloud.

When it was over, Kaneta promised Maruyama that he would return to check on her, then ushered me out of the building.

"So. Kind of intense, wasn't it, Marie? You okay?"

I nodded.

"And you, Tokita, good job, but next time limit yourself to one hour. One hour! That's all the time you should ever give anyone. More than that and you yourself start to go crazy."

"Yes. Okay." Tokita looked exhausted.

"Her problems are not unusual." Kaneta shook his head. "What a god-damned mess."

"I was thinking," I said, "she probably had some problems before the tsunami."

"Undoubtedly. Yes, yes," he nodded. "She comes from a very

good family. But now . . . there is no one." I had felt Maruyama's panic in the tiny, claustrophobic temporary house, and now as I tried to breathe deeply, I also recognized something in her madness: I saw my own grief and the way it had pervaded and unsettled my life for the past three years.

"Do you think maybe a counselor would help . . . ?"

"Everyone would benefit from counseling," Kaneta said, stopping suddenly. He wasn't smiling now. He looked somber. Sorrowful. I worried for a moment that he might cry. His voice dipped in pitch and sounded almost angry. "The best help would be psychological care, plus the kind of activities that I provide. All across Japan people have been suffering for a long time. A long time. And the tsunami has revealed our modern problems, and the limitations of how we now care for each other. This is what has happened to our country."

KANETA PRESSED ON the rest of the afternoon. He seemed to be everywhere all at once; I saw him in a corner with a widow, holding her around the shoulders and gripping her hand, then again with a group of men guffawing in Japanese-man style, and then instructing a group of children to behave and not to cause their mothers any trouble. He told me later that this was his first visit to this particular temporary housing community, and that the number of people who had come to see him had overwhelmed him. He also confided that after visits like the one today, he would be exhausted. He considered his work to be a kind of showmanship. He would not demonstrate anything but strength to the tsunami survivors. But at home, he said, he would sleep and sleep.

I will never forget one of the final things he said to me that day. "You know," he said, "the people who have it the worst are the people who aren't here in the temporary housing. The people I worry about most are the people who are far away, and who saw the tsunami on TV and feel scared, but aren't actually living among survivors. That is who is most afraid. And that is who is hardest to reach."

FOUR

WINTER DEMONS

THE TSUNAMI HIT AT the end of winter, the season that brings the great unknown. The Japanese learned from Chinese cosmologists to associate winter with death, the north, the color black, and the element of water.

You will be hard-pressed to find any hotel in Japan in which the head of the bed faces north. If you stay in a traditional hotel, called a *ryokan*, a maid will spread out your futon, but she will make sure your pillow does not point north. Only the dead are laid out with their heads to the north because this is the direction souls go when they die. There are exceptions, as there always are in Japan. My Japanese grandfather, a colorful but often very difficult character, liked to sleep with his head pointing to the north. He said it calmed him.

The Great East Japan Earthquake struck Tōhoku at 2:46 p.m. on March 11, 2011. At 3:12 p.m., twenty-two-foot-high waves hit the city of Kamaishi, killing over twelve hundred people. Monstrous waves barreled farther down the Tōhoku coast, killing nearly two thousand people in Rikuzentakata and over three thousand in Ishinomaki. The waves were black and composed of what the Japanese call the *hedoro*, the dark, smelly, dirty underbelly of the sea that normally lies dormant on the ocean floor. The last officially documented wave was fourteen feet high, and it struck Ōarai, about eighty-one miles northeast of Tōkyō, at 4:42 p.m. Here, only one person was killed. That evening, the sun set at 5:45, and the temperature in Tōhoku dropped below freezing over night. All told, more than eighteen thousand people died that afternoon and evening, most by drowning. Five days later, with much of Tōhoku still cut off from power, and numerous roads damaged, it snowed, further hampering rescue and recovery efforts.

MY MOTHER SAYS that as a child growing up in Japan, she always knew that winter had arrived because one day the kitchen door would begin to rattle. The winds had changed and now blew down from the north. She was born in 1943, about fifty miles southwest from the city of Nagoya, and was delivered by a midwife; all doctors were at the warfront. Though my mother was very young when the war ended, she still remembers the terror of running from American aircraft and hiding out in bomb shelters. A talented musician, she went to high school in Nagoya and college at Geidai, Japan's Julliard. Further studies took her to Vienna, where she met my American father in the standing-room section at the opera. They ultimately settled in California.

In spite of winter's cruelty, my mother remembers the start of winter with fondness. She liked raking the brightly colored leaves into piles. She and her brothers would set the piles on fire, then toss sweet potatoes into the flames. This was just after the war ended, when millions of Japanese starved to death. My mother and her family did not starve, but they worried about food. The sweet potatoes were a rare sweet treat. If they had enough sweet potatoes, they could take them to an *ameyasan*, a candy maker, and trade the potatoes for sugar and candy. But this didn't happen often. They had to ration their food carefully.

All winter my grandmother fretted about frostbite. My mother remembers losing feeling in her fingertips and color in her hands, which often turned white. My grandmother rubbed her children's fingers and toes to keep the circulation going. When my mother's fingers became itchy, usually in March, she knew then that winter was ending, and she would soon be warm again.

The crops were a more urgent matter than the cold. Winter would determine how my mother and her family would eat come spring, and they would wait out the dark time of the year and trust their future to the earth. In February, if the field of wheat they had planted had begun to sprout, they knew there would be food. All spring, they would watch the wheat grow. In the summer, they would harvest the crop by hand and then take the grain to a mill, which would turn the wheat to flour, for a fee. They then took the flour to an *udon-ya*, a noodle maker, who would turn the flour into noodles. But before all this happened, they needed to ensure that there would be as much flour as possible. And so the children stepped on all the seedlings in February to force the little green shoots to grow back stronger and with more heads. A little hardship—but only a little—makes wheat more productive. This is why stepping on seedlings was a child's job. Adults were too heavy and would kill the plants with their weight.

Because my mother and her family grew their own food—and foraged and bartered when necessary—they were able to survive the lean years after the war. My grandfather, a teacher, had not grown up knowing how to farm. My grandmother, born into an aristocratic family, had not known either. But they learned from other people, and so they were able to raise their three children to adulthood. Others did not fare so well. My mother remembers one family of five in particular: the father, a colleague of my grandfather's, felt that digging around in the dirt was beneath him. The entire family perished one winter.

There was not too much snow in my mother's hometown, located on Japan's Pacific side. My grandmother was from Nagasaki, very far to the southwest, where it rarely snowed. But in Tōhoku at the temple Empukuji, where my grandfather grew up, it was very cold. Temples in general are notoriously cold places because they tend to be old, and even today they rarely have central heating. People in Tōhoku often use something called a *kotatsu*, a thick blanket or futon fitted over a low table, with a heat source underneath. You sit on the floor with your legs under the blanket and sip tea. This is how you stay warm.

I got a sense of the hardship of winter in old Japan when I visited our family temple one February when I was around thirty years old. Throughout my stay, I wore a hat, heavy sweater, wool socks, and two pairs of pants, and still I shivered under the *kotatsu*. It is customary in Japan to bathe before going to bed, but I was so cold, the thought of going out into the unheated hallway and disrobing before I finally sat in warm water was too painful to bear. I said good night and ran from the *kotatsu* to my futon, and bathed in the morning.

It doesn't snow much at the temple. Most of the snow in Tōhoku accumulates in the mountains and on the Japan Sea side, which the Japanese call *yukiguni*, or snow country. When the wind blows the snow, the precipitation sticks to the trees, and the mummified conifers take on the look of monsters. Perhaps this is why Japanese folktales set in Tōhoku are full of stories of snow monsters and demons.

THE ANCIENT JAPANESE came up with numerous rites and rituals to appease the monsters of winter, in some cases trying to prove to themselves that what is harsh can also be entertaining. I think of this as the gift of stoicism. Likewise, my mother remembers the winters of her childhood fondly, even though it must have been a terrifying time for her entire family.

In February of 2003, my mother and I traveled to the Oga Peninsula, a tiny piece of land on the west side of Honshū, about 220 miles northwest of Tōkyō. The year we went, there was so much snow, the bullet trains had stopped running completely. Such a thing had never happened before. We had to take a bus from Morioka to Akita. It was pitch black outside, and the bus grunted up and down the mountain roads, with snow pummeling the windshield. All the passengers were silent. It was as though we were trying to help the driver concentrate. When we finally arrived safely to the town of Ōmagari, where the bullet train was again running, the snow was waist high in places that had not been shoveled. Here and there people had given up keeping the entrances to their homes clear, and they now exited or entered via a ladder propped up to the second floor.

The hotel we stayed in had a hot-spring bath. Japan's location right on the Pacific fault makes it prone to earthquakes, but this seismic activity also means that the country is awash with hot springs, which the Japanese call *onsen*. These hot springs are said to have great healing powers. In Japan, whole hospitals are set up alongside *onsen*, so patients can bathe daily as part of their therapy. A Japanese bath expert may even mix the waters of different hot springs so the bath contains a precise balance of minerals. The Japanese consider themselves *onsen* connoisseurs, and whole conversations can revolve around the very best bath one has ever experienced.

In some cases, as in one of my favorite spas in Kyōtō, Hanaikada, there is just one bath, the water having been mixed precisely so in a simple square tub, shaped like an enormous *masu*, the square-shaped cup used to drink sake. The deceptively simple experience is offered up with the finesse of a master who can do great things with just one gesture. You leave feeling that the very best, most refined part of your inner nature has been touched.

Other spas offer *onsen* as a form of entertainment, the way an amusement park or a cinema multiplex cuts across class and occupation. Stores sell regional treats and toys for children, and other rooms offer video games and karaoke machines. There is usually an assortment of baths—as many as a dozen pools. Some are hot, some are shallow, and some include water jets to help massage sore muscles.

Our spa on the Oga Peninsula was a happy medium between these two extremes. We stayed in a tatami mat–covered room and slept on futons. There was one large indoor pool and one outside in the snow. It was a wonderful thing to slog through waist-high snow and then end the day sitting in a warm bath, looking out at the snow country. The only danger with an outdoor *onsen*, called a *rotenburo*, is that a wild monkey might have beaten you to the waters, as these intelligent animals are known to warm their bodies on the coldest days by bathing.

The following evening, we dressed in snow boots and down coats and set out to see the Namahage, or the demon festival. The path to the shrine was lit by red lanterns, which glowed under blankets of snow. We climbed up a set of stairs, freshly swept, and toward the sound of drums. Up ahead, there was an old shrine made out of wood, where men were beating *taiko* drums on an elevated wooden stage. There was also a massive bonfire in the middle of the shrine grounds, which were rectangular in shape.

The drumming went on for a long time. The night grew darker and darker, and the shrine felt encased in a globe of light generated from the little red lanterns strung along the shrine's perimeter, and fueled by the bonfire. Beyond the protective bubble, the snow continued to fall, sticking to the tall conifers on the hills overhead. Within the bubble of light, the adults drank and ate, and the children ate too. It became darker and colder, and people drank to stay warm and stamped their feet and laughed nervously. All of a sudden, a light appeared up on the hillside. Everyone stopped to look.

The light was a torch, and it was coming down the hill. Another light bobbed behind the first.

One of the adults exclaimed, "It's the Namahage!" It was the demons.

One by one, the demons lumbered toward us. Their faces were red or blue, and they had exaggerated features, with wide, grimacing mouths, protruding teeth, angled eyes, and enormous, bulbous noses. They also had horns. Because demons are not civilized creatures, their hair was long and matted. They wore boots and capes made out of straw. They growled as they came down the hillside, shaking their axes and swords. The children were terrified and a few cried, which only made the adults laugh because they, too, remembered crying at the sight of the demons when they were young. "If you are good," they said, "the Namahage will not harm you. Remember to always be good."

The Namahage came down from the wilderness to the bonfire. The *taiko*-drum masters drummed so hard, the ground shook like a throbbing heart. The demons marched around in a circle, brandishing their torches. Incredibly, the demons seemed to recognize some of the children. They seemed to know which children were disobedient, and they were able to extract a promise from those children to listen to what their mothers told them to do.

When the dancing was over, some of the demons removed their heads. Or rather, their masks. The demons were actually members of Oga township who had volunteered to act as demons for the night. They handed out sesame seeds and rice cakes, foods that would bring good luck for the coming year if eaten. In the spirit of modern Japan, they happily posed for photos. One even lent me his mask to wear for a picture.

Oga is the most famous place to see Namahage, but as you travel through Tōhoku, you will see these demon masks decorating inns, restaurants, and museums, as they are a mark of the culture of this region of Japan. The original Namahage festival takes place on New Year's Eve and is just for the residents of Oga. Then the demons go from house to house, extracting a promise from children to behave in the year to come.

Nobody knows exactly how the Namahage tradition began. Some say that the demons in Namahage are an exaggerated representation of foreigners who crossed the Japan Sea from China. There is also a legend that the emperor of the Han dynasty came to Japan with five demons, who made off with the villagers' wives and children. Quick-thinking fishermen outwitted the demons, though, and now the Namahage festival carries traces of this mythological story.

IN TŌHOKU, MANY other famous snow festivals pay tribute to the power of winter. My mother and I have visited many together. One of the most famous of these festivals takes place in the little town of Yokote, which is about sixty miles southeast of Oga, in Akita Prefecture. Though winter there is cold and harsh, residents have long known that the snow is necessary for their rice crops and for their sake. And so they honor the sleeping water god deep in the riverbed, in the hope that he will wake up in the springtime refreshed and full of vigor.

In the middle of February, schoolchildren build igloos out of snow. These igloos, called *kamakura*, come in all sizes, with the largest ones big enough to house a tatami mat–covered floor and a table that can seat four. Each *kamakura* is lit with candles, and in the back there is a little altar to the river god. Children dressed in traditional clothing made of indigo-colored cloth sit in the large *kamakura*. They serve *amazake*, a warm, sweetened sake, and *mochi*, or rice cakes. My mother and I walked from igloo to igloo, and as we ate and drank, we became warmer and warmer.

In some places, children covered the fields with tiny igloos and placed a candle inside each one. At night, with a field of snow lit up like this, it felt as though we were being reminded that although it was cold, the earth still had a warm heart. Sometimes people placed the candles into the shape of letters and spelled out words like "Life," "Hope," "Luck."

FIVE

Spring Blossoms

In the spring of 2013, I was in a car driving up the Tōhoku coast with a Zen Buddhist priest whom I will call Taniyama. A friend of my temple family in Iwaki, Taniyama was genial and warm, with a seemingly permanent half smile on his face. We were on our way to see his temple, Ryūdaiji, located in Tomioka, in the nuclear exclusion zone. Physically Taniyama reminded me of a *tanuki*, the Japanese badger, in that he was stocky with a round body, round head, and squinty eyes. He did not move with the dart-like precision of the Zen priests I had met so far. Taniyama's gestures were smooth and contained, with a slightly depressed quality, though his alert eyes let me know that he was always watching everyone and taking everything in. I couldn't help but wonder if his prolonged absence from the temple had rendered him a little bored and sapped of energy, or if he had always been so mellow.

Taniyama laughed often about the situation in Fukushima. "What else can I do?" he asked, shrugging his shoulders as he sat slightly slouched in a chair while we drank coffee in a café near the apartment he rented with his wife. "Is this disaster not the most absurd thing you have ever seen? Come to my temple. I'll show you just how crazy the world has become."

Now we were driving north. Aside from the exposed foundations of homes that had been washed away by the tsunami, the scenery on our drive up the Tōhoku coast looked fairly normal. Two years after the catastrophe, most of the debris in the disaster plain had been removed, and any house that could be salvaged had been restored. People were out buying gas, delivering packages, and coming home from work. There were a few newly opened convenience stores, called *combini* in Japanese, that are recognizable across Tōhoku for their squat, rectangular prefab shape. "See," Taniyama said. "The fact that someone put a store there means that people have returned to this neighborhood. Someone is going to make a lot of money with that shop," he chuckled.

We passed the J-Village sports complex, built in 1997 as the training facility for the national Japanese soccer team and used to house soccer camps for children as part of an effort to raise the popularity of the sport in Japan. All of a sudden, every vehicle coming toward us from the opposite direction contained exhausted-looking men wearing pale-blue decontamination suits. Many rode in chauffeured buses, with their heads tilted back and eyes closed; they were too tired to drive their own cars after a day of work. I turned around and watched as the vehicles filed into the driveway of the J-Village sports arena, then disappeared, swallowed up by high fences and shrubbery.

"That's where they all stay," Taniyama said to me in a quiet voice. "No camera crews are allowed. Don't you think that's *strange*? Don't you think the government should show us *something*?" He laughed again, and I realized he was referring to the three thousand or so men who worked around the clock trying to stabilize the damaged nuclear power facility.

As we continued north on the coastal road, the scenery changed dramatically. The houses along the road were still damaged as though the earthquake had happened just days ago. The spines of tile-covered roofs were jagged and cracked, holes hastily covered over with heavy blue plastic tarp anchored in place with bricks. One two-story house on a hillside had been cleaved nearly in two, its halves clinging to each other by shards of wood in the floor and ceiling panels. We drove past house after house whose tattered, shoji rice-paper screens looked as though they had been violently slashed with scissors. Taniyama explained to me that rice paper is easily damaged when it is exposed to direct sunlight for extensive periods. The people in this part of Tōhoku had fled their homes in such a hurry, they had not closed the protective metal shutters used at night and in the early morning on the outside of their windows.

Taniyama carried a Geiger counter with him at all times. He delighted in how the numbers changed as we went up and down hills, or opened the car door or window. He couldn't see the radiation, but he had come to know its behavior the same way a hunter stalking an invisible prey has learned to read the snapping of branches and the rustle of feet on the forest floor. In Iwaki, the reading was respectably low at .1 millisievert. The farther north we went, the higher the number climbed. When the car went over a hill, taking us closer to Tomioka, it climbed to .3 millisievert, then settled back down to .2 millisievert. These numbers would rise higher and higher the farther north we went.

Taniyama no longer wore a radiation suit when he went to see his home. He explained to me that radiation now lingered only in the topsoil and had long ago fallen out of the air. He had one pair of shoes that he wore when walking around the grounds of his house. These were his exclusion-zone shoes. About forty minutes outside of Iwaki, Taniyama parked by an unassuming one-story building off to the left side of the road. He changed his shoes and asked me to follow him.

Inside the building were two middle-aged men behind a rectangular, collapsible table. Taniyama handed them his permit, which stated that he was a resident of Tomioka. While the men filled out some paperwork, Taniyama gossiped with them about friends they had in common and about the weeds growing in his garden. He continued to laugh lightly as he spoke, while one of the men solemnly handed me a hazmat suit.

The suit was made of light white fabric and was not the spacesuit I had come to expect from seeing disaster movies; one didn't just step into a second skin and zip it shut. My suit consisted of many parts, requiring proper assembly and tying. In its intricacy, the suit made me think of old Japanese armor.

First, I slid on a pair of white pants over my jeans. Then I pulled on a couple of what I can only describe as gauze leg-warmers elasticized at the top, around my shins, and at the ankle. I put blue booties over my feet and tied a pair of spatlike coverings over my ankles. Next, I put on a large white zip-up top, then rubber gloves and a shower cap. Finally, I put on a face mask. There was no mirror in the building. Taniyama took a picture of me with my iPhone so I could see what I looked like. Though tidy, the hazmat suit had turned me into the Michelin man. I said this out loud, and no one laughed.

"I'm sorry," I said. "It's an American habit to joke when we are nervous."

The men who had processed our paper work still did not laugh.

"I assure you this is *much* better than the Western suits they originally gave us," Taniyama said. "Those things were terrible." Then he laughed.

The men behind the desk shook their heads in agreement. "I never could get the hang of those things," one man said.

We got back in the car and continued to drive.

The town of Tomioka was largely unchanged since the disaster; windows were broken, roofs collapsed, toys abandoned. Only encroaching weeds and overgrown trees hinted at the passage of time. There was also a speaker, which repeatedly blared that all visitors had to have permission to enter the town and that they had to leave by three o'clock. The voice—a woman—reminded us not to light any matches or turn on the gas, as there was no water to put out any fires. Police cars drove up and down the main road to discourage looters. I had the out-of-body feeling that I was not visiting a town once inhabited by families, but was instead at a theme park riding a nightmare version of, say, the Disney boat ride It's a Small World, where overseers had the right to interrupt visitors when they reached out to touch the dolls on display in the artificial world.

There were also plenty of street signs that repeated the warning about radiation and the lack of water and electricity. Then I saw a few unusual signs, which read, "If you are here to see the cherry blossoms, please remain in your car. Look at the blossoms through the window."

I asked Taniyama for an explanation.

"Oh, that," he laughed. "There is a famous cherry-blossom tunnel in Tomioka. We used to drive through it every year. Some people still come."

The cherry blossom "tunnel" is created when a road is lined on both sides by trees in full bloom. One drives through this tunnel and marvels at the way the sunlight filters through the blossoms, as though the trees are some kind of pink-paper cathedral. On the right day, when the blossoms are in full bloom and the sun is bright, the effect is breathtaking.

"Will you go see the blossoms?" I asked.

"No," Taniyama said. "It's not the same if you can't open your window."

AH, THE CHERRY blossoms of Japan. In all the talk about the nuclear power plant, radiation, and evacuation, I had forgotten about something as simple as trees. How the Japanese love their trees, the cherry tree in particular.

For years I didn't really understand the fuss over cherry blossoms. I knew that *sakura*, the cherry blossom, was on the back of the one-hundred-yen coin, and that Zeami, the famed Noh theater playwright and critic, had compared the perfection of his craft to the beauty of the flower. But I honestly didn't understand why the *sakura*, above all other flowers, got such hype. Then, in April of 2006, my boyfriend and I spent three days with my friends Isao and Nono in Kyōtō. They'd been tracking the impending cherry-blossom explosion on the Internet, plotting itineraries and prime flower-viewing contingency plans with a fervor that initially bordered on fanaticism. Right before we arrived in Kyōtō, Isao sent me a text message: "*Mankai* [full bloom] expected this weekend. Perfect timing!" When they met us at the airport, Nono had a photo on his cell phone of the first blossoms opening up by their apartment complex.

In the morning, Isao prepared elaborate cherry blossom–themed *bentōs*, cutting rice balls into the shape of flowers and entwining our seafood with blossoms. We ate our *bentōs* under the canopy of cherry blossoms by the ruins of an old castle. Later, we went for a late-night walk. Our route—up a hill here, a turn to the right, down a slope, a turn right again—felt haphazard, as though we were stumbling through a maze and not purposely moving toward a clear destination. My boyfriend was tired and hungry, and we wanted to stop to eat, but we were urged to keep walking. It was dark, and men and women were already drunk in the parks and asleep under the trees. The weekend was coming. In the morning, friends would arrive with food and drink. It was the job of the most stalwart member of each party to choose a prime location for blossom viewing and to secure it by sleeping there.

Most of these campers were men; appreciating good food and drink under a cloud of flowers is not just women's work. In the dark, they drank, laughed, and rolled over on their blue tarps, the heavy plastic crackling under their weight. Occasionally an island of light punctured the darkness. Sometimes it would be a cluster of food stalls, selling grilled squid or octopus balls and ringed by red lanterns so the air took on a ruby hue. At one point on this dark walk, a massive, weeping cherry tree had been lit up from below by professional theater lighting designers. The bright-pink chandelier arms hanging down, trembled against the indigo night. It looked like some otherworldly creature, thrust up from the earth to dance in the breeze for us, displaying its flowers and occasionally sending stray petals into our hair. I forgot I was hungry. The adrenaline in my body began to flow.

We climbed up a hill in pitch darkness. The Japanese don't seem to fear lawsuits the way Americans do, and if a street must be dark to maintain atmosphere, then it is dark. We came across a mammoth vermillion *tori* gate, expertly lit up again, a bright, rectangular bulwark against the night sky, like a Rothko painting brought to life. Now we were on a dark set of stairs again, climbing even higher. We were heading to Kiyomizu, a famous Zen Buddhist temple set on a hillside and supported by 139 wooden pillars hewn from the trunks of the zelkova tree. The temple was founded in the eighth century, though its original structures were damaged many times due to earthquakes and fires. The current temple dates from the seventeenth century.

As we rounded the temple balcony, I saw a doorway ahead flanked by massive wooden pillars. Peeking through this, through the darkness, was a shocking bright-pink light. Cherry blossoms. Around me, the air felt electric. We passed through the doorway— through the portal—and were suddenly in another world. The temple seemed like a ship suspended on the waves of hundreds of pink flowers both above and below us. These illuminated cherry trees glowed like the strange, ethereal gases you see in photos of distant nebulae.

"Oh my god," my boyfriend and I said over and over again. This was one of the highest highs I have ever experienced. Here we were, floating on this alien ship, our spirits buoyed by the ecstatic energy of hundreds of other people, all equally awed and excited by the sight of something so singularly beautiful. Below us, the city of Kyōtō spread out and down into a basin, and then up into the hillsides on the horizon.

THE CHERRY TREES of Kyōtō are iconic, but they are not the only *sakura* in Japan. True cherry-blossom aficionados will watch the weather forecast closely beginning in January, to see when the blossoms will first open in Kyūshū, Japan's largest island to the south. They will take their cameras, and go and photograph these blossoms, then follow the wave of pink as it washes over all of Japan, finally cresting in Hokkaido some time in May.

When I was in Japan in 2013, the city of Sendai experienced a rare phenomenon when the cherry trees were not only in full bloom but also covered in snow. Photographers raced to snap pictures of the pale-pink beauties shivering in the cold.

"The poor blossoms," I said to my mother's cousin.

"No," he said. "The snow is good for the flowers. It means they will stay on the trees longer. Like they are in a refrigerator."

The adoration of the flower is a quintessentially Japanese trait. A taxi driver in Kyōtō once said to me, "People who love flowers are kind people." My mother, who was riding in the car with me, nodded vigorously; she understood this feeling implicitly. It's an attitude pretty much every Japanese I have ever met will agree with, for the Japanese obsession with the beauty of nature, and the drive to cultivate it, has its roots in Shintō, Japan's indigenous religion.

No one knows exactly how Shintō got its start. It most likely evolved over hundreds and perhaps thousands of years, as successive waves of immigration settled in the Japanese isles. Shintō is thus not the inspired teaching of a single person in possession of a vision who wrote down one sacred text, but a collection of practices with regional variation.

For the ancient Japanese, life was suffused with a marvelous power they called *kami*. I like to describe the *kami* as ancestor spirits, mythological creatures, gods, demons, the wind, unicorns, the Force—everything powerful but invisible—all wrapped into one. Sometimes a *kami* was felt especially strongly in a specific location: a tree, a rock, a waterfall. Occasionally, a human being could also house *kami*, since people are simply one part of the natural world. Over time, shrines were built on or near these locations to allow humans and *kami* to commune.

It is commonly accepted that there are about eight million gods and demons operating in Shintō at any one time. This is an awful lot of power, and if you consider that not all of the gods get along, and that some are in the air, and some under the earth, in the ocean, on the wind, and elsewhere, and that none are really good or bad, it makes for a land mine–laden spiritual terrain.

Shintō is the reason why, when Nissan first launched its Infiniti car, the advertising campaign included lots of shots of nature, without a single image of a car, a strategy that worked far better in Japan than in the United States. Shintō is the reason why, when you are walking through the woods in Japan, you might see a particular rock or waterfall marked off by a rope and piece of white rice paper, signaling that a god either lives there or once appeared there. Many gods fly in and out of shrines, the most famous of which is Ise, dedicated to Amaterasu, the sun goddess, and from whom the imperial family is said to be descended. But the gods of Japan can be sensitive, and if they are offended, they can cause humans harm.

To ward off this kind of offense, Shintō requires its practitioners to behave properly and to be as clean as possible. Shintō is why you remove your shoes before entering a home in Japan—to leave outside filth "outside." It is why once a year needles and scissors are blessed in Ueno, so the unruly scissor and needle gods do not cause their owners mischief by unnecessary cutting or poking.

The world is alive. If you listen to Japanese, it is full of onomatopoeia. A fire does not just burn; it burns *kachi kachi*. Ice is not crunchy; it is *kori kori*. Glue is not just sticky; it is *beto beto*. As my three-year-old son works his way through Japanese children's books, he is learning a predictable array of cultural manners and customs, but he is also learning more than this. Everything has a face and a sound. Each of the Japanese letters he learns has eyes and a mouth. In the book titled *Ā Ii Kimochi*, which I roughly translate as *Ah That Feels Nice*, by the Japanese children's author Gomi Tarō, the shade of a building has a face; in the summer, when it is hot, one is grateful for how good the shade feels and one can thank the shade as one thanks a person.

The animistic quality of Shintō is why videotape can be haunted, as it is in the horror classic *The Ring*. It's why the single most popular character among young children in Japan today is known as Anpanman, or "red bean bread man." Anpanman flies around the world feeding hungry children pieces of his head. When he runs out of power—when his head is nearly eaten—his caretakers, the baker Jam Ojisan (Uncle Jam) and Batakosan (Ms. Butter), simply bake him a new head. In his adventures against his mortal enemy, Baikin Man or Germ Man, Anpanman is assisted by, according to the *Guinness Book of World Records*, the largest cast of animated characters ever assembled. There is Hamburger Kid, whose eyes peer over a mustache of lettuce that is wedged between the two hamburger buns that form his head. There is Melonpannachan (Melon-Bread Girl), dressed all in green, and Shokupanman (White Bread Man), whose head is shaped like a perfect piece of toast. The Anpanman empire is vast: toys, books, four theme parks, a TV show, and restaurants serving, what else, bread with numerous faces and fillings.

The love of *things*, the belief that the world is alive, is in part what informs modern Japanese design, where things are sleekly, cleverly shaped, almost as though they are repositories for a soul.

UNLIKE THE OTHER Zen priests I had met so far, Taniyama was not born into a temple family. Instead he voluntarily entered Sōjiji monastery at the age of twenty-seven for reasons he found difficult to articulate, but which vaguely had to do with disliking corporate life and a yearning for a more spiritual existence. A few years into his studies at Sōjiji, a matchmaker introduced Taniyama to the woman who would be his wife. She was the oldest daughter of a temple family that had no male heir. She and Taniyama married and had a son, who went to Sōjiji himself. The son, whom I will call Ryūhei, had been scheduled to return home in the spring of 2011, but the March 11 disaster scuttled his plans, and he elected to stay behind at Sōjiji to further his knowledge of Buddhism.

As we drove through Tomioka to Ryūdaiji, Taniyama recalled the days after the earthquake. Not twenty-four hours after the tsunami, Tomioka was ordered to evacuate via a siren and prerecorded voice instructions. The Taniyamas dutifully left their temple behind and went to Iwaki. In the moments when they were able to get a phone to work, Taniyama tried to track down all his parishioners, to see if they were safe or needed help. Taniyama's father-in-law went back and forth from Iwaki to Tomioka, checking on the property; he was in his eighties and didn't see how radiation exposure could harm him.

Eventually the Taniyamas realized they were going to be gone from their home for a long time, and they settled into an apartment in Iwaki, paid for by the government. His wife found work as a calligraphy instructor to children. TEPCO, the energy company that owned and ran Fukushima Daiichi, authored a thirty-page booklet full of legalese on what and how it planned to compensate displaced residents. Taniyama's father-in-law became a community leader among other Zen priests, translating the document into layman's talk.

Now the Taniyamas were planning for a future that might not include their beloved temple. They still went home to set mouse-traps, as there were few cats left in Tomioka; most cats, he told me, had been either rescued or removed. Their son was in his fifth year at Sōjiji and would stay there, while Taniyama attempted to build what is called a *betsuin*, or "temple annex," a small structure where memorial services could be held in Iwaki. It would be more difficult for Taniyama's son to attract a wife if he inherited a temple within the radiation zone.

I had the chance to briefly meet Taniyama's son a few weeks later. Physically he resembled his father in that he, too, had a round head and stocky body. But where Taniyama had a lackadaisical quality, Ryūhei was taut and poised, as though ready to spring into action. He told me how grateful he was to have his family and how much he admired his grandfather, who was working so hard on behalf of so many other people to hold TEPCO accountable. He was grateful to his parents for trying so hard to make his future safe, and he hoped, when he inherited Ryūdaiji, that he could contribute to the restoration of Tōhoku's spirit.

Taniyama and I drove down the main street of Tomioka, then turned left up a steep hill into the temple's parking lot. Taniyama asked me to wait while he opened the temple from the inside. I stepped out of the car, swaddled in my hazmat suit, and looked up at the large, black temple perched on the hillside like an abandoned ship.

Though my family's temple was founded five hundred years ago, the physical structure has been rebuilt an estimated three times; now Sempō was overseeing yet a fourth reconstruction. But Ryūdaiji was that rare and wondrous structure, an actual four-hundred-year-old temple, undestroyed by history. It was beautiful. The proud eaves of the roof flexed in the signature swoop that distinguishes Buddhist temples in Japan from any other kind of building. It was raised up off the ground so it seemed to crouch there like a dragon about to take flight. From the outside, the damage appeared slight: just a few cracked tiles. After a moment, Taniyama slid open heavy wooden doors and asked me to climb up the stairs and enter. "No point taking off your shoes," he said. I walked onto the tatami floor.

In most parts of Japan, February 15 is celebrated as Buddha's death date. Temples unveil statues of the Buddha reclining on his side; this is the final position the Buddha took before his soul became a part of nirvana.

On March 11, 2011, Taniyama still had his reclining Buddha statue out on the main altar, but the earthquake had unceremoniously dumped the gold figure onto the floor, where it still lay upside down, gouging the tatami. Candles, bronze bowls and bells, and other Buddhist implements lay scattered on the floor. Numerous other statues had fallen over, tearing the paper walls. In the room where Taniyama housed the remains of his parishioners who had elected not to pay for an actual burial plot, hundreds of urns and their nameplates had been scattered across the floor. Two years of rain and disuse meant that mushrooms were now growing in through the tatami matting. "See, look," Taniyama laughed lightly again. "Where there is a hole in the roof or in the floor, the radiation level goes up!" The Geiger counter cackled earnestly, and the number rose from two millisieverts to four.

The earthquake had also disturbed many tombstones in the graveyard nestled around the perimeter of the main temple. Japanese tombstones are usually made of granite or marble and can consist of numerous parts: a stone "box," a base, and then a plinth inscribed with the names of the deceased. Many of these plinths had fallen over. Here and there were small bouquets of flowers and unburned bundles of incense. Most likely parishioners had come to visit the cemetery during Ohigan, the biannual Buddhist holiday that falls on the vernal and autumnal equinoxes, when the barrier between the living and the dead thins and the ancestors are said to come home for a visit.

A garden still retained its general shape: azaleas, stone lanterns, and maple trees. But vines crawled across the gravel driveway, threatening to turn the grounds into a Sleeping Beauty–like place of slumber. Taniyama took me to see a giant iron bell hanging in a wooden-framed tower. "This bell," he said, "is the largest in Fukushima Prefecture. For some reason, the earthquake didn't hurt it at all." He gave the bell a big thwack, and the sound reverberated through the trees. "There's no one here to hear us," he laughed. "Just the birds. Imagine that! No one for miles!"

After about twenty minutes we decided to go back to Iwaki. Out the car window I saw fields and fields of large black bags being stacked by cranes. "Radioactive topsoil," Taniyama explained to me. "There's so much, no one knows where to put it all." After a moment he added, "There are a lot of cows in those bags. They were slaughtered, but because of radiation, no one knows what to do with the carcasses."

Regulations required us to visit a checkpoint before we left the exclusion zone. Two young men wearily waved fluorescent-orange batons to usher us into the parking lot of the Number Two Fukushima Daiichi Nuclear Power Reactor. Taniyama stopped to chat with one of the men, a local he recognized from town. Then as we continued on our way, Taniyama said, "He makes a hundred dollars a day waving that baton around. We are a poor town, you see. That's why everyone foolishly thought that the nuclear reactor would be a good thing to build. It was supposed to give us jobs."

Taniyama drove the car inside a mammoth white tent hunched over a broad stretch of smooth concrete, wide enough for half-a-dozen semis parked end to end. All around, signs instructed me not to take any photos. Men wearing decontamination suits waved us forward. Their eyes widened with surprise when they saw my foreign face, but Taniyama put them at ease. "Just showing my friend here what my temple used to look like," he smiled. I sat in the car while a man scanned my feet. Only after I received an all-clear signal did I peel the suit piece by piece from my body and dump it in the garbage. We bowed, then drove back out to the highway.

There was a young field of rice just on the edge of the exclusion zone. Scientists were experimenting to see just how much radiation would taint a new crop. Plants, of course, do not know any better than to come up in the spring, even under a cloud of radiation. If the rice turned out to contain manageable levels of radiation, then perhaps the farmers could once again harvest rice.

"It's just this much dirt," Taniyama said to me, holding his fingers apart by five inches. "If we could just remove that little bit everywhere. Life could return to normal."

"You want to go back," I said.

"My wife grew up there. So did my son."

"Aren't you worried?"

He shrugged. "Nothing terrible has happened to any of us. We haven't gotten sick. I don't see why they couldn't let people past a certain age go home." Taniyama had laughed throughout our conversations that afternoon, in the slightly hysterical manner of someone dissociating from a tragic event. But now I watched a deep weariness cross his face. "I will spend my life restoring that temple. I want *you* to come back and see it the way it is supposed to be."

I promised him that I would.

SIX

Buddha on the Archipelago

A History in Five Lessons

Practically the first thing anyone learns about Buddhism is what is known as the first Noble Truth: life is full of suffering. For many years I had tremendous difficulty accepting this first principle. In a journal I kept at age seventeen, I recorded a conversation I had with Sempō. I told him that I objected to Buddhism because of the first Noble Truth.

"If you say that life is full of suffering, then you're just making yourself suffer." I asked, "Isn't that a self-fulfilling prophecy?"

Sempō listened to me calmly as I confidently laid out my defense of stoicism and the importance of having a good attitude. Then he said, "It is wonderful that you feel this way. But some day, when you are older, you may see things differently. And then you will understand why Oshakasama [the historical Buddha] said what he said."

By the time I had reached forty, the message was very clear.

I. BUDDHA

The story of Buddhism begins around 500 BC, when the prince Siddharta Gautama was born in an area located today in Nepal. At that time, Nepal and neighboring India already had a rich religious tradition, today called Hinduism. Certain key ideas that we associated with Buddhism—rebirth, karma, and meditation—were already practiced and revered by the ancient Hindus.

According to legend, a blind seer prophesized at Siddharta's birth that the baby would be either a great king or a great religious leader. Siddharta's father, preferring the former fate for his son, vowed to keep the boy safe within the walls of the palace. But at the age of twenty-nine, Siddharta ventured outside his cloistered environment. On his travels, he was shocked to encounter a sick man, an elderly man, and a corpse. These experiences revealed to Siddharta that it would be his fate—and the fate of his wife and newborn son—to age and die in the same fashion as everyone else. The revelation shook him greatly.

Siddharta wasn't the only person of his time to be upset by the terror and horror of living. Other men plagued by the same discovery sought liberation from the endless cycle of rebirth and death in which the Hindus believed. These men believed that ascetic practices like starvation, homelessness, and self-flagellation held the key to freedom. Siddharta followed suit, abandoning his family and fleeing into the mountains to find enlightenment.

His early methods were extreme. He starved himself, he refused to sleep, and he cut and burned his skin. Six years later and on the brink of death, Siddharta accepted a bowl of rice and milk from a young woman named Sujata. The food revived Siddharta, and he realized that nothing was possible unless his body was sufficiently nourished. He decided from then on not to harm himself, but to seek a "middle path." He went into meditation under a Bodhi tree. Forty-nine days later, he awoke, enlightened and in possession of the Four Noble Truths and the steps necessary to escape the endless cycle of painful death and rebirth. Siddharta Gautama, now known as the Buddha, or "the awakened one," would spend the rest of his life communicating his insights to as many people as possible, until his death around 483 BC. Mastering the Four Noble Truths would set a person free from suffering, and let a soul migrate to nirvana, a permanently enlightened state. These teachings are the basis for all forms of Buddhism.

The first Noble Truth declares that life is full of suffering. This is followed by the second Noble Truth, which asks followers to acknowledge that suffering is brought about by human attachment. Most people are familiar with the idea of being excessively attached to material goods, but emotions can cause attachment too. In my case, I had been struggling for quite some time with the notion that the Japan of my childhood—the one with my grandparents and my great-aunt, and my young and healthy mother—was already fading when the tsunami struck. What I wanted then, and even now, in my childish way, was to have all of these things back.

These first two steps lead to the third Noble Truth: we can rid ourselves of suffering if we rid ourselves of attachment. Finally, we arrive at the fourth Noble Truth: to end suffering and to cease attachment, one must live correctly, by following the Eightfold Path. In English, these specific steps are called right view, right intention, right speech, right action, right livelihood, right effort, right mindfulness, and right concentration.

In the millennia after the Buddha died, the Four Noble Truths and the Eightfold Path inspired kings and paupers—and prompted many others to ask questions. For example, when the Buddha spoke of entering nirvana, did he mean that all one had to look forward to was nothingness? Should the individual care only about his own enlightenment, or was it important that everyone reached nirvana?

Part of Buddhism's power resides in the concept that attachments—the material, physical, and temporal ones we crave, in addition to the very act and feeling of desire—are all illusory. The world doesn't really have a beginning or an end. And so, when Siddharta Gautama transcended our mundane existence and entered into nirvana, he went into a place that had always been there. But if nirvana has always existed, surely there must be other entities who had also become enlightened in the past. According to Siddharta Gautama, there were precisely twenty-seven beings who preceded him, bringing the total number of Buddhas in the world to twenty-eight. But, said some, if time and space were infinite, shouldn't there be an infinite number of such enlightened beings?

Questions such as these eventually prompted Buddhism to divide into numerous schools. The main divide occurred between what are known as the Theravāda and the Mahayana school. The older version of Buddhism, Theravāda, or Hinayana in Japanese, is now found in Sri Lanka, Cambodia, Thailand, and many other Southeast Asian countries, and it emphasizes the hard work of the individual in reaching nirvana. For followers of the Theravāda school, the Buddha is a great teacher. One strives to be like the Buddha, engaging in the ascetic tradition of living separately from the outside world and attempting to transcend the mundane. Theravāda followers believe in the historical Buddha, and in the presence of twenty-seven Buddhas who preceded him. They also believe in Maitreya, the Buddha of the future.

But the school of thought that ultimately took root in Japan was the newer Mahayana school. We don't know precisely when or how Mahayana developed, though its oldest texts date from five hundred years after the Buddha died. The Mahayanists revere the historical Buddha for what he accomplished and what he revealed, but they believe in the concept of infinite Buddhas, and their temples are often filled with statues of various figures aside from the historical Buddha.

Mahayanists are also taken with the idea of helping others to gain enlightenment. What is the point, they say, of entering nirvana on your own if other people around you are still suffering? Wouldn't a truly compassionate person who is capable of being a Buddha nonetheless remain behind to help others in need? Well, yes, religious scholars said. They gave this compassionate person a name: the bodhisattva. The figure of Jizō, which Kaneta encourages tsunami survivors to make out of clay, is one such bodhisattva, a kind and loving being who stays behind on earth, determined to free humans from their mortal coils.

II. BECOMING JAPAN

The history of Buddhism in Japan is deeply intertwined with the development of Japan as a country. Up until the sixth century, Japan was a kind of wild, wild east, here and there settled by immigrants from Korea and China and mostly inhabited by loosely affiliated tribes of uncertain geographic origin. Because Japan didn't exist as a unified country, it did not start writing its own official history until the sixth century, over a thousand years after Buddhism was born. This means that the earliest accounts of Japan come from the remarkable Chinese historians who had been documenting their own history, and the world around them, as far back as three thousand years.

For centuries, Japan, as seen by China, was one of the "Eastern barbarian countries," known specifically as "Wo" or "Wa," and inhabited by many tribes who were often at war with each other. In 297 AD, a document known as the "History of the Kingdom of Wei" presents the first eyewitness, physical description of early Japanese. The people of Wa are described as short, with a penchant for bowing and clapping their hands at shrines and a preoccupation with ritual purification and bathing. The Chinese also noted that the residents of Wa loved to drink liquor and eat seafood, which is certainly something you can say about Japanese hanging out in an *izakaya* in the middle of modern-day Tōkyō.

In this same document, the Chinese recorded that a queen named Himiko was chosen to rule over the land of Wa, after its many tribes spent years engaged in warfare. Scholars and feminists find the story of Himiko intriguing because it suggests that long after the rest of Asia had undergone by transformation from matri-archy to patriarchy—a process expedited in China and Korea due to the early adoption of patriarchal Confucianism—women in ancient Japan could still hold significant leadership roles. Indeed, Japan's early history is filled with empresses before the men completely take over.

Up until the sixth century, "Wa" is written with the following Chinese character: 倭. Like all Chinese characters, "Wa," or 倭, can be thought of as a picture. To the left, the figure 亻 represents a person standing upright. Then we have the two shapes on the right. The top piece, 禾, represents a grain of rice, with a head bowing over from its stalk. Beneath this is 女, or woman. Together, a "grain of rice" and "a woman" are meant to conjure a picture of a woman bending over her work in a field of rice. Put all these pieces together, and the character 倭 or "Wa," means "bent over" or "submissive" or "docile."

Here is a further description of Wa, also taken from "History of the Kingdom of Wei": "Over one thousand li to the east of the Queen's [Himiko's] land, there are more countries of the same race as the people of Wa. To the south, also there is the island of the dwarfs where the people are three or four feet tall. This is over four thousand li distance from the Queen's land. Then there is the land of the naked men, as well as of the black-teethed people. These places can be reached by boat if one travels southeast for a year." There is no doubt in these passages who represents the advanced, civilized country and who are the somewhat amusing and backward people.

In the seventh century, the Japanese began to compile an "official history," the Nihon shoki, completed in 720 AD. It is believed that large parts of the Nihon shoki preserved stories that had been previously passed on by storytellers. But the Nihon shoki is most certainly a partly fabricated work, written to give the impression that Japan had a long and legitimate history, like the much admired, if also feared, China. For example, the Nihon shoki claims that Japan's first emperor was Jimmu, who ruled circa 660 BC and from whom the current emperor is said to be descended. This picture of a peaceful Japan under the continuous rule of one imperial family does not match the picture painted by Chinese scholars of an island nation inhabited by dwarves with blackened teeth and made up of clans who frequently fought with each other.

Scholars today believe that ancient Japan—or Wa—was in fact inhabited by numerous clans, just as the Chinese historians say. Over time, a few families gained prominence. Ultimately, the Yamato became the most powerful clan. If the name "Yamato" sounds familiar to you, it should; Japan's imperial family is descended from the old Yamato clan, making it the oldest royal household still in existence. Today, court officials help to maintain the fiction that Yamato was always in charge of Japan, though the truth is that by 500 AD, when Buddhism arrived, Yamato had the upper hand but wasn't the exclusive power. Japan was not yet a unified country.

THE GREAT CHINESE emperor Ch'in Shih Huang Ti (221 to 210 BC) is famous for building the Great Wall of China. This massive structure would be destroyed and rebuilt numerous times over the ensuing centuries, but enough of it was rebuilt and repaired in the centuries after Ch'in Shih Huang Ti's reign to ensure that the flow of immigration on the mainland was to the east, toward Japan, and not the west, toward China. By the sixth century AD, Japan and Korea were engaged in frequent cultural exchanges. Korean artisans who'd mastered many of China's sophisticated technologies, like architecture and metalwork, were often brought to Japan, where their skills were prized. There is also evidence that Japan's elite clans were full of Koreans who came perhaps to enjoy the freedom of the "wild east," or perhaps to help ensure the fealty of the powerful Japanese clans, should the Korean kingdoms require aid in the event of a war with China, or with each other. Indeed, in 660 AD, the Korean kingdom Paekche fought with its neighbor Silla, who was aided by T'ang China. Though the Japanese navy was dispatched to aid Paekche, Silla prevailed. History tells us that many royal members of the Paekche family forever abandoned their homeland to live in Japan.

III. THE STATUE

In either 538 or 552 AD—historians still disagree—an envoy of monks, priests, and artisans from the kingdom of neighboring Paekche arrived in Yamato (now not only the name of the clan but also the area it controlled) bearing a bronze statue of the Buddha whose surface was covered with gold. While we don't know the specific location of the Yamato court on this date, we do know it was somewhere near modern-day Nara, which is nineteen miles east of present-day Ōsaka. The Buddha and the envoy were presented to the head of the Yamato clan, King Kimmei, who ruled from 539 to 571 AD. Two other clans were also powerful and influential in Kimmei's court: the liberal Soga and the conservative Mononobe.

The statue of the Buddha came with a tantalizing inscription by the king of Paekche: "This doctrine is amongst all doctrines the most excellent, but it is hard to explain and hard to comprehend. Even the Duke of Chou and Confucius could not attain a knowledge of it. This doctrine can create religious merit and retribution without measure and without bounds, and so lead on to a full appreciation of the highest wisdom. Imagine a man in possession of treasures to his heart's content, so that he might satisfy all his wishes in proportion as he used them."

What happened next tells us a great deal about the Japanese. The open-minded Soga, many of whom were of Korean descent, were fascinated by the Buddha. The clan's main leader, Umako, seems to have believed that Buddhism, with its hierarchical system of reverence, had the possibility of uniting the clans of Wa to create a unified kingdom like Paekche, or even China. Such a vision would have been tantalizing to the educated men of Wa, who were aware of just how powerful the Chinese Sui dynasty had become.

Prior to the arrival of the serene and gilded Buddhist figure, it's likely that no one in Japan had ever seen such a statue. On a recent visit to Tōkyō, I stopped by the Tōkyō National Museum, where numerous versions of Buddhas like this one are housed; the fate of the original is not known to history. Over time, the gold color of these statues has tarnished, but there is one piece, a replica, that demonstrates just how shiny the statue would have been. Even in the sleep-inducing, patina-preserving dark lighting of the museum, this statue is blindingly bright. It was impossible for me not to look at it and think of the power gold once had over the ancient world, before modernity festooned whole buildings with images made out of neon light.

Not everyone was happy with the statue of the Buddha, or with the introduction of Buddhism to the Japanese isles. The Soga's chief rivals, the Mononobe clan, made their displeasure clear. Mononobe leaders did not want this new religion in their land, when there was already a perfectly good religious system in place. Many members of the Mononobe were priests of this older form of religion, which we know today as Shintō, the nature-based religion. King Kimmei finally allowed the Soga to build a temple for the little Buddhist statue. The Nihon shoki, the officially recorded history of Japan, tells us that the ensuing years were a struggle for the little Buddha; it was thrown into the Naniwa river not once but twice, while its temple was burned, rebuilt, and then burned again. Buddhism's future in Japan looked uncertain.

IN 585 AD, a Soga emperor, Yōmei, took the Yamato throne and declared himself a Buddhist. But Emperor Yōmei died less than two years later, the casualty of a smallpox epidemic that raged through the Yamato plain. The Mononobe claimed that Yōmei's acceptance of Buddhism had angered the native gods, and that the fatal illness was his punishment. Shintō, remember, stresses the importance of "purity" and cleanliness. Some historians have wondered if in fact the Mononobe clan poisoned Yōmei. Whatever the cause of death, the stage was set for one final battle between the two impassioned families.

The Mononobe and Soga clans are said to have fought on the banks of the Ekagawa river, in the eastern part of modern-day Ōsaka. The clash was brief, and it decimated the Mononobe almost completely. In the account of the skirmish between the Soga and the Mononobe, the Nihon shoki does something quintessentially Japanese: it celebrates the Mononobe clan member Yorozu, his sense of duty, his loyalty to the emperor, and his warrior spirit, even though there is no doubt that Yorozu was on the wrong side of history. "The guardsmen raced up and shot at Yorozu, but he warded off the flying shafts, and slew more than thirty men. Then he took the sword, flung it into the midst of the water of the river. With a dagger which he had besides, he stabbed himself in the throat, and died." Such beauty in the face of tragedy, such steadfastness, would be the trademark of the Japanese warrior, even centuries later. It is a hallmark of the Japanese to have compassion not only for their own vanquished warriors, but also for anyone who gives everything he has in the face of insurmountable odds.

IV. THE LAND OF THE RISING SUN

In 592, Emperor Yōmei's sister Suiko became empress. She appointed Yōmei's second son, Prince Shōtoku, as her regent. Their long partnership, lasting until Shōtoku's death thirty years later, would mark a period of stability and set the stage for Japan's cultural maturation, when the land of Wa would turn into Japan, land of the rising sun.

Prince Shōtoku is one of those historical figures like George Washington and Queen Elizabeth I, someone who is so romanticized and inspires such passion that it can be difficult sometimes to separate fact from fiction. Among the more outlandish claims: Shōtoku was born in the doorway of a stable (a reference to Christ's birth in the manger and a signal of Shōtoku's historical importance); he was born speaking in complete sentences; he never made a single judgment in error. There is also a more plausible accomplishment, which we can partly confirm with documents: under Shōtoku, and starting in the T'ang dynasty of China (618–907 AD), Japan took on a new name.

In lieu of 倭, the land of the submissive dwarves, Shōtoku used the character 和 for peace, which phonetically sounds the same as 倭, but he went even further. In 607, the Chinese reported that an envoy from Empress Suiko arrived and addressed China as the land "where the sun sets" and Japan as the country "where the sun rises." More specifically: "The Son of Heaven in the land where the sun rises addresses a letter to the Son of Heaven in the land where the sun sets. We hope you are in good health." History tells us that such self-confidence displeased the Sui emperor, who berated the messenger. Over time, however, Japan's reference to itself as the land of the rising sun—it was east of China after all—would be written as 日本, pronounced either "Nihon" or "Nippon" in Japanese.

Prince Shōtoku is also credited with writing and introducing the Seventeen-Article Constitution, which emphasized the moral code that all courtiers were to follow and which made clear that the emperor was the supreme ruler of Japan. He instituted a court ranking system, based on merit, in which officials wore different-colored caps to indicate their status: purple being the highest and black the lowest. The constitution included the declaration that all Japanese should revere the three treasures: the Buddha, his teaching (dharma), and the Buddhist community (sangha). Here we have the clearest, most explicit statement that Buddhism was now the state religion of Japan.

However, in a move that continues to resonate in Japan today, Prince Shōtoku did not eradicate Shintō. In 607, he issued the following edict in the name of Empress Suiko: "Now in our reign, how can one give up the respect and prayers to the *kamis* [native gods] in the Pure Land and on the earth? Hence, all of my attendants should make up their minds to rightly worship the *kamis* in the Pure Land and the kamis on the earth."

The Buddha did not stress belief only in himself as a god; his teachings emphasize a method to escape the pain of existence. And as a result, there is nothing that truly prevents the Japanese from following the Buddhist sect of their choosing while also celebrating the gods associated with their local Shintō shrine. Though there have been tensions throughout history, for the most part the eight million gods and demons of the Shintō pantheon have comfortably shared the sacred space in Japan occupied by the Buddha and his many attendants.

V. ZEN

Japan was forever changed by Buddhism, but Buddhism was also transformed by Japan. Following Prince Shōtoku's lead, generations of emperors built temple after temple, the construction sites reaching out farther and farther from the capital, in a bid to help unify Japan and consolidate the Yamato clan's power. Some temples grew powerful and wealthy and became concentrated centers of learning where the young challenged the old, and Buddhism, as a discipline, developed in complexity.

In the thirteenth century, a boy was born to a low-ranking noble family. His name was Dōgen. Both of his parents died when he was young, but the death of his mother when he was seven particularly affected him. Relatives then took him in and saw to his education. At twelve, Dōgen went to the monastery on Mount Hiei, located today about twenty miles from Ōsaka.

In time, Dōgen started to wonder, If the Buddha claimed that all humans were born with a bodhisattva nature, then why did people have to memorize sutras or answer koans? At that time, these were among the many methods monks used to try to become enlightened. Why, in fact, did anyone have to struggle to become enlightened in the first place? Dōgen also seems to have been frustrated by the bureaucracy on Mount Hiei, which controlled a monk's advancement, often favoring connections over merit. Dissatisfied by the responses he received from his elders, Dōgen ultimately went to China in search of answers. Eventually he met with a monk named Tiāntóng Rújing, who taught him the form of Buddhism we know of today as Sōtō Zen. Like Dōgen, Rūjing too deplored the excesses of the most corrupt temples, claiming that all one had to do to be a Buddhist was to "cast off the mind and the body." And the best way to do this, said Rūjing, was to meditate.

Dōgen returned with this newfound insight into Buddhism and began to teach it to other monks. His following grew, and in 1244 he founded the great monastery of Eiheiji. Though his life continued to be marked by political struggles with priests on Mount Hiei and at court, Dōgen was able to build a formidable following and to leave behind numerous writings. A typical Dōgen saying includes this line: "To practice the Way single heartedly is, in itself, enlightenment. There is no gap between practice and enlightenment and daily life." This stripped-down Buddhist aesthetic pervades all aspects of Sōtō Zen. Most Sōtō Zen temples eschew the fantastic sculptures of bodhisattvas with their jewelry and fluttering robes. Instead, Zen emphasizes rock gardens, green-tea caffeine-infused meditation, and single-mindedness.

Japan's fierce and self-effacing medieval warriors often became followers of Zen. As these soldiers helped to expand Japan's boundaries farther and farther to the northeast, they took their love of Zen with them. The practical, rugged nature of Zen became extremely popular with the residents of Tōhoku, where it remains a majority religion even today.

SEVEN

SITTING TOGETHER

TWO TEMPLES ADMINISTER THE bureaucracy that governs Sōtō Zen in Japan today: Eiheiji and Sōjiji. The latter is located in Tsurumi, a neighborhood on the outskirts of the City of Yokohama. The unpretentious Tsurumi train station is flanked by a liquor store, a discount clothing shop, and a McDonald's; you would not know that one of Japan's great centers of religious training is a few minutes' walk away. But not too far in the distance, you can see a cluster of evergreen trees on a gently rising hill. Walk a few steps up this hill, and you can make out the eaves of a temple roof jutting out between the branches of the trees.

There are twelve structures at Sōjiji. Each is mammoth, with powerful, swooping rooflines that occupy much of the sky, like a flock of bold ravens stretching their wings. Japanese temples project an atmosphere of tense grandeur that I haven't experienced in the stone churches and cathedrals of Europe, with their spires and domes. In a Japanese temple, it's as if the roof itself, with its flexing and stretching, is asking you to remember to stand up straight.

At Sōjiji, visitors are received inside a thirty-foot-tall building that was completed in 1990. It was raining the day I visited for the first time, and I was relieved to enter the cavernous space, even though it was cold inside. I dropped my umbrella in a rack just inside the door (in Japan, there is always a designated place for wet umbrellas), placed my shoes in a locker, and put on a pair of slippers, picked from a pile of slippers stacked by the landing and intended for all visitors to wear; in Japan, one often changes out of street shoes and into slippers when entering a building. At the far end of the room, I saw statues and candles on an altar. The entire area smelled thoroughly of incense. To the right, young monks dressed in black manned an office. Everyone was trim. Some sat at desks answering phones, while others pored over paper work, or stood in little groups engaged in earnest conversation. It looked like the deck of a battleship, staffed by Buddhist priests.

A few minutes later, a young priest named Shiba presented himself as my guide. His head was shaved, and he wore the hallmark dark silk robes of a monk. He also had on a pair of black-rimmed glasses, which made him seem serious yet fashionably modern. Shiba was in his mid-twenties and at Sōjiji for his second year. He had been a math teacher for children aged five to eleven, before he commenced his training so he could take over his father's temple in Chiba Prefecture. I would see Shiba often when I visited Sōjiji.

Like Sempō and Takahagi, Shiba had mastered his monks' robes. The silk billowed about his form as he walked, but he did not fight the excess fabric in the sleeves or in the hemline. Shiba had long fingers, with which he deftly extracted personal effects from the front slit of his robe and just as quickly tucked them away. There was an economy of motion to his every gesture, as though he had long ago learned to do away with expending any excess energy.

As we walked the length of a long, roofed corridor that connected the visitor building to Sōjiji's inner complex, Shiba began his spiel, talking at a business-like clip as if he were a young corporate employee speaking during a PowerPoint presentation. This corridor had been made intentionally long—108 meters, or approximately 118 yards—to separate all the buildings from each other, so a fire could not consume everything all at once, as had happened to the original Sōjiji structures. But, he said, the hallway was also there as a training device, for every day the youngest monks polished the gleaming, chocolate-brown wood; Zen places a premium on physical activity as the gateway to disciplining the mind.

Shiba and his fellow monks rose each morning at three o'clock. They bathed in silence and then immediately went to Zen meditation, which was followed by sutra chanting in the *hondō* (the main hall of worship). After this, they cooked and ate breakfast—before going on to gardening, cleaning, and other chores. They ate very little. Most monks lost anywhere from ten to twenty kilos (about twenty-two to forty-four pounds) in their first two months of training. They were not allowed to leave the campus and were not allowed relaxed moments for chitchat or email. As Shiba talked, he referred to the day he would depart Sōjiji as the day that he would *oriru*, or "come down." One did not graduate, or quit, or leave. One came down off the mountain and returned to the mundane world.

We rounded a corner and stood before the Sōdo hall, the meditation chamber. A low, elevated platform covered with tatami ran the perimeter of the room. At the front of the platform was an apron of wood. Taut, round black pillows had been placed at regular intervals on the tatami. These were the *zafu* meditation pillows, sometimes referred to as *ozafu*, or "honored meditation pillows." Shiba told me that the actual monks' training quarters resembled this public meditation room, and that the wooden portion of the ledge functioned as a table. "Try never to touch this ledge," he said, "as this is the place where I and the other monks eat." Very quietly, a second young monk materialized from a doorway. "Would you like to try to meditate?" Shiba asked me.

From Shiba, I learned that there was a way to walk, a way to remove my slippers, and a way to place my slippers on the floor. I was to use the *ozafu*, and there was a way to position this too. As Shiba guided me through the minutiae of steps, the other priest stood by a gong in the doorway. Something about this other priest's expression unnerved me; he did not smile. I feared that this second priest had been summoned to administer the *kyōsaku*, the bamboo stick that priests use to whack meditators who fall asleep or fail to hold their position properly.

I pulled myself up onto the tatami ledge—doing my best not to make contact with the wooden part—and sat on the hard, round meditation pillow. Then I rotated around to face the wall. The young, scary monk in the hallway struck the gong. It was time to meditate.

I tried to keep my gaze at a forty-five-degree angle as instructed. I found myself counting the number of rows of weave in one tatami mat while listening to the rain overhead. Then I blinked and started counting all over. All too soon I heard the gong ring again. I certainly felt refreshed and calm, but that could have been because the rain had lulled me into a relaxed state. I certainly did not feel I'd reached enlightenment, not even for a moment, but at least no one had hit me with a bamboo stick.

Another monk was waiting for us outside the meditation hall. He smiled at me, and Shiba bowed to him. I was a bit surprised to be handed off to this new young man, whom I will call Hayashi. As Shiba hurried off to his next appointment, Hayashi greeted me in English and asked me where I was from.

"New York," I said.

He told me that he had spent two weeks backpacking in New York. "It's really a great place," he smiled, a little wistfully. "Everyone is happy."

I laughed.

"Isn't everyone happy?" I realized he was serious. "Why would anyone in New York be unhappy?"

"Usually they hate their apartment. Or their job. Or they wish they had more money or were better looking."

"Really?"

Up until that moment, all the young monks I had met had had a slightly hurried and watchful quality to them. Hayashi, in contrast, moved slowly and never pulled out his watch. He also struck me as having the slightly brooding quality that I cannot help but associate with a youthful search for depth. Hayashi had been at Sōjiji for three years, and like Shiba, he had come here to complete his training and to take over his father's temple in Nagano.

I followed him farther into the temple complex, climbing up and down stairs, rounding corners, and every now and then bowing to altars featuring a panoply of Buddhist gods. Other monks passed us by. The monks were nearly always running, as if in a constant state of controlled near panic. They started, briefly, when they saw my foreign face, then quickly recovered with a bow. Hayashi, bemused, bowed back.

It dawned on me fairly quickly that there was a hierarchy to the greetings. There were the deep, shy bows of those who were below Hayashi. These young men scurried away at an even faster pace than they had appeared, as though just seeing us had prompted them to get away as quickly as possible, as though they were afraid of committing an error or felt the need to impress us with their dedication to perpetual motion. Hayashi did not have this kind of near-panicked energy. Even as he seemed to be deeply troubled by something, he also had what I can only describe as a stillness, a term that Westerners often employ when writing about Buddhism. This stillness, a deep and fundamental calm, was a trait that I most often encounter in older priests. For me it is a palpable characteristic, and when I am around it, it is difficult not to feel its force, in the same way that it's hard not to feel the exuberance of someone who moves with great abandon.

As Hayashi and I continued on through an underground corridor, I heard a sound, like the cluttered, undisciplined thunder of a flock of pigeons. A group of young men tumbled into view down another staircase. These boys yanked their sleeves, as a new dog owner pulls on the leash of a spastic puppy. They kicked at their hems, unused to so much fabric around their legs. Some of the boys were fat. They bowed, nervously, and filed into line while their teacher yelled at them to move more quickly. Hayashi and I watched for a while. "First-year students?" I asked. Hayashi nodded. Another group of boys then came down the staircase, moving with distinctly more coordination. "Second years?" I asked. Hayashi nodded again.

We navigated the labyrinth of hallways and stairwells that connected Sōjiji's many buildings until we suddenly emerged onto a covered walkway, just outside Sōjiji's *hondō*. A lattice-like wall separated us from the courtyard beyond, where I could hear worshippers trudging across the gravel while the rain pelted their umbrellas. The *hondō* was enormous, comprising one thousand tatami mats, nearly eighteen thousand square feet. A large gold statue of the Buddha dominated the center of the room, while the back of the room was dark and unlit. Immediately behind us was a large wooden offertory box—every temple has one. I heard the intermittent sound of coins sliding down the angled mouth of the offering container and then hitting the bottom of the box. Over the years, I have thrown lots of money into offering containers. It was an odd sensation to be here—on the inside—with the worshippers behind me, where I normally stood.

Hayashi said, "Tell me. What do you think a priest should do?"

I had been so mesmerized by the coordinated young men, the

statues, and the incense that I'd assumed, naively, that even if Sōjiji had become a bureaucracy with an efficient PR machine, its inhabitants would have a very clear idea of what Buddhism was all about.

"Don't you know what a priest is supposed to do?" I asked.

"Not really," he said.

Hayashi told me that he greatly admired his father and longed to emulate him, but in his first year on the mountain, Hayashi had seen second-year students bully first-year students. One boy was beaten up quite badly. Hayashi thought that this was wrong and wanted to help the injured boy. He did not like himself for not helping, and he loathed that the educational apparatus and the power structure made it impossible to intervene. He felt painfully trapped. He was certain that such a thing would never have happened in New York.

As we were talking, two monks came into the *hondō*, one in front and the other behind. They walked along its perimeter, disappearing into the very back, through a doorway just to the side of the large Buddha. A moment later I heard screaming in Japanese. "*Gomen nasai!*" I am sorry! I am sorry! I am sorry! I jumped. It was a very loud, very anguished sound. Moments later, the men came back out in single file. Like everyone else, they had been trained not to gawk at visitors. Still, they snuck in little looks at my face before they continued around the corner and disappeared.

"What was that?" I asked.

Hayashi gave me a half smile. "Probably one monk has done something wrong. He has to apologize as loud as possible to show all of us that he is really sorry. In my first year, I made a little mistake." He produced a little cell phone from inside the folds of his robe. "Just a little thing. It fell, and I picked it up. And then I had to sit *seiza* for nine hours." To sit *seiza* is to sit resting on your knees. My grandfather continuously scolded me as a child for my inability to correctly sit on the floor; Indian style was the best that I could do. While the older generation of Japanese mourns the loss of the compact *seiza* sitting position, which allows for small rooms uncluttered by chairs, doctors now advise that *seiza* produces numerous health problems in old age. As a result, fewer and fewer Japanese get into the habit of *seiza* from childhood, and very few are able to hold the position for very long.

"When I see young people make a mistake," Hayashi continued passionately, "I don't scold them. I don't punish them. I just point out what they have done. I don't think it's right to hit people. Do you? What would you do if you were me?"

Immediately I thought about my grandfather. Along with his brother, Jitsuo, my grandfather had gone to university in Taiwan, a Japanese colony before World War II. According to family lore, Jitsuo had been sent home from Taiwan because he had developed tuberculosis; this was what eventually killed him. But over the years, reading through family letters, my mother was able to glean the real reason for Jitsuo's "failure" at school. While my grandfather had thrived at university, Jitsuo had spoken out against the practice of corporal punishment employed by the teachers and encouraged among senior students. His challenge to the system had not been acceptable. He was not allowed to return. My grandfather, on the other hand, had gone on to be a successful teacher who whipped his students when he felt it was necessary.

I didn't express any of this. Instead, I asked if there wasn't someone Hayashi could talk to at Sōjiji. He had tried that, but the older priests had just told him that things would get better, and that they were already better than they had been in previous decades. He had to learn to be patient.

"Why don't you just leave?" I asked.

"If I leave now, I will not only hate Sōjiji, I will probably not become a priest at all. Then these past three years will have been for nothing. I am waiting for a turning point."

Here, I began to talk about Sempō and how he had stayed in Iwaki during the crisis with the damaged nuclear reactor. At first, Hayashi was surprised to learn that I came from a Japanese temple family, but he was intrigued and asked me to tell him more. I explained that Sempō spent a lot of time with his parishioners, listening to them and caring for them. Perhaps Hayashi, too, could be the best priest possible for his own hometown without worrying about Sōjiji's approval. If Hayashi admired his father so much, then why didn't he try to learn to be a priest at home?

We drifted back through the hallways, stopping to look at a garden and some of the meeting rooms where high-ranking guests were received to drink *matcha*, powdered green tea. But the romance of the visit had taken on a somber tone for me. Now I felt worried for Hayashi—and the other young men I had seen that day. Daisuke, Sempō's oldest son, had studied here. Had he been bullied too?

We worked our way back to the visitors' center, where yet a third young monk was waiting to take me to lunch. He was very young and very nervous—he had been at Sōjiji for only two months, though judging by the way he looked, either he had been underweight before arriving to study or he had shed his weight very quickly. Before I followed this new guide, I gave Hayashi my business card and asked him to write me. He slipped the card inside a fold in his robe, and then he smiled. "I think, at the end of this year, I will come down off the mountain." I watched him go into the gift shop, where the shop girls flirted with him, and he flirted back.

The third guide took me up to the guests' dining room to eat *shōjin ryōri*, a term that roughly translates in Japanese to "the way of enlightened eating," but which Westerners usually refer to as "vegetarian." Serious monks and priests in training eat *shōjin ryōri* every day.

In the bamboo shoots, a signature dish in springtime, I tasted a gentle sweetness mixed with a trace of salt. A pale flavor. I had taken a few cooking classes at the 350-year-old Pure Land temple Jōkōkuji in Tōkyō, and my teacher, Asano Masami, had told me that the Japanese had a flavor in their food that Westerners did not know about. This was called *awai*, and it meant, roughly, that which is pale but has depth. Each time we finished a dish and tasted it, she asked me if I could discern its *awai*.

It was still raining hard, and in the guests' dining room on the third floor, I had a view of the water plunging through a segmented iron drain pipe hanging from one of the dark wood eaves of the roof. A week earlier, and the large, pale-pink cherry trees in the garden would have been in full bloom, but time and the rain had tattered these once proud blossoms. There was only one tree with blossoms left, a weeping cherry, always the last to flower among the many varietals of *sakura*. I sat and watched the shivering pink tree valiantly clinging to spring in the face of such a gray day. I was pretty sure that this tree was also an example of *awai*, for my mother had told me that certain colors in Japan are known for both pallor and depth. I stared at this tree as I continued to finish the rest of my meal in silence.

When I went home that day, I was exhausted from the effort of trying to see and to taste depth and to understand everything I had been taught. Tomorrow morning at Sōjiji, the young monks would rise at three o'clock while I was still asleep. By the time I woke up, they would have already polished the hallway, meditated, and eaten the first of their three enlightened meals.

A FEW WEEKS after my initial visit, I went back to Sōjiji for a large meditation session. There were about forty of us—all ages and both genders—and I caught tidbits of others' conversations. Most were saying they hoped to learn to relax through meditation.

We were all herded into one of Sōjiji's many meeting rooms.

Here, the man I had thought of as the "scary priest" from my previous visit did a presentation on how to meditate, holding up pillows and slippers, reminding me very much of flight attendants explaining how to use a seat belt, while Shiba spoke into a microphone. Shiba explained that during our meditation, he and a couple other monks would be going by with their *kyōsaku*. If we seemed sleepy or were not able to hold our positions correctly, they would use the bamboo sticks to tap us lightly on the shoulder. He promised this would not hurt. If we felt we needed a smack—a release of energy, he said—we were simply to put our hands together as if in prayer, and one of the monks would happily oblige. I'll bet, I thought.

I spent the entire meditation session determined not to get whacked. As I sat, supposedly deep in meditation, I could hear the sliding of the bamboo stick in the monks' hands as they prepared to hit people on the shoulder. *Slither, slither* went the sticks. I could see and feel the monks' shadows as they passed. The whacking was initially intermittent. But as the minutes accumulated, I began to hear it regularly. *Whack. Whack. Whack.* One man behind me and another off to my left were hit repeatedly. Each time they were smacked, the sound grew louder. I sat up straighter. I estimated that after two hours, very few of us had not been hit. There was the man to my right. And there was me.

Okay, person on my right, I thought. You and me to the end of the line. And this is what I continued to think for the duration of my sitting.

Toward the end of the three-hour session, a senior priest came into the room and spoke to us. "Please," he said. "If you need to stretch your legs, do so." Immediately there was a rustle in the room, followed by a lot of yawning and joints creaking. Still, the man to my right did not move, and neither did I. In a low, sonorous voice, the priest droned on and on about enlightenment and meditation. "You will have been here for three hours," he said. "When you go home, I promise you will feel as if you had been on a holiday somewhere far away. You will feel refreshed." My internal skeptic snorted. So far, I thought the priest sounded as though he were reading from a pre-scripted manual. But then, as though he had heard my skepticism, he said, "Do you think that if any of you meditated at home, you would be able to keep going for three hours? I promise you, you have been able to meditate this long only because we were all together." Three hours? Had it really been three hours? As I write this now, I find it impossible to contemplate sitting for three hours. I can read for hours. I can write for hours. But to just sit, and to sit up straight at that?

At last we were allowed to stand. We bowed to each other. The man behind me, who had been hit so regularly, looked sheepish. The man sitting next to me said in English, "You sit beautifully."

"Thank you," I said in Japanese. I was a little surprised. I, of course, had been paying lots of attention to him, but it had not occurred to me that he was paying attention to me. What was more, the entire time we had been sitting, I had not known what he looked like. I hadn't even been able to guess his age, but now I was curious. He was older—maybe in his sixties. It can be hard to guess Japanese people's age. He had a full head of silver, a somewhat rare sight in Japan, as most people either naturally keep their dark locks or dye their hair. He was very trim and wore expensive, unobtrusive clothing in muted shades of gray, the Japanese version of landed English gentry, who are rich and well educated but would be mortified to display the bad taste of wearing anything too showy.

As we all tumbled out of Sōjiji in a daze, I hurried to keep up with him.

"Goodbye!" Shiba called out to me. The scary priest even cracked a smile. "Come back!"

"Thanks!" I ran to catch up with my sitting partner, as I now thought of him.

"Are you some kind of *star*?" he asked with an arch note in his voice. "Not everyone gets a special good-bye like that."

"No, no," I protested. "That was my first real zazen session. Truly."

He told me that he was a retired computer engineer and that he meditated every chance he got. He was full of recommendations for other places and other forms of meditation I ought to try. He was fond of an obscure form of Chinese boxing. As we talked, it dawned on me that one reason why I had been able to sit still for so long was because he had been sitting next to me, and that he, like me, had not been hit. It was actually as the old priest had said: I had drawn strength from my neighbor. "You should continue to meditate," he said to me kindly. "You have very nice form. I hope we meet again." Then he bowed and walked off briskly.

Outside the temple grounds, a young couple fell into step beside me. It was their first time sitting, and the man had been hit often. "At first it's just like a tap," he confided. "But by the end, I guess they get irritated."

"Bam bam bam!" they laughed together.

I asked if they would consider coming back.

"You know," said the girl, "this is not the way I normally spend my Saturdays. But . . . I do feel really refreshed."

It is often said that the Japanese, like other East Asians, champion the group over the individual. "I want you to remember that in Japan, we know how to work together. But in your country, you know how to be an individual," Sempō had once said to me.

There is a lot of talk these days in Japan about how the nation is losing its sense of community and its ability to work together. I wondered if zazen was one of the vestiges of a time when people had intuited how others around them had felt. Every part of me had rebelled against the actual sitting that day, and yet I couldn't deny that now I felt greatly refreshed and comforted by the weird intimacy of just sitting next to a stranger engaged in the same activity.

I wondered what might happen to me if I were to meditate like that every day, for a year, as young monks did when they trained. I wondered what else I might be able to do that I had been sure I could not do before.

EIGHT

EATING TOGETHER

LONG AGO, WHEN I was a teenager, Sempō had suggested that I go to Eiheiji to better grasp the meaning of Zen. He had offered to sponsor me for the visit; you have to have an affiliation with a Sōtō Zen temple to be allowed to stay overnight at Eiheiji. Instead, I chose to go to college and read lots of books on religion, convinced that classwork was the best way for me to learn anything. After having spent time at Sōjiji, however, I understood that learning from books was not at all the same as actual practice. Now I was here at Eiheiji to try to better understand what had shaped priests like Kaneta and Sempō.

Today Eiheiji trains as many as two hundred monks at any one time. Most of these young men are like my cousins, children of priests who are expected to take over their family temple. Occasionally someone comes along who is drawn to Buddhism solely out of a sincere interest, someone who wants to study at Eiheiji for the experience alone. Such a candidate must still have a *rōshi*, a "master" who runs his own temple and who can vouch for his pupil's aptitude. For these people, Eiheiji is the only place to study; this is where their idol, Dōgen, lived and taught. In its remoteness, its history, and its age, Eiheiji has a mystique and, for many, an authenticity that Sōjiji can never match. Everyone I had met at Sōjiji told me that if I really wanted to get at the heart of what Dōgen had taught, I needed to go to Eiheiji.

TWICE A YEAR, in April and November, young monks who wish to train at Eiheiji arrive early in the morning, stand outside the main gate, and ring a bell. This is how they ask for admission. Two stone tablets inside the gate bear the following inscription: "Only those concerned with the problem of life and death should enter here. Those not completely concerned with this problem have no reason to pass this gate."

If it is April, it is still very cold outside, and there will likely be snow on the ground at Eiheiji. These young monks dress simply and traditionally in black tunics, which are belted and flare into a short skirt. They also wear white leggings, straw hats, and straw shoes and carry a simple bag on their backs. They are made to wait, often for hours, before a senior monk opens the door and yells at them. They wait some more until they are allowed inside. Then they are made to wait some more. Finally, a senior monk quizzes them: Did they read the tablets? What do the tablets mean? How can they expect to become priests if they did not even notice the tablets? Everything— even waiting outside in the cold—is part of their training, and they will be expected to subject themselves fully to their education.

Eiheiji, whose name means "Temple of Eternal Peace," is in a remote part of Fukui Prefecture, which is located about two hundred miles northwest of Tōkyō and faces the Japan Sea. The Eiheiji compound is composed of more than seventy buildings that climb up the side of a mountain and are connected by a series of covered staircases and walkways. In between the fortress-like buildings, centuries-old cedar trees shoot skyward, some as tall as one hundred feet, while brooks run alongside the wooden staircases. There is a deep feeling of permanence, as though the temple has always been a part of the mountain. The day I visited, pausing by the old gate, I watched a young monk dressed in black run from left to right across an elevated wooden walkway balanced partway up the mountain. He looked like a raven in flight. Before flying out of view, the monk paused to bow toward some altar so far up the hillside that I could not yet see it. I felt like I was about to enter some other realm populated by mysterious beings who swooped from branch to branch on trees that supported a wood and stone fortress.

Guests who spend the night at Eiheiji are nominally treated as though they are in religious training. The more nights you stay, the more intense the training. The day I went, there were twelve of us, all with our own rooms on the same floor in the guest center. The hallways and stairwells of the facility were very institutional looking—fluorescent lighting, a whining elevator, and beige linoleum tiles. But on the inside, the guest rooms and practice rooms were suffused with atmosphere. Each room was seven to eight tatami mats in size, and warm and inviting. I had a balcony too, with a view of the courtyard below and the dark-green cedar trees and moss-covered rocks. By contrast, the monks have neither air-conditioning nor heating, though it's hard to know exactly what the dormitory looks like, as photography is never allowed.

I was asked to wait in my room until someone returned to attend to me. I sat for a few minutes, but the long trip in the toilet-free, one-car train I had taken to get here meant that I was very eager to go to the bathroom. I didn't see how anyone would mind if I slipped out.

As it happened, people did mind very much. On my way out of the bathroom and back to my room, I was intercepted by two monks who seemed flustered that I was wandering about on my own. One

ushered me back to my room. There was a "way" to go to the bathroom, they explained. It involved bowing to the small statue of the
Ususamaryō bodhisattva in an altar just outside the bathroom door.
Had I even noticed the altar? Before I took a bath, I was to bow
before a different altar, home to the Battabara bodhisattva. I was
not, under any circumstances, to talk while I was out in the hallway,
in the bathroom, or in the bath. As I circulated these public spaces,
I was also to keep my arms and hands in a specific position—the
relaxed *gasshō* position—in which my hands were clasped in front.
Just now, I had done everything incorrectly, though I had at least
managed to properly exchange my hallway slippers for the ones in
the toilet, and then exchange them back again.

Years of training in dance classes led me to immediately try to
mimic the *gasshō*. "Like this?" I clasped my hands and held my arms
out stiffly.

The monk look troubled. He was very young and from the
countryside in Aichi Prefecture, not too far from where my mother
had been born. His family temple dated back to the Muromachi
era (fourteenth century). Unlike Hayashi or Shiba from Sōjiji, this
young monk had not the slightest whiff of city about him, and he
did not seem to know how to behave in any way other than with
complete sincerity. "Well, don't let anyone know I told you this,
but you don't have to be so stiff. You can relax. But please, don't let
anyone know I told you."

There was more. My bed had been laid out for me, but in the
morning I had to fold up the mattress, remove the sheet and the
pillowcase, and put them out in the hallway. The mattress had to
be folded in thirds. The pillow went on one specific shelf, and the
mattress on another.

It was 3:30 in the afternoon, and we would be leaving for zazen
meditation in two hours. I was encouraged to take my bath now

and to remember to bow and not talk. There would be no lock on my door, and I should take my valuables with me. With a bow, and arms in perfect *gasshō*, the monk retreated from my room.

THERE WERE THREE women in the bath. One sat perfectly still in the water, a paragon of erect and silent fortitude, her back to the door. When she left the bath, she bowed and never once showed any sign of discomfort, but she made a great display of drying herself off in the bathing area so she would not drip in the changing room. My twitchy Western self was immediately irritated by her calm and her perfect consideration for others.

The other two women were mother and daughter. Though we had been instructed not to speak, they began to talk to me as soon as the Perfect One had departed. They were staying in the room next to me, they said. They were nervous. They had never done this before, and now that we were all here and committed to staying overnight, there would be no escape. I told them I was nervous too.

"I forgot to pack snacks. And coffee," I said.

"Coffee!" the daughter cried. "I forgot coffee too! And we will be getting up at three a.m. to meditate!"

I told her I had some Excedrin, and I would be taking that, at which point she laughed. She had noticed that her room had come with a complimentary cookie. I ought to check my room for a cookie too. We all swore to save our cookies for the 3:00 a.m. wakeup call. Our secret alliance sealed, we settled our imperfect bodies into the water, and it occurred to me for the first time that here I was in the company of women, all of us trying to do our best to follow the rules of a religion that had been established by men.

At 5:00 p.m., a monk rang a bell, and the great wooden gate of Eiheiji was closed. Just like that, most visitors were shut out. Almost immediately, the temple took on a different atmosphere. All I could

see out the window were the shapes of slim, young, black robe–
clad monks. The lumbering, photographing tourists were gone. I
was reminded of the times I had gone to see dress rehearsals at the
ballet in New York. On stage, there were stagehands checking the
lights and the props, while dancers jumped up and down to warm
up. Then the lights dimmed, and when they came back on, only the
dancers remained, and the stage suddenly was fraught with tension.

At 5:30 p.m., we were summoned from our rooms and asked to
stand in two lines in the hallway. There was a range of ages—from
single guests in their twenties, to a few married couples in their
fifties. Everyone stood with arms in the *gasshō*-relaxed position, and
then we were marched away to dine. No one spoke a word.

We were going to eat *shōjin ryōri* for dinner in a formal, Japanese-
style room. We were to sit on our knees on a square pillow on the
tatami floor and eat with chopsticks while leaning over a lacquered
table only a foot off the ground. There were additional rules. There
was a way to pick up a bowl and to eat from it. When I put the
bowl back down, I was not to make a sound. Not a single clink. I
must never eat from a bowl while it was still on the table; I had to
hold it. I was to keep my mouth closed. I should not talk, I should
not slurp, and I should try to eat any noisy foods, like pickles, as
silently as possible. Everyone would hear me if I made any noise.
When I needed to put down my chopsticks, I was to place them at a
forty-five-degree angle on the bowl on the lower righthand corner,
with the eating end pointing out. We were to eat absolutely everything; there should be no leftovers. Living things had given up their
lives so we could eat, and we were not to do something as wasteful
as to leave even a grain of rice. There would be a way to stack the
bowls, and we would be guided in this, but we were to do it silently.

And then there was the most important thing: we all had to
finish eating at the same time.

The food was delicious, but I chafed against the rules. I was certain that because of my foreign face, everyone would be looking to see if I could eat correctly. It was spring, and so the menu included some seasonal foods, like bamboo shoots, which crunch in the mouth. I chewed these very slowly. A bowl clattered. Our eyes darted to the source of the noise; the mother I had met in the bath had dropped her bowl. I looked around the room to see who was eating what, as though to get permission to start another dish; there were nine bowls in all. And then an odd thing happened. I could, in fact, sense exactly where everyone was in the process of eating his or her meal. I could feel that the woman next to me had eaten only a third of her food, and I slowed down accordingly so she would not be left behind. I could feel that the man all the way to the left had finished—too early. I could feel that everyone noticed he had finished too early. I could feel that everyone was alarmed.

The monk who was watching us eat told us that we had two extra pieces of food by our tables: a banana and a sweet. We were allowed to take these to our rooms to eat later. I looked at the girl from the bath, and she winked at me. I winked back. The monk then talked us through the exact order in which we were to silently stack our bowls and push them to one end of the table. Now, said the monk, it was time to rise and to go to meditation.

Despite having sat on my knees for the last twenty-five minutes, I was able to stand up in one motion. Around me, everyone else shot up. But in the corner of the room, there was a problem. A young man—the one who had finished eating at least five minutes before everyone else—could not stand up. His legs were stuck in the *seiza* position. He pushed his arms off the floor to free his body, but his feet would not cooperate. We all began to gather around him, waiting for him to stand.

He was a good-looking guy whom I guessed to be in his thirties. He was tan and extremely fit and either worked out regularly or played some kind of sport. He was also quite tall, at least six feet. I wondered, absent-mindedly, what a jock was doing at Eiheiji.

The monk attending to us suggested that the man relax and stretch out his feet. Everyone was waiting, he said, and by just waiting here for the man to stand, we were wasting time. It was fine that the young man could not sit *seiza*. Even I, in Japanese, suggested that he stretch out his legs and wake them up. He ignored us. "*Daijōbu.*" I am fine, he said. "I want to stand up properly."

The seconds ticked. We continued to wait. I felt the agonizing pain of knowing that someone was doing something *wrong*. Can't you see this is *wrong*, I wanted to say to him. Again the monk asked the young man to please stretch out his legs and to stand up. The point of dinner, he said, was to move together. To learn to move as a group. But the man persisted. I grew increasingly tense and frantic. Finally the man was able to hoist himself up. There was an audible sigh of relief from the group. Off we went to our rooms, before we were led to meditation.

THE JAPANESE HAVE a phrase: *kūki wo yomu*. It means roughly, "to read the air" or "to read the atmosphere." If you use this phrase in Japan, everyone knows what you mean. To be truly Japanese—one of the characteristics that supposedly make the Japanese so special—is to have an ability to immediately sense a change in the atmosphere and to adjust accordingly. But this man, with his not eating on time and his holding us back because he could not stand up, had not been able to read the air. Occasionally I heard from older people that the Japanese were unlearning this ability and that this was a problem. Reading the air had been so necessary when most Japanese had been farmers and had relied on cooperation to make their rice crops grow. "Now we are becoming too much like you," relatives said, by which they meant "too Western" and unable to read the air.

I was alarmed by my reaction to this man. I had wanted him to get up and in fact had been deeply frustrated that he couldn't. I had even decided that this man—this jock—was *difficult*.

I recalled my conversation with Hayashi when I first visited Sōjiji, and how he had been troubled by the bullying he had witnessed during his three years of study. In my impatience with the very tall jock, I saw the seeds of a bully.

One of the things that Dōgen stressed repeatedly in his teaching and writing was that the body needed to be trained and that the mind would follow. My dance teachers had always said something similar: "how you dance is how you are." This was always a great irritation to me because while I am a competent dancer, I am not a great dancer. And I have met plenty of wonderful dancers who left much to be desired as people. A bookish sort of person at heart, I had always believed that it was what I thought that mattered most, not how my body moved. And yet, weirdly, in the eating-together exercise, a great deal about myself had been revealed to me, including excessive pride.

Not long after dinner, we were recalled to the hallway, and from there we walked silently as a group to the meditation room. Once again we were instructed in how to walk and how to remove our shoes and climb up on the elevated meditation platform. As I sat, I listened intently for the sound of the *kyōsaku*, but I didn't hear it. In fact, the entire time we were sitting, no one was hit at all. I started to relax into the zazen position and focused simply on the sound of my breath.

A few minutes before our meditation ended, I heard someone enter the room. He was breathing loudly, and I wondered if he were ill or had some kind of a lung problem. Then the visitor began to talk. His voice was warm and kind, and he asked us to stretch out our legs if we were uncomfortable. Around me, bodies began to melt. The man said that even if we were able to meditate for only a few minutes a day like this, we would learn to be more comfortable within our own skin. The world today did not teach people how to be comfortable with their own bodies. Modern people treated their bodies like objects. A moment later, he asked us all to stand up and to come join him in an adjoining room for a talk.

His name was Maruko Kōhō, and he was a priest from Nara. He congratulated us on having completed our session, and said that we might think that meditation would be something we'd get better at doing as we got older, but in fact this was not true. Maruko had learned recently of a study conducted at Tōhō University by the scientist Arita Hideo, which revealed that the brain waves of a novice meditator were identical to those of a veteran. Meditation could help us immediately by raising our levels of dopamine. Science had proved that Dōgen was right; all we needed to start down the path of enlightenment was our bodies. Even a body as sickly as Maruko's had been helped by this discipline.

Maruko was born just after the war, during the great famine. The youngest of seven children, he was very weak as a child. His mother remembered him as being too quiet and never causing any trouble. In his youth he developed rheumatoid arthritis. This admission took me aback. He was nearly the same age as my mother, who also suffers from the same illness.

Maruko was not from a priestly family, and he might not have become a priest were it not for his parents' taking him to the mystical mountain Dewa Sanzan. There, a healer tried to rid Maruko's body of pain. The healing didn't work, but Maruko met a priest from Nara who happened to be on a pilgrimage to Dewa Sanzan. They hit it off, and the priest invited him to Nara to become a disciple. The daily meditation greatly relieved Maruko's pain. Today he was a believer in the healing power of Zen. Were it not for his illness, he might never have learned about Buddhism. He now trusted in the great wisdom that life was full of suffering and happiness and that wisdom lay in this tension.

I loved listening to Maruko Kōhō talk. He was small and slight, and one of those people who seemed to be both young and old at the same time. I could see the child in him, even though his hair was gray and he dispensed the kind of worldly advice that only an older person can give with conviction. His emotions were extremely close to the surface, as though there was a candle burning inside him, just under his skin. When there was no wind, the flame grew very strong, and his eyes brightened, and his voice became robust as he emphasized an important point. If he was disturbed, a breeze rushed over his face, and he became dark and troubled, and you felt the absence of his light. Just as quickly, he would brighten again. The effect was captivating, and I avidly took notes during his entire talk.

Maruko wanted to discuss the true meaning of the middle way, the concept at the heart of Siddharta Gautama's teachings. He sensed that people today didn't really understand what was meant by the middle way, because we now lived in a world in which people thought they had a right always to be comfortable.

His gaze settled on the man who had had such difficulty standing up in the dining room. "You, for example. Are you married?"

"Divorced."

"Ah."

A pause.

"That is too bad. It is too bad for you. And for your wife too, isn't it. And now you have come here to Eiheiji."

The man nodded.

Maruko said that in the past, when a young man got married and brought his wife home to live with his family, there were often tensions between the mother and the daughter-in-law. This was one reason why young people no longer wanted to live with their in-laws. Very often, the older woman was attached to her role as the great beauty in the family and did not like ceding power to the new wife.

"And then," said Maruko-sensei (*sensei* means "teacher" and is often used as a sign of respect), "one day that old woman is sick and is dying. Is she able to thank her daughter-in-law for caring for her? Is she able to be grateful in that moment?" He wanted us to imagine the moment of death and of the final parting, when we all say good-bye to each other. He used the word *owakare*, the great parting, the term that Kaneta had also used when talking about his job at the crematorium after the tsunami. As a priest, Maruko had seen many people die, and he had seen many families just after a loved one had passed away. The very worst thing was when someone forgot to say "thank you" before dying. If only the dead could see the pain they left behind when they died selfishly. He often counseled the living on this inherited pain and tried to get them to put it into context.

In Japanese: わたしが、わたしになるためにじんせいのしっぱいもひつようでした。"In order to become myself, my mistakes and hardships were also necessary." This was an essential way to view life. It was only by keeping this in mind at all times that one could live in the present. The practice of Zen, he said, was about looking forward and living in this way.

I SLEPT POORLY that night. I knew we would be roused at 3:00 a.m., and I had the same kind of anxiety I often get when I need to be up early to catch a flight. I had meant to save my banana and my bean cake to eat at 3:00 a.m., just before the morning prayers, but by 9:30 p.m. I was hungry, and I finished them off. Finally, around eleven, I fell asleep.

I had set my alarm but needn't have bothered. Just after 3:00 a.m., there was a great clattering. Outside, a young man ran up and down the wooden hallways of Eiheiji, hitting a metal bell with a mallet and exhorting everyone to get up. Not long after, a monk in the hallway outside our rooms asked us to please come out and line up for zazen.

A monk would later say to me that at Eiheiji, one woke even before the birds. He said it was an unnatural time to be awake, and it made him feel as though he was operating outside of the natural order of things, as though just getting up when it is still dark is powerful enough to force you to think more clearly.

AFTER ANOTHER GENTLE meditation session, we all climbed up the slick wooden stairs toward the apex of the complex. It was extremely cold outside. All around me, I heard a great commotion of flying robes and slippered feet scaling the staircases to the top. Every few seconds or so, a bell rang out the same note over and over.

One monk was chosen to stand on top of a pole and to hit a gong every time someone new approached the *hondō*. I can still picture his face. He was beautiful, almost too beautiful to be a man, or perhaps more accurately, he had a kind of beauty we no longer see or are perhaps unaccustomed to seeing in the modern world. Later, I would tell Kaneta about this young boy, and he would laugh. "The Eiheiji *bijin*," he chortled. The Eiheiji beauty. "It's all the rice they eat. Their skin turns white! They become as beautiful as princesses."

Now we were at the upper reaches of a building called the *hattō*, or the dharma hall. We sat down in the very back and were urged not to stick to the painful *seiza* position, as the morning service would be quite long. Around us, monks exhaling white breath began filing in from the cold. They wore no socks. To the right, senior priests began to assemble, their ranks betrayed by their slightly more colorful robes and their age. Some of the eldest sat in low chairs. The very back of the *hattō* had a statue of the historical Buddha seated in meditation. Overhead were several large gold chandeliers whose individual pieces were made up of bells and lotus flowers and wheels. It was an abstract representation of Buddha's paradise.

What I saw that morning is called the *hōyō*—the morning sutra reading—which includes prayers for the dead and the living. It involves physical coordination and closely resembles a very carefully rehearsed dance or pageant. The effect was stunning. Young monks—those who had been at Eiheiji over a year—were chosen to go and get portable bookshelves, about two feet long and one foot high, filled with tiny compact books. Holding the shelves sharply to the side, as though the wind were pulling the books behind them, they half crouched and half walked in between the lines of monks, who each deftly nabbed a book. The hands of the seated monks darted in and out, one after the other, in rapid succession like successive typewriter keys hitting a sheet of fresh paper. When the bookshelf-carrying monks came to the end of a row, they turned, pivoting on the balls of their feet like dancers do, then continued back down another row. Again, hands shot in and out. The monks with the bookshelves kept their heads perfectly level, never once bobbing, and the overall effect was of a human loom weaving an invisible tapestry. Sometimes a monk would present an important figure—like Maruko—with a table on which there was an instrument or a document. This too required the same dramatic pose—legs bent, arms outstretched, and head kept level.

The chanting was enormous and swollen, an early-dawn Mormon Tabernacle choir in the mountains. As soon as one sutra ended, another began. Sometimes the monks whipped little books out of their robes and held the tomes up straight in front of their eyes, elbows at a ninety-degree angle. Some monks knew the sutras by heart and didn't need their books. The style of chanting varied: now fast, now slow. The pitch went up and down. There was one unusual style of chanting: it did not rest on a tone but sounded like the scattered, slightly crazed chanting of bees.

The tightly coordinated, purposeful manner in which the men chanted and moved reminded me very strongly of ballet and the inner discipline dancers require to keep the body under control. But unlike dancers, these monks had not auditioned to get into a touring company; most were born into their roles due to an accident of fate. I was accustomed to thinking that talent was the decisive factor in whether or not someone could dance or move with arresting agility. Was it, in fact, possible to teach anyone to move with such graceful precision?

I recalled an incident I'd witnessed a couple of months earlier. I had just arrived in Japan and was at the Odawara train station on my way to see my relatives. It was rush hour, and the train station was full of young people on their way home from work and school. Suddenly, a young man who couldn't have been any older than eighteen dropped a handful of change. Instantly, men and women stopped and began to pick up the coins. The reactions were spontaneous, and though completely unplanned, they had the look of an organized effort, like a flash mob. In less than thirty seconds, a dozen people, all of whom were unrelated, had picked up the change, handed it to the young man, and then continued on their way, melting back into the flow of rush-hour pedestrians. Later I wondered if I would have been able to seamlessly join the coin-collecting effort, which seemed to be coordinated by nothing more than instinct.

The rest of the morning at Eiheiji continued with a tour of the lower grounds—Dōgen's grave, a smaller temple, a meditation room—and breakfast, during which the divorced jock again finished eating too quickly and again had difficulty standing up. Then my stay came to an end. The great gate was opened. A few tour buses were already parked outside.

In my room, there was a little notebook for guests to record their impressions of Eiheiji. I sat and read some of the entries. One after another, previous visitors praised Maruko. More than one person wrote that he or she was going to leave Eiheiji with the resolve to live a better and happier life. One person wrote that he had decided not to kill himself. Although it is difficult for me to write in Japanese, I added my lines of praise. There was a knock on my door.

A young priest came by to let me know that Maruko had asked to see me. He had noticed my avid note-taking. He thought perhaps we could sit and talk.

MARUKO HAD A small office on the same floor as the registration desk. One wall was completely lined with books and a few photographs and mementos. The center of the room was dominated by a long, low table, which Maruko apparently used both as a desk and as a place to drink tea. When I entered his room, he was seated compactly on a square pillow. With sparkling eyes, he greeted me and asked me where in America I was from. I gave him the usual spiel: I was from California but lived in New York and had family with a temple in Iwaki.

Maruko reciprocated with a brief story of his life: His own temple was erected by Prince Shōtoku, which meant that it was very old. But it was destroyed in the nineteenth century, during the Meiji Restoration, when the emperor was reinstated and the feudal lords thrown out of power. That struggle loosened popular resentment against numerous temples in Japan, many of which had grown wealthy and corrupt in feudal years. Maruko's temple was not much more than a ruin when he took it over, and he spent the next seventeen years begging in order to raise enough money to restore it. He now divided his time between his own temple and Eiheiji, where he was one of a number of senior priests, rather the way a corporation has many vice presidents. When he was finished talking, he asked me if I had any questions.

I said I had two. I asked him why priests at Sōjiji had been so willing to use the bamboo stick, while no one had been hit at Eiheiji. Instantly, Maruko's face flitted into hardness. The *kyōsaku* was something he never used, and he trained the young men who worked with him never to use it either. He liked to oversee guests at Eiheiji because he wanted us to leave with a positive and true impression of Zen. The *kyōsaku* was an invention of the Edo period and had nothing to do with Dōgen. There were priests—particularly at Sōjiji—who abused the *kyōsaku*. This bothered him tremendously because zazen meditation was here to help us and should not require any physical beating.

I asked him then about the word *gamman*. Among the articles I had read in Western newspapers about Japan's ability to deal with the March 11 disaster, I frequently ran across the assertion that people from Tōhoku were particularly good at *gamman*, a kind of Japanese stoicism. Somewhere I had read that *gamman* had entered the Japanese language via Zen Buddhism, and that residents of Tōhoku were good at *gamman* because Zen was widespread there. I wanted to know if this was true.

Maruko's eyes brightened. He grabbed a book off the shelf, and his taut, thin fingers whipped through the pages. The book appeared to be a dictionary of Buddhist terms. "Hmm. Hmm," he said. Then, "Aha. Here it is. Here it is. Yes. It came into Japan via Buddhism. *Gamman* is not a good thing." He shook his head. "Not a good thing at all." He neatly slid the book back on the shelf.

Did I know the story of the historical Buddha? In his early years, Siddharta Gautama subjected his body to extreme hardship until

he discovered that such methods were not at all a path to enlightenment. In choosing the middle way—the Buddha's way—people
should not abuse their bodies. When Japanese people did *gamman*
and tried to endure that which cannot be endured, they were harm-
ing themselves. "It is better," Maruko said, "to speak up and to
express oneself. We must learn to do this in Japan."

He went on to say that Japan was undergoing tremendous hardship now. In recent decades, Japan had also experienced great wealth.
But it was nature's course for great wealth to be followed by days of
relative poverty; neither extreme could be maintained forever. He
also expressed strong opinions about nuclear power, in keeping with
Eiheiji's stance as an organization. The United Kingdom had about
five earthquakes a year, and the United States two hundred. Japan,
on the other hand, endured around four thousand earthquakes each
year. It was irresponsible for such a country to have nuclear power,
and it ought to be eradicated.

Then he paused and gathered his thoughts. "You have to think of
time differently. Time is not just *your* time," he said. "Time doesn't
just belong to humans."

ON THE BUS out of Eiheiji, I sat with some of the other people
who had stayed overnight with me. This was the first chance any
of us had to talk to each other, aside from the one encounter in the
bath. It turned out that everyone else had been just as tense as I
had been. No one had slept well. No one was sure they would ever
repeat a visit, let alone stay for three nights. Everyone was hungry
and regretted not bringing snacks.

We all spoke of the man who had eaten dinner and breakfast so
quickly.

"Do you think he ever noticed that he finished eating early?" I
asked.

"Not that kind," one of the women shrugged. "They never learn."

"No wonder he is divorced!" another woman exclaimed. Everyone laughed.

THE VISIT TO Eiheiji continues to affect me. Early on, it provided me with a way to talk to Buddhist priests with a greater understanding of what they do. On a visit to my family in Iwaki, for example, I told Daisuke about the man who had not been able to finish eating his meal at the same time as everyone else.

"Yes," Daisuke laughed. "Now, imagine what it would be like to eat that way every day for a year."

"Did you change?" I asked him.

"Yes," he said, seriously. "You have to. You change in all kinds of ways that you aren't even aware of."

Nearly everyone I met who had trained at Eiheiji knew who Maruko was, and brightened when I recounted the conversation I had had with him. One young man who had just "come down" from Eiheiji told me that while he had endured a very difficult year, he had been extremely lucky to have had Maruko as his main teacher. Other boys had not been so fortunate. When I asked him to elaborate, he merely shook his head. Another priest told me that when tourists and guests were not looking, the monks who failed to perfectly carry out their instructions were dragged down the long wooden stairways by the hem of their cloaks and berated for failure. The teachers at Eiheiji, this priest told me, were much stricter than the ones at Sōjiji.

Kaneta, himself Eiheiji-trained, laughed when I repeated these stories. The hardships made the young men stronger, and men needed hardship. It was something I, as a woman, could not understand. There was a reason why Japanese corporations and the Japan Self-Defense Forces emulated Eiheiji's training. A big part of me agreed with Kaneta's assessment; I didn't understand and didn't want to. There is an aspect to Zen that is very male and very martial, and it is at odds with my essentially peaceful nature.

But I also found that when I considered meditation, I longed to be either at Sōjiji or at Eiheiji. I wanted to be able to sit with other people, buoyed by their strength and perhaps lending a hand back. I also did not want meditating to be too easy or relaxing. Difficult experiences make us grow, and I had come to like the feeling of growth.

One evening, many months later, I had a conversation with Nagaoka Shunjo, the heir to Daianji temple located to the extreme north of Tōhoku. Growing up in this remote part of Japan, Nagaoka had sworn he would never become a priest. He'd escaped provinciality by entering prestigious Waseda University in Tōkyō. Then he'd worked for a corporation and used his vacation time to travel internationally. At age twenty-seven, Nagaoka had the sudden realization that he could not live in a city the rest of his life. Even though he was married and had a small child, he entered Eiheiji and stayed for a year. He spent the next years going back and forth between Tōkyō, where his wife and child still lived, and Tōhoku, to help his father care for Daianji. The 2011 disaster crystallized his commitment to Buddhism and to continuing his father's work.

A thoroughly modern man, Nagaoka was alert, athletic, and learned. Sometimes when I talk to older priests, I feel the tug of generations, a shade of my grandfather, for example, who could not understand why I could not sit correctly on the floor. This was not so with Nagaoka, who was in all ways my generational peer. He wore a neat, fashionably minimal pair of black-wire-rim glasses. He drove a Toyota hybrid. He grasped irony and sarcasm.

The training at Eiheiji had been difficult, Nagaoka said, but it had made him feel that he could do anything. When the tsunami struck on March 11, he did not hesitate to get in his truck and drive to the coast to see what he could do to help. It didn't matter that people were afraid of priests or thought that priests only showed up for funerals—things I had often heard from other priests when they explained to me why they did not immediately go to Tōhoku to volunteer. Nagaoka was able to focus on his desire to help, and help he did. Even now, once a month, he drove to Kamaishi to read to children in the elementary school. On other occasions, he assisted Kaneta with Café de Monk. Nagaoka credited his training at Eiheiji for giving him this resolve. The temple training meant he could respond to the world now not just with his mind but also with his body. With action. And this, he said, was the great gift of Buddhism and, specifically, of Zen. He wanted to use this training to see through the restoration of Tōhoku, and he was grateful he was born in a position that gave him the chance to be helpful to others.

Nagaoka also told me that there were many similarities between the different forms of Buddhism. "But," he said, "the one thing that Zen cannot tell people is where the dead go."

Pure Land Buddhism had an easy answer: the dead went to Amida's Western Paradise, otherwise known as the Pure Land. In paintings, the Western Paradise is bright gold and everyone is smiling and happy, and the interiors of Pure Land temples strive to re-create a miniature version of this golden splendor with lots of bright paint and a gilded altar. These temples are warm, comforting, and beautiful. There is a reason why even today, when you go to old villages in Japan, the temples located within the town proper are often Pure Land; they were intentionally constructed to be accessible to the common person. Zen temples, on the other hand, are often up on hillsides, which is the case with my family's own Empukuji, and have a sense of being just slightly out of reach of the mundane world.

My *shōjin ryōri* teacher Asano, who had married a Pure Land priest, scoffed at Zen priests and their followers, who are always urged to meditate. "Who has time to meditate every day like they do? Most people have to work." While Zen priests in training at Eiheiji and Sōjiji eat *shōjin ryōri* three times a day, Asano serves it only on special occasions; she considered it unrealistic to eat *shōjin ryōri* so often. For her, there was no point if Buddhism could not be accessible.

I had by now met several Pure Land priests, including young Tokita, who had volunteered at Kaneta's café and who had spent so much of his time trying to help the distraught woman Maruyama. I always liked Pure Land priests because they were kind. I also liked that their temples were unapologetically beautiful; there is always something stark about Zen temples by comparison. And if there was one thing I wanted after my father had passed away, it was comfort and release from grieving. But I had learned that grief could be so persistent, it would not easily bend to cheerful reassurance, no matter how much I might want it to. In the harshness that is Japanese Sōtō Zen, I wondered if there might be the seed of true wisdom.

NINE

The Little Princess

A T THE BEGINNING OF June in 2013, I arranged to participate in Kaneta's next available Café de Monk. He was particularly pleased that I planned to bring my son, Ewan, who, at three and a half, would help to cheer up the elderly women in the temporary housing community. I would be visiting the Minamisanriku community, which, Kaneta wanted me to know, had suffered two recent tragedies. First, a woman had lost her son in Algeria; he had been working as an engineer at the Tigantourine refinery before terrorists had infiltrated the plant, killing him in addition to thirty-eight other hostages. Then, a three-year-old girl had died, just six months ago.

I HAD BEEN to Minamisanriku twice since the disaster. Like all badly damaged towns, Minamisanriku had been built on a flat plain that opened up to the ocean. This made it an attractive place to live if you were a fisherman. After the tsunami, when everything had been destroyed, it was easy to see how vulnerable the plain was to the sea. The area literally looked like a bomb had dropped on the town and flattened it.

The towns built on the tsunami plain in the southeast of Japan can give you a feel for what Minamisanriku would have looked like before March 11, 2011. The city of Odawara, for example, is about forty miles southwest of Tōkyō and located on the Pacific Coast. If you were to drive through Odawara in a taxi, the city would look cramped, but solid and stable, the way numerous Lego pieces clustered together can make a secure structure. There are banks, sushi restaurants, and fish shops all huddled together and on top of each other. The ocean is nowhere in sight. But you would see regularly spaced signs warning "Sea Level 1 meter," or "Sea Level half a meter," and "Tsunami Evacuation Route this way." In 1923, the entire city of Odawara was destroyed by a tsunami.

In Minamisanriku, waves from the 2011 tsunami reached fifty-two feet in height, and they destroyed over 95 percent of the town and over 50 percent of the population. The water demolished nearly every single building in the tsunami plain, except for three. A government building was stripped of its walls, so only its twisted red metal ribs remained, along with the ruins of the fire department, which became a shrine for dead emergency workers. Off-duty firemen still visited often to pay their respects. Off in the distance, there was a hospital where 74 out of 109 patients had been killed. Those who lived had managed to make it to the roof.

Minamisanriku is also famous for the story of Endo Miki, a twenty-five-year-old city worker who sacrificed her life to continue broadcasting the message that the tsunami was coming, and warning her fellow townspeople to flee. Among the lives she saved was that of her mother, who, in one of the city's safe evacuation zones, listened to her daughter's voice until Endo stopped speaking completely.

There are several temporary housing communities for former residents of Minamisanriku. The one I visited that day was in a peaceful little valley, just over the hill from the remains of the town. Once again, there were identical, rectangular houses standing side by side, with laundry racks to the back. Inside the community building, which was much smaller than the one in Ishinomaki, a dozen elderly women were already hard at work making rosaries and folding origami flowers. My son was a momentary distraction, as he chattered in Japanese, before he ran outside to play with another boy who lived in the community. A couple of kindhearted Pure Land priests who had driven up from Chiba Prefecture offered to oversee an impromptu game of soccer.

This group of survivors had already been through Kaneta's Jizō-making class, and they were now receiving their finished statues. Kaneta pulled out a small Jizō—no more than two inches high—and placed it on the table next to a grandmother holding a six-month-old baby. "There you go," he said, gesturing to the clay figurine. "There is Hina." Then he turned to me and made a quick introduction.

The name "Hina" most often means "sunshine" when it is given to a Japanese girl. Hina had been just a baby when the tsunami struck. Her grandmother had been taking care of her, and she immediately strapped the baby to her back, headed for the hills, and literally hiked over the mountains to safety. Fortunately, Hina's mother and father had been out of town the day of the tsunami, and both were safe. But the family lost its home, and was forced to move to the temporary housing unit.

Just over a year ago, there was good news. Hina would have a baby brother. The entire community was excited. So many people had died at Minamisanriku, and the impending arrival of a new addition gave everyone a feeling of hope. In November of 2012, Hina posed for her "Shichi Go San" portrait, which commemorated a special Shintō rite in which girls aged three and seven, and boys aged five, receive blessings at the local Shintō shrine and dress up in traditional outfits.

In December, Hina's baby brother was born. About a week later, Hina had a fever—nothing too high, but certainly high enough that her parents and her grandmother kept a close eye on her condition. And then she died. It was a freak incident. Hina had contracted a respiratory illness caused by the RS virus. Children frequently get infected with this virus around the age of two, but their bodies are usually able to fight it off. For reasons unknown to doctors, Hina was unable to do so. An autopsy was performed at the hospital, and doctors initially assumed that little Hina died of MRSA, the antibiotic-resistant staph bacteria. In the end, it was simply a virus.

Kaneta explained this to me while Hina's grandmother cried silently, as she rocked her baby grandson, whom I will call Kasugi. "I'm so very sorry," I said, chastising myself for not having looked up more phrases to say to the grieving.

"Now you take this Jizō," Kaneta said to the grandmother, "and you put it on the altar for Hina. And then we are going to have to let her go."

The grandmother nodded. She had big round liquid eyes, like a deer, and gave herself over completely to crying. Beside her sat a family friend who occasionally took over care of the baby.

The day proceeded quietly. Some of the women tried to bring out another of the community's boys to play with Ewan, but the boy would not come out. "PTSD," they all said to me; the term is the same in Japanese as it is in English. Kaneta briskly went in and out of houses to check on people. Ewan continued playing outside with a new friend and with the priests, who were now folding paper airplanes with oversized origami paper. One of the ladies gave me a little charm in the shape of a princess, made out of *chirimen*, or scrap fabric. "For your boy," she said. "For protection. We make these things here when we are bored."

Finally I asked Ewan if he wanted to go for a walk with me. As we were strolling through an alley separating two rows of houses, a voice called out to us. It was Hina's grandmother. "Hello," she said wistfully. "Won't you come in and play with Hina?"

I hesitated only for a moment. "Yes, of course," I said. "We'd be delighted." I took Ewan's hand and explained we would be going inside the nice lady's house to play. We worked our way over to the entrance, took off our shoes, and went inside.

AT THE END of February in Japan, you start to see a special kind of doll displayed in the windows of department stores and traditional shops and homes. These dolls are called *hina*, and they are part of the tradition of honoring Girls' Day on March 3. The dolls—figures of the emperor, empress, and their attendants—are placed on a stage covered with red cloth, and they are dressed in elaborate and multilayered silk robes that mimic those worn in the Heian era (794–1185 AD). Even today, the reigning emperor and empress of Japan dress in a similar fashion when posing for formal portraits. The most elaborate of the *hina* dolls include miniature tangerine trees, cherry blossoms, and diamond-shaped rice cakes, foods traditionally associated with late winter and early spring.

For most people, the dolls are a chance to honor a treasured daughter, and to admire a family heirloom, as many of the doll collections can be several hundred years old and passed down from mother to daughter. After March 3, the dolls are swiftly put away for another year; it is considered bad luck to leave them out.

Some parts of Japan still remember what the dolls were actually supposed to do. The month of March could be very cold and potentially dangerous for the young and vulnerable. So the old Japanese used to make straw dolls, and people prayed for the bad luck and evil spirits to attack the dolls instead of their children. The straw dolls were later sent down the river, taking everything evil with them. The modern-day custom of displaying *hina* dolls originates in the tradition of creating evil-attracting dolls by hand.

Some parts of Japan, like tradition-preserving Kyōtō and the city of Tottori, which is three hundred miles southwest of Tōkyō, on the Japan Sea side of Honshū, still practice the doll-floating tradition, called *hina-nagashi* or *nagashi-bina*. In Kyōtō, the ritual is formalized, with actors dressed in Heian-period costumes sending elaborate straw dolls down the Kamigamo river. In Tottori, the feel is more rustic, and local children and visitors do the floating themselves. It is cheery to be outside in the cold and to see young children, brightly dressed in colorful kimonos, sending homemade dolls down the river.

The lingering effects of winter are less of a concern to modern people, so perhaps it's not a surprise that people have forgotten the original reason for displaying dolls in March. Doll-floating is also a nuisance, as too many follow the tide out into the ocean and become caught in fishermen's nets. These days, in towns where the dolls are floated, city volunteers wait downstream from the launch site and catch all the "bad luck" dolls before they make it out to sea. The dolls are later burned, after a Shintō priest recites a prayer.

HINA'S GRANDMOTHER BECKONED us into the second of the two rooms. This was the living room, set up with a low table, and a TV off to the side. The family friend whom I had seen in the community center sat quietly on a *zabuton* pillow. Beside the TV was a shrine to Hina. The shrine was homemade, a stair-step structure covered in red cloth, like the platform used by the *hina* dolls. Hina's Shichi Go San portrait had been placed in the middle. There were candles, a bell, and several clay Jizōs; the one Kaneta presented today was apparently not the first Hina's grandmother had made. The multiple levels of the shrine were festooned with large bags of candy and toys. In the very center, under the portrait, was a rice ball, colored pink and shaped to resemble the face of the superhero Anpanman.

"Anpanman!" said Ewan, recognizing his friend, the red-bean-bread superhero whose theme park we had visited only a couple weeks before.

"Every day, Hina's mother makes her a new rice ball and puts it there for her to eat," said the grandmother.

"Anpanman candy!" said Ewan.

"Go ahead. Have some candy with Hina," said the grandmother. Ewan looked at me for permission.

"I don't want to take your candy," I said.

"Please. Have some candy. And please play with the toys."

Ewan impulsively picked up the bell and rang it. He smiled at us and then began to dismantle the shrine of its toys.

"I have a video," said the grandmother. "Let's turn it on. You can see Hina while Ewan is playing with her." A camcorder was attached to the large-screen television. The grandmother began to cry softly again, while caring for little baby Kasugi.

Ewan looked at Hina's photo. "*Kawaii ne.*" She's very cute, isn't she, Mommy? he said to me.

"She's beautiful," I said.

On the television, Hina was laughing at the camera, then running across the room of the temporary housing unit. Her voice was the bright, energetic voice of a healthy and happy toddler. "She *was* healthy," the grandmother said to me. "Just as healthy then as your son is now."

The grandmother told me how delighted Hina had been to have a baby brother. She had been a little jealous at first, but then after Kasugi was born, she instantly transformed into the perfect older sister. This was the hardest thing about losing Hina. The grandmother began to cry harder. When Hina came down with the fever, she went to sleep with her grandmother because her parents naturally wanted to keep her away from the newborn baby. "But why can't I see the baby?" Hina cried. And then, said the grandmother, she went to sleep, and then . . .

While we were talking, my son found an unopened box of Anpanman figures. He held out the box with a look of triumphant delight. The grandmother told him to open up the box. Then she asked me to tell the story of how Ewan was born. I told her how he had been due in January, but that my water broke suddenly in December. I called the doctor, who asked me to come to the hospital. We tried for forty-eight hours to induce labor, but my body would not cooperate. Ultimately Ewan was delivered by Cesarean.

"Isn't that fascinating," the grandmother said to me through her tears. "Isn't life so strange? The start of life and the end of life are so strange. You can't understand the meaning at the time. Only later, when someone dies, do you understand their story. And even then sometimes you *don't* understand . . ."

She trailed off again and handed Kasugi to her friend. "Has anyone in your family died?"

I told her how I had lost my father six months after getting married, and just over a year before my son was born. I explained that my father had been my best friend and that I still struggled without him. I had spent much of my pregnancy crying. I had tried not to cry because I hadn't wanted my son to be sad. I still found it incredible that my father would never know Ewan. He loved children. She nodded. She said she could not understand how or why Hina was not going to be an older sister.

There was a sudden change in the air. I looked up and saw Kaneta standing in the entry to the room. He had been so quiet, I hadn't heard him come inside. He saw me sitting on the floor, and Ewan surrounded by an array of toys and unwrapped pieces of candy, and the video camera playing back a recording of Hina laughing and smiling. He started almost imperceptibly at the sight of us, then nodded once to himself. "So," he said to the grandmother, as he sat down at the table. "You're still doing this kind of thing with the video."

Ewan went over to Kaneta and stood next to him.

The grandmother nodded, the tears flowing freely.

"You know you've got to stop it. Otherwise she can't move on from here. She's still here right now. That is your first challenge—to let her go."

"I know," the grandmother sobbed.

"Your second challenge will be how to explain Hina to little Kasugi. He's just a baby right now. But soon he will begin to notice that you are crying. And he will be able to talk." Kaneta looped his priest's apron over his head and looked over at another priest who had come into the room. "Which sutras do you know?" As I had seen him do before, Kaneta consulted with the volunteer to determine which ones, if any, the two of them knew, despite their different schools and their different training.

While this was going on, Ewan did an odd thing. He seemed to understand that they were about to perform a memorial service, and so he picked up the mallet used to ring the gong and began to hit the bell. He rang it a few times, looking around for approval, which Kaneta, utterly nonplussed, gave him. Then Kaneta took out some incense and lit it, and Ewan immediately took one of the sticks and waved it around in the air, as he had seen me do, to extinguish the flame but keep the end burning. "Whoah!" Kaneta exclaimed, as he took the incense from Ewan's hand. "That's enough now."

We all put our hands together, and Kaneta and his assistant began to pray.

The last time I had thought about the connection between life and death was when my son was born. I remember thinking about the strangeness of watching consciousness develop in my son while, if I was to believe the Buddhists, my father's consciousness was fading. Sometimes my son laughed or nodded his head exactly the way my Japanese grandfather did. It's genetics, of course, that account for this. I remember my father saying to me the only thing that ever lived on in humans was their DNA.

Kaneta finished chanting his sutra, and as if he could read my thoughts, he said, "Isn't life a strange thing? I just don't know why things happen sometimes. Look at you," he said to the grandmother. "People from all over the world come here now to see you because of the tsunami."

She brightened just slightly and looked at me. "I wouldn't have met you if it weren't for the tsunami. And Hina got to play with Ewan today."

I smiled back at her, but inside I was raging against the injustice of a three-year-old girl dying, after having been saved from the tsunami by her grandmother. If Hina were alive, she and Ewan could *actually* be playing together with toys, instead of in this imaginary space.

"Where is she buried?" I asked.

"At Daitokuji," said the grandmother. "A nearby temple. It's an amazing place—hundreds of years old with a large statue of Fudō Myō-ō. Our family had no burial plot. No place to go. But Daitokuji took us, and I can visit her any time. I am so grateful. So grateful." She began to cry again, and I hugged her.

"That's where you should take Kasugi," Kaneta said. "That's where he should play with Hina when he is older."

It was time to go. I was taking a train back to the city of Sendai. After the tsunami, the train ran very irregularly, and I would need to hurry to catch it, or risk paying an exorbitant amount for a taxi. The grandmother would not let us leave until we took a pack of Hina's candy.

I picked Ewan up in my arms. Kaneta was staring at the shrine.

"Anpanman," he said. "You know, the other day I had to do another funeral for a child. That one was Anpanman-themed too. This seems to be the trend for children who die."

"*Sore ike!*" I said. Let's go! This is what Anpanman and his flying friends often say right before they depart for new adventures.

"That's right!" Kaneta said brightly. "And you know what? One day, we will all take off! We will all take to the sky!"

Before I left, I promised the grandmother that my son and I would return to see her. Then I gave her a hug. People don't usually hug in Japan; even now, people mostly bow when they say goodbye. But it seemed wrong just to bow in this context. The grandmother hugged me back.

"And I'll be back, you know. I'll see you again very soon," Kaneta promised. "In the meantime, take care of that baby." And with that, Kaneta ushered me out.

TEN

Parting the Atoms

I HAD ALWAYS ASSUMED THAT my family in Nagasaki had been very lucky to be out of town the day the atom bomb was dropped. My mother's aunt and cousins had evacuated to the countryside. My great-uncle had been out fishing. That's what I had been told.

One morning in early spring a few years ago, I was sitting with my mother's cousin, Ryūnosuke, and drinking coffee in his living room. Very casually, he started to talk about the bomb. He told me that his father—my great-uncle—had actually been conscripted into the military and had not been home in three years on the day of the bombing. Ryūnosuke's father was physically weak, and thus he was in the last group of men scheduled to be sent to the front; had the war not ended when it did, my great-uncle would surely have been killed.

Ryūnosuke was nine at the time of the bombing. He was standing outside the family home, mesmerized by a strange plane flying too low and far too slowly. "The Japanese say *pika don*!" he exclaimed ruefully, referring to the onomatopoeia the Japanese reserve for nuclear explosions. "Well, I saw the damned *pika don*. I went into our house, but it was falling apart, so I ran back out into the nearby shelter with the rest of my family." When they emerged hours later, the city was on fire. After about a week, their next-door neighbors were dead. He could not understand why his family had survived and others so close to them had died.

I realized then that I hadn't been told the truth about my family's experiences, in part because no one wanted to make me, the American, feel bad. Nor did they want to hurt my mother, who had married an American. But I suspected there were also more complicated social reasons for the revised version of the truth we'd been told. In Japan, it is one thing to have been located in the vicinity of the explosion. It is another thing entirely to have been showered by radiation. The latter can make you a social pariah.

Ryūnosuke is a handsome and successful man. He has never traveled overseas, but he loves American jazz, Impressionist paintings, and Somerset Maugham. When I was twelve, I listened to Stevie Wonder songs and transcribed the lyrics so Ryūnosuke could sing along. In his retirement, he paints beautiful watercolors and contributes to his town's historical preservation society. He has been kind to me since childhood, though I've seen his personality change as he has aged. The bombing continues to haunt his life. He told me that he used to protest the U.S. occupation and all forms of nuclear power in Japan, but that time has made him more pessimistic. The government that drove Japan into World War II was irresponsible. The war liberated many Japanese from their inherited feudal position as serfs to the emperor. This is an attitude that more than one Japanese has expressed to me in private. But the fact that human beings continue to wage war against each other, while being fully aware of what the atom bomb can do to the innocent, made him highly skeptical of our worth as a species.

He spoke matter-of-factly, but there was an underlying urgency to his words, and I realized that for a long time he had wanted to unburden himself of his memories and his feelings about the war and about people. Behind him, his wife stared in shock; she had never heard him talk about witnessing the nuclear bomb. My mother, who had been sitting with us, was also stunned.

I asked, "Is there anything transcendent you believe in? Isn't there anything good that we have done?"

He said that his mother had become a Christian as a young woman and had turned fervently to her faith after the war, but Christianity did not suit him. He was not sure that any religion did. He paused. And then he said to me that there was a form of Buddhism that greatly intrigued him. It was older than Zen and certainly far older than Pure Land. Though it originated in China, it has all but disappeared there, but it has been preserved in Japan for over a millennia. Its teachings had been veiled in secrecy. Up until the twentieth century, nothing had been written down about this form of Buddhism, and to learn anything about it, one had to work directly under a master. In the West, scholars categorize this form of Buddhism as "esoteric," a reference to its secret and somewhat mystical reputation. Its name was Shingon.

"I've heard it said that Shingon explained the Big Bang long before we knew about atoms," Ryūnosuke said to me. He told me that I ought to consider going to Mount Kōya, the home of Shingon, to find someone to teach me the Shingon form of meditation, called *ajikan*.

MOUNT KŌYA, OR Kōyasan, is not really a mountain, but a basin in the middle of a constellation of eight different peaks that is said to resemble a lotus flower. Founded in 819 AD, Kōyasan developed from a small and remote complex to become a Buddhist mecca akin to Lhasa. At its peak, Kōyasan housed about a thousand subtemples and numerous shops, becoming a sort of Buddhist Disneyland where samurai and aristocrats could relax and gain inspiration, while serious clergy trained to become priests. Fires and revolutions reduced Kōyasan to nearly 120 temples, and while women were not permitted to climb Kōyasan until 1872, today everyone is welcome.

Kōyasan is also home to the most famous cemetery in Japan. A walk through the Okunoin cemetery puts you face-to-face with a who's who of Japan: the great heroes, the villains, the *daimyō* (Japan's feudal rulers), and Japan's greatest corporations—all have either a monument or an actual mausoleum there. In fact, the number of mausoleums dedicated to samurai and the number of those erected for the employees of corporations are roughly equal, with about a hundred devoted to each category. Were nothing else to remain of Japan but this cemetery, scholars would have a snapshot of twelve hundred years of Japanese history: from emperors, to kamikaze pilots, to Panasonic employees. As of 2013, the newest memorial, commissioned by an anonymous nun, was built of pink marble to pay tribute to the victims of the 2011 Great East Japan Earthquake.

Shingon was founded by the great Buddhist teacher Kūkai, who, to the Japanese, is an early historical figure of mythic proportions, like Prince Shōtoku. Kūkai was born in 774 AD to an aristocratic family on the remote island of Shikoku, but the history of his early years is not definitively known. His family seems to have tried to educate him to become a bureaucrat, but Kūkai was more interested in Buddhism. In 804 AD, thirty-year-old Kūkai went to China in search of a Buddhist text he'd seen in a dream.

In China, Kūkai was greeted by the Shingon master Hui-kuo, who said, "How excellent, excellent that we have met today at last! My life is ending soon, and yet I have no more disciples to whom to transmit the Dharma. Prepare without delay." Three months later, Hui-kuo was dead, and Kūkai was his spiritual heir. In 806, Kūkai returned to Japan and set about sharing what he learned.

His accomplishments are legendary. It was Kūkai who was said to have developed the kana script—the Japanese phonetic alphabet still in use today. Kūkai was a great engineer who also constructed the Manno reservoir, still the largest irrigated reservoir in Japan today. His calligraphy was so beautiful that Ryūnosuke would stare and stare at it in museums, trying to figure out how one person had created such beautiful letters. Kūkai was beloved by the emperors he served, who always asked him to help stop droughts and plagues. But it was his Buddhist teachings that most distinguished Kūkai and made him so beloved by his followers—and also by nonbelievers—even today. While my cooking teacher, Asano, was not a practitioner of Shingon, she had tremendous respect for Kūkai. "He helped establish the roots of Buddhism in Japan," she said. "It's impossible not to be in awe of him."

In 835, after a long illness, Kūkai died, and his followers interred him in a mausoleum deep in the woods. Several years later, a priest opened the tomb and found that Kūkai's remains had not decayed. The great Buddhist teacher had not died at all. He was still alive, deep in meditation and awaiting the arrival of the future Buddha, Maitreya. To this day, senior priests on Kōyasan proceed into the mausoleum, where they are said to change the great master's clothes. They also bring him two meals a day: one at 5:40 a.m. and a second at 11:00 a.m. Both meals are, of course, *shōjin ryōri*.

Over successive centuries, Japan's elite competed to build their mausoleums close to Kūkai to ensure their salvation. Some could not afford an actual tombstone, so they made arrangements to send a lock of hair or a nail to the communal crematorium located just off to the right of Kūkai's mausoleum. The important thing was to be near the great master. From time to time, people even encountered Kūkai. I had read a particularly moving story about a World War II veteran who encountered Kūkai in the fog in the cemetery. The great old priest looked exhausted, and the soldier realized that the great man, too, was weary, after struggling to save as many people as possible during the war.

. . .

IN 2004, KŌYASAN was designated a World Heritage site by UNESCO, and it is now a popular overnight stop among foreigners. There are no hotels on Kōyasan. If you stay here, you must spend the night in a temple.

With over seventy temples to choose from on Kōyasan, I had no idea which one to select. On a whim, I phoned a place called Shōjōshinin because my guidebook had starred it, noting its lovely medieval-period gardens. Shōjōshinin was located just before the entrance to the Okunoin cemetery. I couldn't see Shōjōshinin when I first disembarked from the bus. Only after I crossed a stone bridge suspended over a canal did Shōjōshinin unfold in overlapping layers of gray, brown, white, green, and pink. There was a wooden gate just on the other side of the bridge, flanked by two large wooden buckets of water; samurai had once visited Kōyasan on horseback, and the buckets for watering the horses are today maintained out of respect for tradition. It was late April when I visited, and spring had long since passed in the Tōkyō area. But here, behind a low wall made of white stucco and neatly pieced together pieces of wood, two large cherry blossoms spread up and out like geysers.

In the office, a priest named Yanagi greeted me. He had been at Shōjōshinin for seven years. Though he was married, he spent most of his time on Kōyasan, flying home once or twice a month to see his wife, who lived on the island of Hokkaido. Yanagi wore an allergy mask over his mouth. This isn't so unusual in Japan, but during conversation, the masks are often removed. Yanagi didn't remove his mask at all, and I had the uneasy feeling that I was being kept at a polite arm's length.

I asked Yanagi the same questions I ask every priest I meet for the first time. Did Shōjōshinin have a head priest? The answer he gave me was so bizarre, I was certain I had misunderstood. Yanagi seemed to say that while Shōjōshinin had a head priest, this man had not been recognized by the Kōyasan bureaucracy, a fact that made Yanagi very angry. Even when his face was flushed red and hot with anger, Yanagi did not remove his face mask to breathe easier. I quickly apologized for asking questions. It was no matter, Yanagi said, and then told me to follow him to my room.

Though no one used the original kitchen anymore, it remained intact and untouched, with no rope or glass separating it from the hallway as we passed by. The floors were slick and black, the legacy of hundreds of feet polishing them smooth. There were mammoth pots over kiln-sized stoves, once used to boil rice and soup for guests and monks-in-training. Overhead, an open-air chimney stood ready to release smoke and hot air. The chimney was angled to collect water in a basin that would have been used for washing. There were shrines to the Shintō goddess Amaterasu and to the god Daikokuten; in true Japanese fashion, it was perfectly acceptable for one to honor the native Japanese gods and the Buddha at the same time.

The door to my room could not be locked from the outside; from the inside, one turned a screw in a hole to keep the door permanently shut. My grandparents had locked the sliding glass doors in their house like this. In the room was a *kotatsu*, the blanket that fit over a low table, like the one I had used at Empukuji. The windows opened up to a view of the Momoyama-period garden in the back of the temple, with a little pond and neatly manicured trees. A wisteria was just off to the left, though it would need another month to bloom.

AT 5:50 THE next morning, one of the priests rang a bell, and I rose and wended my way through the labyrinth of passageways to the *hondō*. It was time for morning prayers. Five priests in brightly embroidered robes, including Yanagi, sat on the tatami floor in front of the altar. There was a lot of chanting and bell ringing, and at one point I heard Yanagi give a special prayer for the victims of the tsunami and their families.

At the very end, one of the priests turned and bowed to everyone in the room and said in English, "Now we have concluded our morning service. Please join us for breakfast." The guests, all foreigners, rose to leave. A moment later, Yanagi said in Japanese, "If anyone would like to visit the other rooms in the temple, they are currently open, and contain several fine sculptures of great historical importance."

I realized he was talking to me.

The rest of the Westerners began the tricky business of putting on slippers, while I, and a Canadian girl I had befriended, made our way over to Yanagi, who stood in a doorway just off to the side.

There were two small rooms beyond Yanagi, and these were connected by a doorway. In the first room, there was a stunning Amida Buddha from the Kamakura era that had originated from the workshop of Unkei. I was shocked. Unkei is often referred to as the Japanese Michelangelo. In 2008, for example, a twelfth-century statue by Unkei sold at auction for a staggering $14.37 million.

"Technically, it's just the studio of Unkei," Yanagi said to me.

"But still."

There was also an exquisite small statue of the warrior god Bishamonten. "For many years," Yanagi said to me, "our temple was associated with the Uesugi clan. Have you heard of them?"

I certainly had. The Uesugi were one of Japan's most famous families, and in the sixteenth century, the warlord Uesugi Kenshin was famous not only for his prowess on the battlefield but also for his wise governance over his fief. Once upon a time, Yanagi explained, each of the temples on Mount Kōya was associated with a powerful clan, and if I looked closely, I would see that many temples still flew the banner of their feudal patron.

The next room contained an even bigger surprise, for here stood a Heian-period statue of Fudō Myō-ō, the Buddhist deity whom I had most loved from childhood. Temple lore indicated that the statue had existed around the time of Kūkai himself—that he would have seen it. "And now you are seeing it too," Yanagi said.

Instantly I thought about my father. Fudō was without question his favorite deity too. We both loved how Fudō always appeared to be at once charming but ferocious, and whenever we ran into a Fudō statue in an art gallery or museum, we instantly tried to copy his expression.

I should note here that while my father listed his occupation as "farmer" on his tax returns, because he had inherited a family wheat farm in Nebraska, he was in reality a sort of jack-of-all-trades, extremely skilled with his hands and enthusiastically curious about everything. He had always loved all the arts, and in the 1960s, he rented a car and drove around the Balkans and on to Greece and Crete and then to Italy, in a pilgrimage to see some of the world's great art treasures. He hadn't known too much about Japanese art as a young man, though his mother had a collection of *netsuke*, little ivory figures in whimsical shapes that the Japanese used to help attach containers to their kimonos, since traditional Japanese clothing did not include pockets. Once he met my mother, however, my father's curiosity led him to investigate Japanese art, which in the 1970s and '80s could still be collected for a reasonable price.

My father liked to find damaged and undervalued antiques and to repair them either for us to keep or to resell. Mostly he kept what he found because we were unable to part with the treasures he nursed back to life. Our house was full of Japanese screens that he had patched up, Buddhas who literally needed a hand, and porcelain ewers requiring a lid. My dad would supply all these pieces with new parts. Though he always looked for and hoped to find a Fudō, he never had.

Yanagi asked me to continue to follow him. He paused just outside a small building, perhaps no larger than six tatami mats. The doorway was quite low, and I had to stoop to enter the dark space. Inside there was another altar, with gold cups and bells and the intricate trappings to associate with Shingon. At the back of the room was a closed box, the kind that holds a statue.

"This," Yanagi explained, "is the true *hondō*. The original." The room we had inhabited for morning prayers, while still a *hondō*, was not the original one that had existed in Kūkai's time. That room was for visitors. This room was the real thing. And it had a history.

Yanagi chose his words carefully. He said that this *hondō*—this little room—was very important in the history of Shingon, and for true believers. This marked the spot where Kūkai had once built a little hut for himself. Later, the hut was replaced by a small temple of the same dimensions—this very temple—which explained why the room was so small. Before Kūkai was taken off to his mausoleum in Okunoin, he spent the night in this room. While alive, Kūkai had also told his followers that if they were troubled and felt they needed to speak to him, they could come to this little *hondō* and he would be there for them. The closed box contained a statue of Odaishisan, or "the great master," as believers refer to Kūkai, on view only one day of the year—April 20.

"So, Kūkai died in this room?"

Yanagi waved his hand, the way Japanese do to negate something you have said in error. "No no no. Odaishisan is not dead."

I WAS LATE for breakfast, the last to start eating and the last to leave. The cleaning crew had begun to remove the abandoned dishes and tables while I was still chewing my bamboo shoots. I engaged one of the men in conversation.

His name was Furuie. He was middle-aged, and seemed to be in charge of the kitchen staff. He was a civilian, he explained, born and raised on Kōyasan. Once upon a time Shōjōshinin had had many pilgrims, but now he mostly served foreigners, many of whom did not understand the food they were eating. Consequently, there was tremendous waste. Once, he and the kitchen staff had tried to serve Western-style food, but there had been complaints. The foreigners wanted the authentic experience, even if none of them actually wanted to eat the food.

After commiserating with Furuie about the wasted food, I asked if he knew where I might find some coffee. "There are many cafés in town," Furuie said cheerfully. "Priests love coffee!"

Not long after, I was about to leave the temple to go sightseeing when I ran into Yanagi in the large hall with the ancient rice pots. He had heard that I was in search of coffee, and had made a pot for us to share, though he asked me to make sure I did not let any of the other Westerners know. The coffee was just for us.

We sat in the reception area together, and Yanagi poured me a cup. Then he took off his face mask to drink. The coffee was excellent, and I told him so. Yanagi beamed, and I felt relieved to see his entire face. Yanagi said he was partial to good coffee and had ground the beans himself. He looked at me expectantly again.

I wasn't quite sure what I was supposed to do, so I simply said the first thing that came to mind. I told him that I was interested in trying to learn the esoteric form of meditation called *ajikan*. Might it be possible to do *ajikan* at Shōjōshinin?

At this, Yanagi perceptibly started. It was possible for me to try to meditate here, Yanagi said, but proper training would need to be done by the temple's *jūshoku*, or the head priest. Unfortunately, the *jūshoku* was often quite tired late at night. The previous evening,

Yanagi had attempted to teach *ajikan* to a foreign guest, but she had complained that meditating so late in the day had not left her enough time to take a bath. Also, the meditation session had taken place immediately after dinner, and the foreigner had not liked being hurried through her meal just for the sake of making an appointment. She had been sleepy during the meditation. I, too, might not particularly like to meditate in the evening, though it was the only time the *jūshoku* had free, if he was even free at all. If he wasn't, Yanagi himself might be able to teach me, but then he was also very busy. Perhaps, Yanagi suggested, I could try to sign up for an *ajikan* meditation class at Kongōbuji, Mount Koya's main temple. It ought to be available there. And if it was not, I could phone him back and let him know, and he would see if my *ajikan* session could be arranged without interfering with everyone else's work.

There were now so many "coulds" and "woulds" and "mights" that I felt completely flustered. I had fallen in love with Shōjōshinin— with the dark hallways, the intricate garden, the irrepressible cherry trees. I loved the oversized Shintō shrines by the kitchen, the bustle of the monks and the staff moving throughout the grounds, and, of course, the special little *hondō* and the statues.

But I also felt that I had inadvertently been clumsy and perhaps even offensive. Maybe I ought to just get through my stay, like all the other foreigners who were clearly regarded as ignorant, and just skim the surface of the experience, instead of trying to probe any deeper. I was so uncomfortable that I decided I would most certainly not call Yanagi in the event that I needed his help. He was clearly busy, and I had no desire to add to his stress and to become stressed myself as a result.

At Kongōbuji, the ecclesiastic head temple of the Shingon religion on Mount Koya, I was told that no *ajikan* meditation was available. No one I asked seemed remotely interested in helping me to find an alternate teacher. It was a rainy day, and I wandered around from building to temple before finally coming upon the visitors' center. Once again, I asked a woman at the information desk where I might receive *ajikan* instruction.

"Unfortunately, there is no public *ajikan* available right now. They don't do it till May. Where are you staying?"

"Shōjōshinin."

"Oh. Well." She paused, then continued speaking rapidly. "Your temple's *jūshoku* can help you. Or Yanagi. He knows *ajikan* too. You call and ask them. Do you have the phone number? Do you have a phone?" She didn't wait for me to answer, but instead plunged ahead, barking out to her assistant to help me with the phone number, reiterating that one of the two men ought to be able to help me.

I protested. "Yanagi sounded like he was very busy. And apparently the head priest is . . . often busy."

"Nonsense. They can teach you. Call them. Or I will. Where else have you been on Kōyasan? Did you go to the cemetery?"

"Partway. I didn't go all the way to Kūkai's grave."

"Mausoleum. He doesn't have a grave . . ."

" . . . because he isn't dead."

"You should go there," she said. "Then meditate with your priest tonight. Now. We have a purification ceremony here starting in five minutes. You should go do that. Guests were supposed to be in the waiting area ten minutes ago. Hurry!"

There were three of us in the waiting area: a very thin Japanese man with extremely long white hair, carrying a weathered backpack and a walking cane; the young woman from Canada; and me. The information woman had given me a pamphlet written in unusually accurate and detailed English. It explained that parts of Jukai, the purification ceremony, would take place in complete darkness, rendering the document completely unreadable once the service was under way. The pamphlet also went to great lengths to assure visitors that participating in Jukai did not mean one was swearing off God in favor of Buddha, and that one would not accidentally swear oneself to be a Buddhist.

A few moments later, two priests, wearing black frocks with gold-and-scarlet over-robes, glided out of a back room and made their way toward us. They looked roughly the same age—early forties or late thirties—and moved with uniform grace. One of the men caught my attention. He was trim, with alert, very round eyes that darted about, quickly taking in information and assessing it. He had an intelligent manner about him. At the same time, he let show, just briefly, his irritation that among the people who had come to attend the morning's purification ceremony were two foreigners. This dissatisfaction seemed to confirm an inner confidence that bordered on arrogance.

"Let's go. Come on. Come on!" The arrogant one waved us out a door, as though we were puppies in need of our daily walk. The Japanese pilgrim, who had brightened perceptibly at the sight of the two men, turned to me and gave me a wide, tooth-missing smile, his eyes sparkling. With his long, white hair and a long moustache dancing off the sides of his mouth like tentacles, he looked like one of those five-hundred-year-old carp you see in ponds on the grounds of ancient temples. I smiled back, a little startled that he had engaged me.

The priests repeated the instructions given on the information sheet: We would be in a dark temple room and would not be able to read a thing. At the end of the ceremony, we might receive a special diploma. If our names were called, we were to walk carefully to the front of the room. There would be very little light, and we would need to climb a set of stairs. Then they asked us to rub our hands with special incense.

"Thank you," I said in Japanese.

Most of the time when Japanese people realize I speak their language, they are either happy, relieved, or, most often, impressed. But the arrogant one seemed even more irritated. "Is your phone on? Make sure your phone is off. I don't want any phones going off in the middle of the ceremony. How about your friend?" he nodded at the young Canadian woman. I assured him that our phones were off. "You are sure? No photos either. You aren't claustrophobic, are you? Because it will be dark. And we won't open the door for you if you are scared." I assured him that I would be just fine, and told myself that I would be here only for half an hour. I ought to be able to withstand anything for half an hour. The tatami floor was quite old and very worn. Clearly, many hundreds of people had been here before me and had survived. The arrogant one rolled his eyes, and his partner swung the heavy doors shut, sealing us in. I had said I was not claustrophobic, but in the dark the air seemed heavy and thick.

Before long, the two men came in again from a side door. It was still quite dark, but I knew them from their silhouettes. They crept onto the altar, then sat off to the side and started chanting after inviting us to chant too. One phrase was repeated constantly: "*Namu Daishi Henjō Kongō.*" Later, I would learn that in repeating this, I was vowing to take refuge in Kūkai.

A third figure, large and shadowy, now strode onto the altar and sat in the throne. We couldn't see his face. There was just enough light to make out his profile—I could see his ears, but I couldn't really see him. I couldn't even tell if he was facing us or facing the back of the room. He looked, instead, like a living statue.

We were lectured in Japanese on the Eightfold Path, the rules one needed to follow to achieve enlightenment, but it was not a version of Buddha's teachings that I had ever heard before. The man in the middle—the man on the throne—said that humans had cravings and that it was impossible to remove desires and cravings, but that day by day we should think about the things we wanted and try to make it a habit to respond to our hungers in the best possible way. In doing so, over time, we could be closer and closer to Buddha. "Avoid gossip," he repeated. It seemed like an odd thing for a Buddhist priest to say, but it struck a chord with me. I was far too old to worry about what people thought about me, and yet I did all the time.

All too soon, the man in the middle began to read our names. The older man with the long hair climbed up to the altar first. He was from Hokkaido, the very north of Japan, which only confirmed for me that he was on a pilgrimage. Then it was my turn, and finally the girl from Canada. The priests departed, and a moment later the doors were opened and we went outside into the pouring rain. We crossed from that hall to another larger temple room and then back into the visitors' center.

I stopped by the information desk to thank the lady for having helped me, but before I could say anything, she waved her hand emphatically. "Hey! Ryūshin-san!" she called out. "This girl is staying at your temple and she wants to meditate."

I turned around and looked. It was the arrogant priest from my Jukai session. It was now lunchtime, and he was chewing on something. "Hmm?" he mumbled, his large, round eyes open wide in disbelief.

"You go and talk to him," the information lady ordered me.

I very much did not want to talk to this man, this priest who assumed all foreigners were rude enough to keep their cell phones on and who was apparently working so hard at his day job, that Yanagi and all the others at Shōjōshinin had to work doubly hard to make up for his absence. And why was he absent all the time anyway if he was the *jūshoku*? The fact that he was even better looking up close made the situation even more annoying.

Before I could say anything at all, Ryūshin swallowed his food and spoke to me. "Yeah, I heard there was a request for meditation. So have you ever meditated?"

I said that I had done zazen but had never tried *ajikan*. I explained that I had relatives in Tōhoku who ran a temple, and that they weren't sure I really understood Buddhism, and that I thought I owed it to them to try to be better educated. I said I was the sort of person who liked to read and always thought it was possible to learn everything from books, but that I now was not so sure. "There's almost nothing written down about Shingon," I said. "There must be a reason for that."

"I don't read many books myself," Ryūshin said cheerfully.

He told me that at its core, Shingon required followers to put certain practices in the body. It was only by inhabiting these behaviors that one would understand Kūkai's teachings. Perhaps in the future I would come back and do sutra copying. It was an entirely different thing to chant a sutra out loud, let alone read it silently. If I wrote it down, I would have a deeper understanding. There was a distinct shift in the way he spoke to me now. A genuine warmth, mixed in with a gentle curiosity. He would be very happy, he said, to teach me the basics of *ajikan* meditation after dinner.

IN THE AFTERNOON, I went to Kōyasan's museum to look at the treasures accumulated over the centuries. Kūkai was particularly interested in the mandala, a depiction of nothing less than the entire universe. There are two kinds of mandala: the "diamond" mandala, which is square in shape, and the "womb" mandala, which is round. The diamond mandala represents the outside world, and the womb mandala the inner world. Most of the time, mandalas are depicted through very colorful, geometrical paintings featuring rows and rows of Buddhas and bodhisattvas seated in meditation.

Unlike Zen altars, which usually house the historical Buddha,

Shingon's prime being of worship is known as Vairocana in Sanskrit, or Dainichi Nyorai in Japanese. Guidebooks often explain that Dainichi Nyorai is the "Cosmic Buddha"—he has always existed and always will exist outside the confines of time. By contrast, Shakyamuni, the historical Buddha, was born a man and became an enlightened being, and thus has a specific beginning. In nature, the Dainichi Nyorai appears like the sun, which accounts for his brilliant jewelry and elaborate clothing. He is also often surrounded by a motley crew of other Buddhist deities who have dozens of arms and sometimes extra eyes and heads. Intellectually, I knew that these many-armed and -eyed creatures were supposed to represent the Buddha's ability to be everywhere all at once, but I always found statues such as these to be more amusing than enlightening.

THAT EVENING, THE mood at Shōjōshinin was fraught with excitement and expectation. "Hello! Welcome back!" Furuie greeted me. For the first time, Yanagi seemed relaxed and happy. Ryūshin was coming! Ryūshin would be here tonight, and I would have the chance to meditate with him! They were ecstatic, and I wondered again what exactly was going on in the temple. I had an hour before dinner, so I took a bath. Then, since Shōjōshinin offered free Internet access, I sat down and began to do a little digging. It didn't take too long for me to find what I was looking for.

A decade ago, Shōjōshinin had been in the care of a priest called Yamagishi Shungaku, who had passed away unexpectedly in 2003. On Kōyasan, temples are not handed off to the eldest son but instead follow the old way in which the current head priest chooses a successor from among his disciples. Yamagishi, the old head of Shōjōshinin, had wanted Ryūshin.

However, another priest named Kuri, who already had one temple of his own, submitted a claim asserting that *he* was the designated heir; the paper work did not clarify how or why he came to make such a statement. In the initial settlement of this dispute, the Kōyasan bureaucracy allowed Kuri to look after Shōjōshinin for a year. Then the position was to go to Ryūshin. In the meantime, Ryūshin could keep his room at Shōjōshinin while working a day job at the visitors' center and also acting as a "priest for hire." But Kuri never signed the agreement. Instead he submitted yet another document to Kōyasan, asking to be paid a fee equaling the amount of $280,000 to release his claim. And here is an example of the kind of "nuance" that the Japanese prize in their communication; Kōyasan responded to this claim with silence, which meant that the bureaucracy condoned Kuri's behavior.

The other priests at the temple—Yanagi and others—were Ryūshin's followers, which accounted for their feeling of brotherhood and for the fierce way in which they at once protected him and were suspicious of newcomers. They kept Kuri away and welcomed Ryūshin home when he was able to take a break from his other responsibilities. For ten years, the men had kept this delicate equation in balance. Later, when I indignantly told Ryūnosuke about this situation, he nodded indulgently as I carried on and on. "Marie," he said, "in Japan, such an important thing like bloodlines can never be decided in court. It is a matter between the different temples to sort out on their own."

A little voice in my head reminded me about the purification ceremony and how we had been advised to avoid gossip. I was now not avoiding gossip. I was very actively seeking out gossip and taking sides in a dispute that had nothing to do with me.

AFTER DINNER, FURUIE intercepted me in the hallway. "Wait right here!" While I waited, I watched young men slide open the doors to the kitchen with one hand, while balancing little dish-covered tables stacked one on top of the other. They moved like acrobats. A moment later, Ryūshin came out to meet me. He had changed into a set of mustard-colored robes. "Hello," he said cheerfully, then glided off toward the *hondō*. I quickened my pace to keep up.

"I'm forty-five years old, and I've been here since I was eighteen. That means I've been in this place for twenty-seven years. Can you imagine?" He laughed, as if to say he understood how the very idea that a forty-five-year-old man spending twenty-seven years in a monastery in this modern world was an absurd thing. He said he'd come to Shōjōshinin as a result of connections between his family's temple in Nagasaki and the temple here. He was the second son—his older brother got the family temple.

Ryūshin's eyes were large and round. In this, he was like my mother, whose own mother was from Nagasaki. "I have family in Nagasaki," I said. "I went there often as a child."

"I understand your family owns a temple in Tōhoku too." He paused and smiled at me. "*En desu ne?*" It's fate then, isn't it?

I apologized that it had taken me so long to understand his circumstances.

Ryūshin kept smiling. "Everything around us is here to teach us something. I wasn't tough enough when I was younger, and now I have to be. Please don't worry. I'm all right. And I am *very* happy you are here."

He ducked his head and went into the *hondō*—the real *hondō*. I was going to meditate like a true pilgrim. Everything had been prepared. There were two pillows catty-corner to each other on the floor. The overhead light had been extinguished. Warm candlelight and sparkling gold dishes gave the small room a powerful luminescence. Here in this little space, with its hidden Buddha and its link to Kūkai and history, I felt a presence that comes only from a powerful and carefully managed intimacy. I did not feel like a guest visiting a beautiful space kept out of reach; I had been allowed on the inside.

On the floor, a two-foot-high easel displayed a square painting of the Sanskrit character for "A." The "A" had been painted in black ink inside a white circle, with a lotus flower drawn very lightly on the bottom. The rest of the paper surrounding the circle was black. Candlelight illuminated the painting from behind, so it glowed like a small moon. Now I didn't feel like I was in a room at all, or at least not an ordinary room. I was in some kind of planetarium, and the world had been stripped away, and around me stars and planets trembled. "Have a seat." Ryūshin patted the pillow next to him and started to talk.

"The point of Zen, as I understand it, is to be nothing. To be in the void." He scoffed. "What is . . . *nothing?*"

He picked a dish up off the altar—the gesture was meant to seem casual, but it was full of dramatic flourish. Look at this dish right here, he said. Will this be here in a million years? No. So it is here. But it is not here. You know about atoms? Kūkai thought about atoms long before we were able to see them. If we had a thread that was thin enough, we could thread it through the cup and it would go out the other side. And so the cup is here, but it is not here. If enough time were to go by, the cup would not be here, but if we were to look for its atoms, we would find them scattered around the universe, which means the cup would be everywhere. And in the same way, the Buddha is everywhere. The point of Shingon is not to be nothing, but to understand that everything is and is not actually concrete. That's it.

Twelve hundred years of history, thousands of pages of ink

spilled on the subject of what the Buddha meant by entering the "void" and "nothingness." For me, this was the simplest, clearest explanation I had ever heard.

"Do you have a pen?" he asked.

I did. He wrote down two phrases in Chinese from the Heart Sutra:

心是得色

色是得心

I have only a rudimentary ability to read Chinese, but I knew these characters. The character 心 means "heart," with the two little marks in the upper right corner acting as little heart beats. The second two characters can be translated to "are very." The third means "color." For me, the phrase seemed to read, "Your heart has many colors. There are many colors in your heart." Ryūshin smiled indulgently. He said that a closer translation would be, "Matter is in your heart. Your heart is in matter. Everything is the same thing. The point of meditation is to feel this deeply. Within your heart." He touched his left breast.

He told me about his friend who had started out as a freelance cameraman, and who had gone to India to photograph homeless people, and then he decided to live like a homeless person in order to get their point of view. He started sleeping on the streets, and he learned that for homeless people, the air six inches above the ground is different from air that is higher. People who sleep on the streets sleep within that six inches and know about a quality of air and size of space that most people do not. The world was full of such seemingly hidden spaces.

Then the friend decided to go to Tibet. He hiked through the mountains and became extremely hungry and asked to join a monastery. The monks there told him to bring some water up from a nearby stream. They gave him a bucket, and he did as they asked. For days he brought the monks water, until he was finally invited to join the monastery.

They taught him to meditate. His focal point was a small window with no glass. Ryūshin held up his hands to show me how small—just a foot across. "This small!" Out the window was a view of the Himalayas. The monks told Ryūshin's friend to "go to the mountains," but they didn't mean that he should physically go there. They meant that he should fly there. And so he did. Ryūshin's friend noticed that some monks had lost fingers due to frostbite. Done correctly, however, meditation aided circulation and kept most of the monks' fingers warm and dry. Even though they were up high in the Himalayas and there was no heating and the meals were sparse and they wore thin robes, the monks were comfortable.

The man came back to Japan and became a Rinzai Zen priest and continued to pray and prostrate himself every day, not for enlightenment, but for everyone else. He taught meditation too, and Ryūshin considered him to be a master. He asked me to visit his friend someday.

Then Ryūshin talked a little bit more about Shingon. Kūkai once said that if you are a doctor and you walk along a mountain path, you will look at the plants and will know how they can be used to cure different ailments. A different person will walk along the same path and not know any of this, but that doesn't mean the plants don't have this power—they still do—it's just that the person doesn't know about them. A mineralogist will look at rocks and know that a precious stone is buried deep inside, but another person will look at them and just see rocks. In the same way, the Buddha is always inside a person, but that person has to recognize it.

The Buddha will lead you to the water, Ryūshin said, but you are the one who will have to force yourself to drink. All difficulties that are placed before us are placed there to teach us, and we must try to learn from them. When we do not like people, we must ask instead what it is in the person we are supposed to see that is good and what the situation is trying to teach us. That is why, he said, he had been able to persist at Shōjōshinin, despite the fact that the Kōyasan bureaucracy did not want to recognize his right to inherit the temple.

Kūkai said that if you come to a lake, you can be the kind of person who looks up the word "lake" and tries to figure out what it is based on its properties. Kūkai suggested it was better to go straight into the lake and figure it out as you swim.

Ryūshin laughed a lot as he talked, as though he was aware of how absurd he sounded. But he also seemed quite fond of absurdity, gleefully asking me if I wasn't amused, too, by the prospect of meditation preventing frostbite, or that sleeping on the ground within a six-inch space could reveal one of earth's secrets. Gone was the jaded, irritated man who had performed the purification ceremony. He was in his element—a teacher who enjoyed making the difficult questions of Buddhism easy and manageable. After he spoke for a while like this, in the dark room with all the fluttering candles and the green leaves on the altar, he said it was time to meditate.

He said that Kūkai knew that people needed beauty in order to focus and to learn, and that this was why in Shingon, one looked at a mandala with the Sanskrit character for "A," pronounced "ah," which was the first syllable in Sanskrit, English, and Japanese. He said that when a baby is born, it exhales and cries. And when we die, we take in a breath and then die.

I said I thought that people exhaled when they died. No, he said, we just breathe in. The air leaves us only when we are already dead. And this is why, he said, the breath is so important when you meditate. He asked me to visualize a large cup in my torso. And then he asked me to breathe.

First, I exhaled all the air in my lungs. Then, as I inhaled, I imagined filling my lungs with a pure liquid like milk. I imagined exhaling all the way down to my diaphragm, and then inhaling to my diaphragm. Then I exhaled harder, emptying everything from all over my body. I imagined the new air filling up my lungs and going through my veins and into my capillaries. Then I closed my mouth and breathed through my nose and focused on the mandala, with my eyes half closed.

At first, I would just stare at the letter "A." One day, I would close my eyes and see the symbol in my imagination. Eventually the letter would float out at me. It would enter into my body, and it would fill me up and I would be in it, as though I were sitting in the moon. Then I would practice sending the letter back out to the painting. Much later, I would be able to bring the letter back into my body, except this time we would both travel out into space.

Ryūshin told me that it was okay for my mind to be skeptical, even clouded. Meditation was supposed to be like looking at the moon. Occasionally, a cloud would come in front of my mind. But this was just fine. No cloud stayed in front of the moon forever. Something, he said, always blows a cloud away.

So we sat together and looked at the Sanskrit "A" suspended on the easel. The whole time, I had this strange feeling of being in the forest and looking at Kūkai's mausoleum from a slight angle, from the left and as though I was a bit up in the air. The letter "A" did not float into my body—it did move, but it seemed to want to go at my head. It dawned on me that at this moment, on Kōyasan and maybe even at Eiheiji, or in Tibet, other people were meditating. We were all sitting together. If you did a Google Earth satellite photo of the world, and put in little people-shaped icons where everyone was sitting, it would look an awful lot like a modern version of the mandalas I had seen in the museum that afternoon. And what if I added in everyone praying? Everyone in a mosque or a church? There would be more little people-shaped icons sitting together.

All too soon it was over. Ryūshin told me to exhale hard three times, with my hands above my head, and then lean over onto the floor. My fingertips tingled.

"Today," he said, "was just the beginning. Over time, everything else will just happen as I described. You just have to train your body."

He told me that Shingon was the only branch of the Buddhist faith in which it is acceptable to ask for material things and to receive them. "But what," he asked, "is that thing for? Is it just for you? Or is it for other people? If it's for other people, then that's okay."

He reiterated something I had heard at the purification ceremony that day. Kūkai had insisted that there was no point in not having desires or in trying to stop desires. It was important to desire something for the good of others.

I did not want the evening to come to an end. I had that same feeling as a young adult when I played the violin in the pit orchestra for community-theater shows in the summer. How I loved those evenings with show people, and how I mourned the end of summer, the end of the shows, the start of school. Then, as now, I didn't want to leave this magical space. Even now, months later, I can describe my time at Shōjōshinin, but there is a certain ineffable quality that escapes language, as there always is with things that shake us deeply.

I WOKE EARLY for morning prayers, led this time by Ryūshin. The door to the special *hondō*—the real *hondō*—remained closed, as did the doors to the side rooms containing the treasures. There would be no special viewing today. At breakfast, Furuie stopped by my table and told me he knew that I was leaving, and that he and the staff were most sad. I promised him that I would return, and that the next time I would bring my son.

I was reluctant to let go of my little room, with its view of the garden. One day, I thought, I would like to return here to this very room; I made a note of its number. As I was packing, there was a knock at my door. I opened it to find Ryūshin sitting on the wooden floor just outside. I sat down too, on the tatami in my room. I felt like a character in a Japanese novel, or in a film, for in the world of historical dramas this was the only way that men and women could converse—with a wall between them. Ryūshin had brought me a book he wanted me to read. It was written by his friend, the man who had gone to Tibet to become a priest. Ryūshin promised to keep in touch with me, and vowed to continue fighting the bureaucracy on Kōyasan.

I asked Ryūshin if he thought Shingon could have a practical application for the modern world. I asked him if he or any of the monks he knew had gone to Tōhoku to volunteer after the disaster.

He told me that after the tsunami, many priests—including Yanagi—had wanted to volunteer to help with clean-up efforts, but many of the men he knew had been discouraged by the experience. Priests were not welcomed. People thought they were harbingers of death. While the Christians had allied themselves with the Red Cross and were able to go right away to volunteer, the Buddhists had no such system. Many monks had left Tōhoku, discouraged.

But, he said philosophically, the priests had only themselves to blame for things turning out like this. They had not been treating their profession properly for many years—and now people were uncomfortable around them.

"We are too much at peace in Japan. We live in a bubble." The human heart, he said, had to have something to strive for or against in order for it to maintain a straight path. Without any friction, people simply wandered. "Shingon came from China. When Kūkai went to China, he was greeted by the master Hui-kuo, who said that Shingon would die out in China. And it did forty years later. We have managed to keep Shingon alive in Japan for twelve hundred years. If you think about it, the next stop eastward for Shingon would be . . . your country."

CRITICS OF SHINGON complain that it is an elitist religion. To attempt to understand Shingon is to immerse yourself in an aesthetically rich world, and to be taught by one teacher in an intimate relationship. Most people don't have the time or resources to commit themselves to a lifetime of this kind of intense and impractical study. It's no surprise that the Japanese aristocrats loved Shingon; nor is it a surprise that Pure Land Buddhism, with its populist message, supplanted Shingon in the hearts of commoners.

Yet I was deeply moved by my experiences on Kōyasan in a way that I was not with any other form of Buddhism. After my visit to Shōjōshinin, Buddhist sculptures and paintings looked completely different to me. Prior to going to Kōyasan, I'd looked at statues of many-armed Buddhas and just seen a human form with too many arms. They might as well have been identical to those unfortunates featured in a supermarket tabloid who required an operation from an expert medical team to remove extra arms. Now the many-armed Buddhas reminded me of twentieth-century statues by Giacometti or the Cubist pieces by Picasso, in which a human body seems to be everywhere all at once. This is what medieval Japanese artists had been trying to convey—nothing in life is static. These statues are physical expressions of all a body's desires, and the fact that one can't actually predict at any moment where a body, let alone an electron, will go next.

ELEVEN

WHERE THE DEAD GO

A CCORDING TO THE JAPANESE, when children die, their souls gather on a riverbank called Sai no Kawara. In the Pure Land sect of Buddhism, it's believed that children are sent to Sai no Kawara as punishment for causing their parents the deepest possible grief. Other schools teach that the souls of the dead children are unable to cross the river to the other side, where they can be reborn, because they haven't accrued enough karma in their short lives for anyone to judge what their next turn on the wheel of fate should be. While stranded, the children build little pyramids out of rock and stone; this Sisyphean task is supposed to help them either accrue a little bit of karma or build a scalable ladder they can climb to get out of the underworld. But there are demons lurking nearby, and these malevolent beings are always knocking over the rock piles so the children have to start all over again. Overseeing this never-ending drama is a cruel old hag known as Shozoku no Baba.

Fortunately, there is one particular bodhisattva who is dedicated to helping these children, and his name is Jizō. Unlike other bodhisattvas, Jizō wears simple robes and no jewelry. He often carries a staff. Sometimes you will see a small boy and girl hiding just inside his robes. On temple grounds and in cemeteries, such as the one on Mount Kōya, you may see dozens of Jizō statues made out of stone but dressed with a red bib and a red hat; red has long been associated with the power to ward off evil in East Asia. The extra fabric also helps give Jizō more hiding places for the lost children, because when he can, Jizō sneaks across Sai no Kawara and gathers children into his robes. Before Shozoku no Baba can figure out what is going on, Jizō brings these little children back over to the other side of the river, so their souls can go through the necessary process to be reincarnated.

You can visit Sai no Kawara. In fact, there are many Sai no Kawara all over Japan, though the majority are located in Tōhoku. They are sacred places, cherished by locals, and the site of unofficial pilgrimages for grieving parents who worry about how their lost children are doing on the invisible journey to the next world. Most are located next to a body of water, such as a river, or by the ocean. Though I grew up knowing that such places existed, my mother had never taken me to any of them. They were so sad, she said, and there were so many other things about Japan that were more important. But the 2013 Japanese documentary in which I participated included a visit to a Sai no Kawara located in Iwaki. And so early on in our filming, I went to the underworld for the first time.

THE EVENING BEFORE the documentary shoot at Sai no Kawara, I was at dinner with the film crew. The conversation, fueled by excellent sashimi and sake, turned to religion. The cameraman, Usui, wanted to know the main difference between Japan and the West.

It was an enormous question. In a lighthearted effort to simplify, I pointed out that the orthodox Judeo-Christian god is a man, that he is often portrayed as a father, and that he tolerates the existence of no other gods. In Shintō, the indigenous Japanese religion, the top spot is reserved for Amaterasu, the sun goddess. Indeed, by the time the documentary was completed and broadcast, there were two versions: one for Westerners and one for the Japanese. In the version shown internationally, the narrator was a British male. The version shown in Japan was narrated by a woman.

One by one, the crew professed not to be religious at all. But even as they said this, almost all of them had opinions about the side-by-side existence of Shintō and Buddhism.

"It's very convenient," said Okisa, our driver. "If one god doesn't work out, then you can just go to another shrine!"

"There's always another god," Usui, the cameraman, agreed.

"It would feel very strange to have just one god," Okisa said. "Like, how would that work?"

The men gazed into their beers, and the table grew quiet. I realized they were trying to put themselves *there*, in that place where there was always only One God with One Point of View and that He was a he. It made them uncomfortable, and presented an inflexible worldview to which even they, unreligious and modern Japanese men, were not accustomed.

In a very short amount of time, I had grown quite fond of the crew. All of them, except for Okisa, had traveled around the world for NHK, the national broadcasting company of Japan, and belonged to a far more worldly generation of Japanese than my older relatives. But it was moving to see how quintessentially Japanese they still were in the way they checked to see how everyone else was doing. Did everyone have a beer or need more? Okisa, who hailed from Tōhoku, in particular kept an eye out on the communal food we shared. "Usui, you haven't had any sashimi, so this is for you," he would say, his ability to keep track of who had eaten what apparently remaining an indelible part of his character even after five beers.

"Endo," Adachi, the soundman, confided to me, "always makes sure we eat well. And if he can, he makes sure there is a bath in the hotel."

Usui was broad-shouldered, a little swarthy and earthy, and with a low voice and an eye for attractive women. His earthiness made him a skeptic. Had I *really* spent that much time in Japan as a child? Would I please smile at the camera like I actually wanted the survivors of the tsunami to be happy? A practical man, he had a quick eye for excellent lighting, setting, and storytelling.

Adachi was routinely teased by the team for being an *otaku*, which roughly translates to being a geek, and for having a house filled with toys and anime paraphernalia. In true Japanese style, the teasing mostly went on at night when we were eating and drinking (a lot), and was never truly mean. He didn't seem to mind the teasing too much.

"When I play video games with my wife, she is the navigator," he said proudly one evening.

"I've always wondered," said Endo, the director, "how an *otaku* like you got married."

The men laughed uproariously.

"Well? How did you meet your wife?" I asked.

"Skiing."

"What?" everyone exclaimed. It is perhaps worth noting here that Adachi was not exactly athletic-looking, partly the result of pursuing the latest anime-tie-in pastries for sale at the various convenience shops we visited. In fact, he even reminded me of an anime character, though I'd probably put him in the company of Totoro or Rirakkuma or other large, cuddly animals.

"Hahaha," Adachi chortled. "You didn't know I could ski." Throughout our trip, Adachi paid careful attention to me because I had a cold and was sick and coughing often, which he could hear on his headset. It was Adachi who began giving me medicine from his own supplies to stop the cough. At night in his room, he would play back the sound recorded during the day, and consult with Endo over the quality of the audio. He was precise, superstitious, old-fashioned, and modern all at once. During a visit to a tsunami debris field, I found an intact teapot and declared that it was a shame to leave it there, unused. "That teapot belongs to someone," Adachi scolded me, his voice rather low and with an edge to it.

Okisa was still in his twenties and pure Tōhoku; he reminded me greatly of my cousin Takahagi. Okisa had been a taxi driver before the tsunami. In the evenings, he told us stories about how his life had instantly changed after the disaster, and how he and his friends had immediately loaded up a car full of cigarettes, alcohol, and medicine and then repeatedly snuck back and forth through military checkpoints to distribute care packages, and to do more grocery and medicine runs as needed. In the wake of the disaster, he had started ferrying media people around Tōhoku with such efficiency and expertise—many of them had never been this far northeast in Japan—that he eventually got a job as a driver for NHK. The tsunami had damaged numerous gas stations and convenience stores, and Okisa knew what was open, what had moved, where the new convenience stores were, and where the best food was. The latter was important. I've never met a Japanese person who isn't obsessed with good food.

Then, there was Endo, whom they all respected but also loved to tease for his having gone to Waseda University, which is sort of like going to Princeton. A bright, curious, and worldly person, Endo was also imperturbable, endlessly polite, and driven. He walked just slightly on tiptoe, as though he was always buoyed by some idea or thought; wore large, round practical glasses; and was often in his default expression—the half smile. Unlike Okisa, who dressed fashionably in muted but well-tailored clothes made of denim and cotton, Endo paid little attention to aesthetics in fashion. His vision was large scale. He was passionate about big ideas, and he loved the thrill of unraveling a new mystery and presenting information via the precise art of the intelligent documentary. I'd often see him in the morning, having finished eating before anyone else. He sat with his cell phone and whipped through notes and Web links with a quickness that reminded me of my grandmother's students flashing through abacus exercises.

That evening before we went to Sai no Kawara, the conversation turned from religion to ghosts. One by one, everyone admitted to having seen a ghost—except for Endo. He was far too practical and modern to have seen one, but he was fascinated and perhaps even a little envious that everyone else had a ghost story. He did, however, have a related worry.

Before he left home for the filming, Endo had approached his film editor. He had explained the proposed content of the documentary to her, and she had blanched. She had said that since her youth she had been troubled by an ability to see ghosts. They always made her sick. Since the tsunami, she had worked on a few programs that had been filmed in Tōhoku, and had become violently ill. She had asked Endo to please be careful while on this particular shoot, and he, ever the rationalist, had listened to her fears and calmed her down.

"Are you worried about ghosts now?" I asked him.

"No," he said. "I'm only worried that she might not be able to do her work." He politely asked if it might be possible to see if Sempō would be able to perform an exorcism. I assured him that this would be no problem at all.

IN THE MORNING, the sky was a brilliant blue and the water at the beach a shifting prism of liquid light. Okisa explained that before the tsunami, no one had been allowed to surf off Iwaki for reasons that were unclear; they simply hadn't been allowed in the water, and so they had to travel to points north and south to surf. After the tsunami, when everyone was feeling particularly loyal about their hometowns, the surfers volunteered to help clean up the beach, and then they petitioned for the right to surf in their own waters again.

"I don't know if I would surf in that water," said Usui.

"But it's their home," Okisa explained.

Ordinarily the ocean would be full of fishing vessels, but because we were so close to Fukushima, no seafood was being harvested. I walked along the road that ran parallel to the beach. A long row of cylindrical black bags made of heavy vinyl lined the water-break. Each had been spray-painted with a number. Adachi saw me looking at the bags and said in a low voice, "They contain radioactive topsoil. The numbers refer to the date that the bags were sealed, and to the location where the soil came from. If we knew how to decode the bags, we could figure out exactly where they came from and when they were packaged."

"What're they doing here?" I asked.

"They have too much waste," he said softly. "No one knows what to do with them all. So they use them in places like this, to reinforce the seawall. I was on the film crew that learned about this. But it's not really widely known."

We got back into the van, and Okisa drove us past the long, flat stretch of coast that had once been thick with houses. Here and there on the concrete remains of a wall was graffiti, all of it uplifting. In one area, someone had taken the time to paint hundreds of lotus blossoms, a Buddhist symbol. On another wall was the word *Gambatte*, which loosely translates to "Hang in there."

Okisa drove down a hill and then stopped by a small inlet. We had not been parked for more than a few seconds when I suddenly recognized where I was. Off to the left were a few low boat ramps and a concrete water-break. Behind me was a house whose face had been torn off. This was where Sempō had brought me on my first visit to Iwaki after the tsunami. We had been just feet from the entrance to Sai no Kawara.

A bulldozer hammered through rubble, and men in hardhats and gloves stood in the sun, continuing the daily chore of cleanup and restoration. Endo asked me to follow him toward a large headland that formed one of the arms of the bay. Scattered all around the front of this headland were hundreds of identical figures of Jizō, each about two feet high. A path threaded between the statues. Hanging over the path were large banners in the shape of carp. These were *koinobori*, the carp banners that are hung up as a symbol of Children's Day in Japan. In other locations, the *koinobori* signified the pride of having a child; here, the *koinobori* marked the entrance to a cave where the soul of a lost child might be lingering. To get into the cave, I had to walk past the Jizōs and pass under the banners, then go down a slope toward the mouth of the cave. To someone watching from the outside, it would have looked like the earth was swallowing me up.

We inched our way down the rocky entrance into the grotto, and then we were inside. Almost immediately, there was a shift in the atmosphere. The air was moist like breath. It had a voice. Soon I would realize that this was because the cave was actually a cavern that led all the way through the rock and out to another entrance, which opened up to the sea. As the wind rushed in from the ocean, it was compressed, and it roared. But the effect was unnerving.

Endo explained to me that this cave had been worshipped for a great many years—no one really knew how long—but that the tsunami had rushed through and eviscerated the Jizōs once neatly arranged inside the cave, along with a host of other objects that grieving parents had brought for their children: stuffed animals, bottles of juice, changes of clothing. A sign said that people were not to bring flowers or anything else, but people did anyway. Then the tsunami had ravaged all these offerings, decapitating numerous statues in the process. Just like one of the demons that haunt the tales of Sai no Kawara, the water had also knocked over the numerous pyramids of rock that visitors had patiently assembled over the years. After the tsunami, volunteers had worked carefully to try to sort through the mess and restore the cave so worshippers could use it, but the cave was still pockmarked by tiny grottos where the statues had once stood.

Endo asked me if I was scared, and I defiantly told him that I was not. The truth was that I was deeply unsettled. I could hear the ocean outside, but I could not see it, and the thought occurred to me that if a tsunami came at this particular moment, I would not see the water rushing in, and we would all be trapped. There was very little natural light and no vegetation. The rock had a wild anthropomorphic quality to it, like it was the hide of an animal. The floor was very rocky and uneven. I climbed up and down over the boulders, feeling very ungraceful, while the camera followed me.

I felt claustrophobic, but up ahead I could see some light and I began to work my way through to the other end. Here and there unrescued statues of decapitated Jizōs lay in the sand. In one area, there was a tangle of toys mixed in with flotsam and jetsam—a Pooh Bear, a Mickey Mouse, and a plastic toy car. Then all at once I could see the ocean. I hurried toward the mouth of the cave and stepped out onto the beach. The air changed, as though the cave had exhaled and sent me back into the bright light of the living. Behind me, the crew was preoccupied with filming additional location footage.

I wasn't really in a hurry to go back. What I really wanted was to find a way to get back to the van without going through the cave again, but the beach didn't continue around back to the starting point; it hit a wall of rock. I was standing on the beach, with my back to the water, when I noticed that the tunnel I had passed through actually had a second chamber. It angled off to the side, and I had missed its entrance because I'd been so intent on getting out. I went over to investigate.

This second grotto also had remnants of the statues and shrines that had been there. The walls were pockmarked with little indentations, each of which still bore the shadowy imprint of its former inhabitant, the Jizō, the shadows created from layers of accumulated dirt and dust. Because the floor was pure sand, this cave felt simpler and even kinder; I didn't have to struggle to pass through. I started to wonder which cave was really Sai no Kawara: the first one that had been a challenge to climb through, or this one, which was so much easier to enter? I went back out to the beach again.

This time I noticed that off to the right was a natural bridge in the rock, a window through to the main beach. With some effort, I could completely avoid going back through the cave again. Instead, I could go through this window, then up to the beach and the waiting van. But there were waves and the water was rough. There was no telling what the walk through the window would be like, or whether I could even make it through before the water got to me. Still, it was really tempting. Anything to avoid the hot, sticky breath of the cave again.

I stood there for a while, looking at these three holes in the rock: a window straight through to the main beach, a cave that bore deep into the headland but had no exit, and another cave that was the only safe exit, though uncomfortable. I felt like I was in one of those fairy tales where you had three choices and only one would be correct.

Around the world, folk stories featuring the underworld often make the point that humans should not go to the afterlife until it is truly their turn. In the Greek myth "Orpheus and Eurydice," the musician Orpheus goes to Hades to rescue his dead wife. He is allowed to do so with the caveat that he cannot look at his wife until the couple is aboveground. Orpheus, however, succumbs to curiosity and turns to look at Eurydice before she makes it out of the underworld, and she immediately dies a second time.

My feelings about "Orpheus and Eurydice" changed after I saw the Paris Opera Ballet perform the Pina Bausch version. I'd been grieving the loss of my grandparents and my father and nursing the worst of my depression for a good four years. Toward the end of the ballet, Orpheus turns to look at Eurydice. She dies as soon as he sees her, and he dies soon after. It suddenly occurred to me that the point of the story was not so much that the underworld was to be avoided, as it was that you should not look at grief for too long.

So here I was, at Sai no Kawara, on the other side of the land of the living, trying to figure out how to go back. I often felt in those days that to be stuck in grief was to feel kidnapped against one's will and forced to go to some foreign country, all the while just longing to go back home.

But maybe it was wrong to look at this place as being quite so menacing. Maybe the point was not that too much grief was dangerous, but that like these different grottos, I was supposed to remember that life and death were connected, that those people I loved were gone but still retained a connection to me. My world was connected to theirs. Was this the point of Sai no Kawara?

I turned around and went back through the first cave, through the moist air and out to the parked van. The crew continued filming the cave from various angles. When they returned a few minutes later, they were troubled. The camera had not worked consistently. The film had flickered. The sound had gone on and off. The men quickly assured me that such things happened from time to time, but the problems had clearly added to everyone's unease about having gone into Sai no Kawara for the purposes of filming it for TV. Without saying anything out loud, all of us—educated people in our thirties and forties—felt that we had been trespassers.

. . .

THE NEXT STOP on the itinerary was Empukuji in Iwaki. In the finished documentary, Sempō and I have an earnest conversation about Buddhism, the tsunami, and the temple, but a truly interesting portion of our trip never made it to film.

After Endo stopped interviewing me on camera, Usui and Adachi took some location shoots. Sempō had long since retired to the house. Endo then took me aside. Might now be an opportune time to talk to Sempō? I agreed that now was indeed a good time to discuss problematic ghosts and auras attaching themselves to us, and we threaded our way through the house to find Sempō lying on his side on the tatami floor of the living room and watching television. I said, "Endo has something to talk to you about."

Endo explained that while he himself was not afraid of ghosts, and did not even particularly believe in them, he was concerned about his friend, the film editor who from childhood had been plagued by extrasensory perception. Sempō listened, and soon a half smile flitted across his face. He sat up and said he understood the problem. He had encountered it before. Sometimes people just had the ability to see spirits, and it was always a nuisance. There was little anyone could do unless a priest was able to help, or an ancestor intervened and removed the "special sight." Mostly, this kind of thing was best treated by a Buddhist priest.

In the past, Sempō had been hired to remove illness-triggering evil spirits or to clear construction sites of lingering ghosts. This difficult work exhausted him. Most of the time he was successful in clearing ghosts or removing evil spirits, but sometimes, he said, there was nothing he could do. Sometimes people died.

One day Sempō was chanting and communicating with an evil spirit who had possessed the body of a young girl. He looked down and saw his feet turning to smoke. He was dissolving. He was giving so much of himself to the removal of the spirit that this contact was taking its toll on his own health. He drove home and was in bed for days with a high fever. After that, he promised his wife he would perform no more exorcisms.

"Wait a minute," I said. "Were you . . . did you do this kind of thing before you became a priest?"

"Oh no," Sempō said. "Nothing like this had ever happened to me." He had been a prosecutor before becoming a priest and had lived fully in the world of the law and reason. It was just the nature of his job as a priest that over time, after attending so many funerals and listening to people talk about their problems, he found himself seeing things that he did not know existed. "Anyway, the easiest thing for me to do would be to teach you how to do an exorcism yourself. Would you like that?"

"Yes," Endo nodded, immediately pulling out a notebook. I pulled mine out too.

There followed perhaps fifteen minutes during which Sempō tried to remember how to do an exorcism. It had been a long time, and he wasn't sure he had all the hand gestures and the syllables. "Let me see. *On basara on.*" He snapped three times, making a zigzag from right to left. "No wait. Maybe it was the other way." He made the zigzag again, this time from left to right. "No, I'm not sure."

I said, "I think you've taught me this before."

"That's right," Sempō rolled his eyes. "You with all your strange interests, like shamanism. I thought you would need to protect yourself, so I taught you this a long time ago. And you forgot, didn't you? You snap, like this"—he snapped again, certain that one made the first snap in the upper right corner of a "Z," before moving down to the lower left corner for the second snap, and then over to the right for the final one—"and that clears the spirits out of a room. That's the short-cut exorcism." He frowned. "No, wait. When you make the zigzag, you don't snap. You use three fingers." All at once, Sempō laughed boyishly. "I can't remember!" He leapt up neatly from his kneeling position and pulled a book off a shelf.

I pulled out my cell phone and prepared to take a photo of the tome.

"Put that away."

"But I want to remember the book . . ."

"You are not allowed to look at this book," he said.

"Is it a Zen book?"

"Of course not. Zen doesn't teach exorcism. Anything weird like this comes from Shingon."

He flicked through the pages and very quickly found what he was looking for—strict instructions on how to do a Buddhist exorcism.

Sempō snapped the book shut. "Tell you what," he said. "Best thing is for me to do the exorcism for you. Then you won't be bringing along any ghosts to upset the film editor. I'll give you the abbreviated version now, and you can take notes. But then get your crew, and let's go back to the temple for the full treatment." Endo and I furiously took notes, then prepared for the exorcism.

A few minutes later, all of us, except for Okisa—who was down by the van; we had inadvertently forgotten to ask him to join us— were at the *hondō*. Sempō had changed from his official casual priest's clothing into his formal, gold thread–embroidered robes for the occasion.

The new *hondō* was roughly two and a half times larger than the old temple. The old *hondō* had withstood the earthquake on March 11, 2011, but a subsequent aftershock had rendered it unstable and dangerous. Sempō hoped in time to transform the empty space into a garden. The inside of the new space smelled of fresh cedar, pine, and tatami and was bright blond in color, a steady contrast to old temples, which are a glossy, molasses brown, the legacy of smoke, incense, and time. There was an antechamber in the back of the new *hondō* that housed boxes of bones stored for family members who did not have the means, or perhaps the desire, to bury the remains in an actual cemetery. A robotic vacuum cleaner moved across the wood floor of the antechamber, then disappeared from view.

"I have two of them," Sempō said a little sheepishly. "It's hard to keep a large temple clean."

The vacuum cleaner proceeded across the floor again. It was round, perhaps only six inches high, and made very little noise.

"There's a funny thing with this vacuum cleaner," Sempō said. "It moves at an angle. You would think that the best way to clean a room would be to go from side to side. But this robot moves in an X." He strode over to the vacuum cleaner, knelt down as one does when approaching a small dog, and waited for the vacuum cleaner to collide with his foot. It started with surprise, backed away, and then gingerly moved around the obstruction. Sempō laughed with delight. "Did you see that?" He knelt down to intercept the vacuum cleaner again, and the little machine started once more.

Sempō stood up then and walked over to the large altar. The four of us were still standing in a line. Sempō lit three sticks of incense and handed one to each of the men. "You don't need one," he said to me. "You've held a lot of incense lately."

Then Sempō transformed into a priest. He dropped the boyish, amused expression he had while playing with the vacuum cleaner. He stood up straighter, and his voice dropped in pitch till it took on the burnished, cavernous quality that I so loved. *"Namu nyorai ongu . . . ,"* he began. I looked at the men. They were standing very straight too.

Sempō cut the air in front of us three times, his silk robe hissing as his arm sliced the air. Then he came behind us and touched our backs and our spines, as though to release some invisible being that might have taken up residence inside.

It was over very quickly, and Sempō relaxed and smiled at us again, the corners of his eyes crinkling up. "Remember," he said. "If you can't sleep, try the lion pose and face north. That's what the Buddha did. It might be that you need to release something in your body to the north." The lion pose referred to sleeping with the right side down, with the heart farthest away from the floor. It was so called because this was how a lion slept. Sempō said there was ample research to show that if you slept with your heart away from the floor, it was easier for the body to wake up. Lions slept like this so they could wake up instantly and escape from any predators.

"I thought you aren't supposed to face north when you sleep," I asked.

"I said if you *can't* sleep, you should face the north," Sempō responded. "That will encourage whatever spirit is bothering you to continue on its way. Cut the air three times like I taught you, do the lion pose, and then face north."

Sempō wanted to treat everyone to dinner. He knew a place run by one of his *danka*, and he offered to take us there. It took a few minutes for Sempō to change back into his relaxed priest's clothing. Then I met him by the parking lot, and we got into his car. At the bottom of the hill we could see the little figures of the crew members earnestly demonstrating the exorcism for Okisa. Endo had his notebook out and was consulting it. Okisa was nodding earnestly. Sempō laughed. "Boys are always boys, Marie," he said. The crew looked up when they heard the car engine, and then scampered into the van. Sempō laughed again, then pulled up next to the van and waited until the crew was ready to follow us to dinner.

Two months later, when the documentary ran on television, I had an email from Endo. He told me that his film editor had been comfortable during the editing process. She hadn't gotten so much as a headache. The scenes of Sai no Kawara had scared her, but ultimately she didn't see any ghosts on the film. Later that summer, Sempō would be traveling to Tōkyō for a Buddhist priests' convention, and he offered to meet with the film editor and give her a complete exorcism so she might never be plagued by ghosts again.

TWELVE

UNDERWORLD

IN THE DAYS WHEN Prince Shōtoku was championing Buddhism and Kūkai was learning the secrets of esoteric Buddhism, the Shimokita Peninsula was inhabited by a people today called the Ainu. There are traces of Ainu DNA in some of the current Shimokita inhabitants, and vestiges of the old culture still remain in the place names, in folk beliefs, and in certain words. It is said that the Ainu did not fear the dead or death quite as much as the ambassadors of the Yamato clan who pushed north from Kyōtō to colonize the Japanese archipelago.

To the Ainu, one place on the Shimokita Peninsula was more sacred than any other: an extinguished volcano, believed to be the spot where beloved ancestors paused before disappearing from the visible world. There is a lake in the bed of this old volcano, called Lake Usori, a word that does not exist in Japanese. Scholars believe that *usori* was eventually transliterated into *osore*, the Japanese word for "doom" or "fear." Today, the extinguished volcano and its surrounding environment are collectively referred to as "Osorezan," which roughly translates to "Mount Doom." This ancient hallowed site is one of Japan's three most sacred places. For unlike Sai no Kawara, which is geared to only children, everyone who dies passes through Mount Doom.

The Shimokita Peninsula, as nearly every English guidebook will tell you, sticks out from the northern part of the main island of Japan, and is shaped like an axe. To reach the peninsula, you have to cross a narrow stretch of land—the handle of the axe—passing hamlets and down-at-heel inns, before the land spreads out again to form the blade of the axe, which is nearly thirty miles across at the widest point. Once you are on the peninsula, it's hard not to feel that you are in a space that is very separate from the rest of Japan. The air there is crisper; the cherry trees routinely blossom a month later than they do in Tōkyō; and Buddha's birthday, celebrated on April 8 at most temples, is celebrated a month later so it is warm enough to go outside. There is no bamboo. Rice fares poorly. Historically, the losers of major battles were sent there to live out their days as punishment for being on the wrong side of history.

When I visit the peninsula, I always stay at the same place: a magical inn called Yagen Sō, located in the Yagen Valley at the base of Mount Doom. The inn is owned and run by Hara Sanaeko, a woman in her fifties who was born and bred in the wilds of Tōhoku. I like to call her the Mountain Woman. The inn reminds me of the TARDIS, the time-travel device on the British television show *Doctor Who*, because from the outside, the inn looks far too small to comfortably house more than one or two people. Inside, however, the space seems to magically open up into an inviting array of lovingly tended rooms, hallways lined with practical amenities like a washing machine, special rooms for guests traveling with dogs, and one glass case displaying a stuffed peacock that had once been a pet. Then there is the bath, which delivers pure, clear, *onsen* water into a blue-tiled tub, and which the Mountain Woman will tell you has the power to cure almost any illness. In the event that you are not ill, the water will reveal any tiredness that you have been suppressing in your body, and render you exhausted and unable to get out of bed for twenty-four hours. After that, says the Mountain Woman, you will feel greatly refreshed.

There are actually four different inns in the Yagen Valley, and each inn has an *onsen* that draws water from the same source: the Yagen hot spring, whose name means "medicine tool." Different historical figures are credited with finding the hot springs—and being healed by the waters. Recently, New Age fanatics have become enamored of the Yagen Valley because it is said to be home to the mischievous and mythological creature called the *kappa*. Adding to the otherworldly feel of the place is the old-growth forest, whose ancient, immense trees seem to hush the wind, so the moment you enter the valley floor, the air abruptly takes on a serene and still quality.

As a child, the Mountain Woman had stayed at Yagen Sō with her family, when it was just a camping site with an outdoor *onsen*, but no facilities. She had learned from her father to forage for wild vegetables in the old-growth forest and in the hills surrounding the valley. Such delicacies are called *sansai*, or "mountain vegetables," and the Mountain Woman still picks and serves an assortment of wild vegetables to her guests today. Over the years, her father built a cabin, then added rooms to the original structure, always preserving the bath in the center.

Some guests who stay at Yagen Sō come for the water in the bath, or to go hiking in the primordial forest, or to look for spirits. But a great many people visit Yagen because they are struggling with an unshakeable grief, which they hope can be relieved by a pilgrimage to nearby Mount Doom. Because of this, the Mountain Woman has become an expert on the various forms of grief and in consoling those who are in mourning.

One time, I overheard the Mountain Woman talking in the hallway to a male guest. His wife had been dead for two years after a car accident, and he was having trouble moving on. His wife's ghost was around all the time. He had decided to go to Osorezan to speak to an *itako*—a blind medium—to learn what the ghost wanted, or what he should do for her.

The Mountain Woman said that there was nothing wrong with a ghost sticking around for a while. The man didn't need an *itako*. He just needed a priest to read a sutra, and then he should move on with his life and enjoy all his grandchildren, whom he was lucky enough to have. The Mountain Woman's own husband died five years ago, and his spirit stuck around for two years as well, mostly because he was worried about her. In time she realized that this kind of mutual worrying, while nice, wasn't helpful, and in her practical way, she told him to get going. She, in turn, renewed her focus on local activities. Anyway, there were only two blind mediums left on Mount Doom.

I have heard her administer this advice time and again to her guests. They ought to enjoy the magic waters of her bath. They could go to Osorezan if they wanted to receive a special sutra from the priest. But they should not expect too much more. "An *itako* cannot really help you." Still, people came to see the only two remaining blind mediums.

Once upon a time, part or all of the Japanese islands were ruled by female shamans, and Chinese scholars noted that a powerful queen named Himiko temporarily brought peace to the otherwise uncivilized land. Tōhoku and Okinawa—Japan's northern and southern extremes—preserved the tradition the longest, even after the arrival of Buddhism. Scholars believe that the blind mediums on Mount Doom are the last vestiges of this fading period in Japan's history.

Historically, the mediums were blind women who were trained via a harsh regimen involving hunger, cold, and freezing baths to learn to "channel" the dead. Modern medicine and women's rights have today made it possible for those born blind in Japan to seek treatment and an education, and to have more choices regarding their future.

Twice a year, the few remaining *itako* gather at Osorezan to commune with the deceased for a fee, setting up tents just inside Osorezan's main gate, while the male priests hold their own far-grander celebration within the temple structures. The lines to see these last remaining mediums are significant, and people wait patiently for up to six hours for a consultation. No new *itako* are reported to be in training.

IN THE EVENING, I left the primordial forest where Yagen Sō is located and turned up a mountain road to begin a serpentine climb. The narrow road switched back and forth through a tangle of evergreen and deciduous trees, before descending down the other side of Mount Doom. Suddenly I was hit with the strong smell of sulfur; the underworld does not smell like the land of the living. The road descended on a steep angle and rounded a curve. The grounds of Osorezan stretched out in alternating shades of white and gray, while a yellowish and burbling stream ran parallel to the road.

To the left there was an arched red bridge. In the old days, before bullet trains and tour buses made Osorezan easier to reach, one had to cross this bridge, a representation of the bridge the dead cross on their way to the underworld. The river is commonly called Sanzu no Kawa, which translates to the "River of Three Crossings," and you can think of it as being a bit like the River Styx. The virtuous have no problem traversing the bridge, provided they are wearing clothing and have six coins to pay Shozoku no Baba, the old hag. In addition to terrorizing little children, Shozoku no Baba waits on the other side of the bridge to strip the dead of their clothing and to take their money. If the dead arrive naked, because their relatives were too poor to cremate them with clothing on, Baba takes their skin. Those with too much bad karma must cross the river at a shallow point; the worst people are cast straight into hell.

The red bridge at the entrance to Osorezan is now more ceremonial than functional; a nearby turnout accommodates cars so tourists can take photos of each other standing on the apex of the rounded bridge. I passed the bridge and headed to the large parking lot outside the temple proper. It was evening. By the time I got out of the car—the Mountain Woman dropped me off, while my mother and son, who had been traveling with me, stayed behind at the inn—and headed to the information booth, only a few tourists were left on the grounds inside. I explained to the ticket taker that I had come to spend the night, and then with instructions on how to find the guest quarters, I crossed the gate into the underworld that is Mount Doom.

Once upon a time pilgrims stayed together in shared quarters, all sleeping in the same room. Now Osorezan boasted an imposing guest facility, which the Mountain Woman likened to a hotel. In its comforts and its sleekness, it was very much like a hotel, though not of the ordinary nature. The entry foyer was all black marble, with an array of slippers and a white, backlit Jizō waiting for guests. If the way station to the afterlife had a hotel, it would look like this.

I was told that I would be having dinner at six o'clock with the other guests—there were two other women. One was from Kanagawa Prefecture; she had just up and decided to take the overnight bus to Osorezan. She was twenty-four and dreamed of being a Celtic singer. The other, a fifty-six-year-old woman from Hokkaido, was divorced, though still living with her husband.

The Hokkaido woman was quite small but plump, and she had large round eyes and tanned skin. As we got to talking, I asked if she knew about her family background, and she confided in me that a DNA test had revealed that she was part Ainu. She had a best friend, she said, from the island of Okinawa who had also had a DNA test and discovered she was Ainu.

If I had expected to experience the camaraderie of mourners who had come to Osorezan to face their grief directly, I was disappointed. The hotel staff assured me that in other seasons, Osorezan was full of mourners, or families who traveled in groups. Off-season—now—Osorezan was also a landmark for those on a spiritual quest.

Dinner was *shōjin ryōri*, and quite good. Though we were not supposed to talk, it was clear very quickly that we would break all the rules. The woman from Hokkaido spoke the most. She said she knew we might not believe her story, but that did not bother her. She wanted to show us the photos she had taken of Osorezan the day before. Here, she said, was a photo of Lake Usori. She handed her phone to the Celtic-singer-to-be. "It's *michi no hikari!*" the young woman exclaimed. A street of lights.

I took a look. My skeptical eye saw a photo of the lake, taken directly into the sun, which had caused the picture to take on a glare. Then again, if I looked closely, the resulting glare did indeed look like the triangular shape of a road receding into the horizon. "Wow," I said politely.

"It's okay if you don't believe me. I don't need you to believe me," she said.

The old priest returned to the dining hall. "Women," he scoffed. "You aren't supposed to talk."

"Sorry," said the woman from Hokkaido.

"Well," he grumbled. "Anyway. Now is a good time for a bath. Just take a flashlight when you go outside."

"Outside?" I asked.

"That is what I said. Yes."

Osorezan's position on the bed of an extinguished volcano accounted for the ubiquitous smell of sulfur and for the strange yellow river I had crossed to arrive here. All this plus the wind, the chill, and the fact that I had developed a cold were enough reasons for me not to take a bath outside. But I would not have the full Japanese experience if I did not take advantage of the subterranean hot springs.

There were two small wooden shacks on the approach to the *hondō*: one for women and one for men. Pilgrims regularly stopped here, had a dip, and then continued on. The lady from Hokkaido insisted that the baths were much more enjoyable in the evening when there were no other tourists.

I couldn't help but be spooked. Everyone had told me that Osorezan was full of ghosts, and though I did not expect to see anything otherworldly, the mere suggestion was enough to make me want to stay in my room. Still, I put on my *yukata* (a lightweight kimono), grabbed a towel, and met the other two women in the lobby.

The wind was quite strong, and though I could not see much, I could hear the whir of countless plastic pinwheels all around. Pilgrims brought these pinwheels to entertain the spirits of deceased children, and then they left the toys next to statues of Jizō or at altars. We crossed the gravel courtyard and then went into the creaking, wooden shed and began to strip off our clothing. There is a phrase in Japanese—*hadaka no tsukiai*—that means "naked friends." The concept is not at all sexual, though it does imply intimacy. When you bathe together, you are in a vulnerable state and you can't help but share confidences and become closer.

Three years earlier, after a breast-cancer diagnosis, the woman from Hokkaido had begun to receive messages that she needed to undertake a spiritual journey. In her previous lives, she had been

a shamaness, and many of her previous forms had been killed—
usually by men. She needed to do a pilgrimage to as many "power
spots" as possible to appease the angry spirits of her former selves.
The term "power spot" in Japanese refers to locations said to harbor
strong *reiki*, or "healing energy," and are a reflection of Japan's growing New Age movement. Conveniently, a great many power spots
are on the sites of traditionally sacred temples and shrines. She was
quite convinced that there was a reason—some act of fate—that
had brought us together in this same spot. We must have met in a
previous life.

At 6:30 in the morning, we went up to the main *hondō* for the
morning prayers. Then, after breakfast, we three women went for
a walk.

The word often used to describe the grounds of Osorezan is
"lunar," because once you move past the temple structure and onto
the plains behind it, you find yourself surrounded by white and gray
rock, the exhaled detritus of a volcano. There is something decid-
edly otherworldly and alienating about being in a place that is composed of the earth's innards. Because of the high sulfur content, few
things can live in and grow on Osorezan, save for crows, an unusual
species of fish in Lake Usori's poisonous waters, and a rare fungus.
Beyond that, there are a few patches of grass, but no trees, no flowers, and no insects.

The grounds roll gently, with congealed towers of rock, under
which sulfuric hot springs burble and steam. Punctuating this terrain were tall statues of Buddhist deities, often in the form of Jizō,
forming a skyline of mourning and longing. Along the pathways
were brightly colored pinwheels, offerings, piles of coins, and bouquets of daffodils. There was my old friend Fudō Myō-ō, the Buddhist deity whose form I had seen at Shōjōshinin, and whom my

father and I had so loved, and one odd pile of rocks with a pair of chopsticks. It was a *harikuyō* shine, a place to pay respects to broken combs and pins and needles. In the old Japanese tradition where everything was animated, one had to pay respects to the pins and needles, lest they harm you.

I began to notice a pattern. People had left little offerings in front of the statues. Usually they were worn river rocks on which someone had written with a permanent marker. But sometimes someone had done something more personal. There were three wooden figures in front of a Jizō, which I assumed were representations of the people who had died. I picked one up and turned it over. It read, "For Taki. Fourteen years old. *Sake.*" There was also a smaller statue: "For Kiyo. Two years old. *Miso* soup." And then: "For my one-year-old. Yogurt and a park." Someone, perhaps a parent, had made these little dolls to represent the deceased and, on the bottom, had written out offerings to their spirits. It is common in Buddhist temples in Japan to leave an offering for someone who has died. At Empukuji, for example, offerings to the deceased children were grouped together, and parents usually brought little bottles of milk or packages of candy—just as Hina, the little girl who had "played" with Ewan, had had on her altar. Such actions aren't meant to be taken literally, but figuratively, so the living feel they are doing something constructive on behalf of the person whom they miss so much.

We saw a hexagonal building filled with clothing and a few portraits of the deceased. Outside the building, there were more handkerchiefs and towels. In the desiccated, sulfuric landscape, the abandoned garments looked less like an accumulation of offerings and more like the shredded remains of people who had disappeared.

Of all the things I saw at Osorezan, none moved me more than a half-dead grassy field, located not too far from the lake's waters. It was customary to tie two fistfuls of grass together, a gesture indicating that though the living and dead are separated, they are still connected. I found two untied tufts and bound them.

The climax of the grounds of Osorezan was the lake itself, a quiet, eerily still, pale-blue caldera. It was ringed with mountain peaks, one of which housed a tall radio tower for Japan's Self-Defense Forces that was shaped like a mammoth walkie-talkie. During peak visiting times, the shores of this lake are covered with flowers and piles of stones, as those in mourning help the departed by building stone towers the demons have knocked down. Sometimes people picnic here, offering part of their meal to the spirit of the dead.

In 2013 a new monument, dedicated entirely to victims of the March 11 tsunami, was erected along the lake's shore. The woman from Hokkaido had been there the day before, but she hadn't dared interact with the shrine. It had felt too powerful and overwhelming. She'd been afraid of it. I went to take a look.

The monument was composed of three parts: First was a large, granite lotus blossom, shaped like an igloo with a wide-open mouth, in which sat Jizō, and a baby boy and girl. Directly in front of this was a granite altar with half-burned sticks of incense and piles of flowers. On either side of the altar was a pair of rectangular pillars, about three feet high, each of which held a "bell of hope." We took turns ringing the bell, then walked around to the back of the statue. It was here, said the woman from Hokkaido, that she had become nervous, for the back of the large igloo-shaped lotus blossom was covered with handprints of all shapes and sizes, a reminder that the tsunami had killed people of all ages. We were to find the handprint that most nearly matched ours in size, and then put our hand in that spot and pray.

I stopped to look at the front of the statue one more time. I had missed a small detail in my initial examination: someone had placed three round river rocks on the base of the lotus blossom, and written the names of the deceased on the stones. Accompanying this were also a handful of coins, one of which was an arcade token for a video game.

IT WAS CLEAR to me from childhood that Buddhism was wrapped up in the grim business of death. This gave me the impression early on that the Japanese were unnaturally obsessed with death. Every home we visited had an ancestor shrine, with large-scale, solemn, black-and-white portraits of the deceased person, who never smiled. When we visited my mother's friends, the first thing we did was to pay our respects to the dead relatives, many of whom my mother had known. She would tell me stories about them—about how Dr. Yamaguchi had fed her after the war when she was hungry. One night we stayed in the home of her former boyfriend, who had died but left behind a wife, with whom my mother was friendly. I couldn't sleep that night. Our futons had been laid out in the "most honored room" in the house, which included a large black-and-white portrait of the dead man solemnly staring down at me from the wall. I couldn't take the directness; I was too accustomed to the dead being tucked away, as they are in my own Western culture.

My grandparents' Buddhist altar was hidden in the back room in a corner. Hanging on the wall above the altar were photos of people unknown to me—my great-grandparents, and great-uncles and -aunts. Their names were etched on black-and-gold *ihai*, or funerary tablets; the inscribed labyrinth of esoteric Chinese characters only reinforced the idea that death was a singularly serious and incomprehensible business. Every morning we lit incense for these people, and if my grandparents received a special treat from a former student—a box of cookies or a flat of apples—the sweets were always put on the altar so the ancestors would get to "taste" the delicacies first.

Empukuji, with its large temple hall, had a mammoth altar, with a two-foot-high Buddha, and a golden chandelier hanging from the ceiling. This was in addition to the private altar Aunt Shizuko had in her home just for relatives. Early in the morning, Aunt Shizuko would offer prayers to the Shintō gods at her Shintō shrine, then give incense to the ancestors and then to the Buddha. Any gift of fruit or cookies were given to the Buddha first, and I had to bow to him when I removed a watermelon from his dais (watermelons in Japan are much smaller and rounder than their American counterparts). This was seriousness of the utmost.

To my own eyes, Aunt Shizuko was a kind of Japanese person—and woman—I'd never seen anywhere else. When we went into town together to see Aunt Shizuko's friends—a doctor, another priest, a shopkeeper—you could see how they reverentially deferred to her. One of Aunt Shizuko's best friends was a pub owner named Yuriko, who owned a sprightly poodle and made tasty meals in the three-hundred-square-foot kitchen of her pub, Hisamatsu. Yuriko had a sharp wit, and she effortlessly teased the men who came to drink at her restaurant after work. But around my Aunt Shizuko, Yuriko was restrained and dignified.

I asked my mother about Aunt Shizuko's seriousness, and her response was, "Aunt Shizuko did not have children." Over the years, I have often heard this as an explanation for why someone has seemed "off" in Japan. To have children is to be allowed access into a particularly happy and life-affirming viewpoint. Not to have children—or to lose them—is to be in danger of losing hope for the future.

Here in Mount Doom, all these things—respect for the dead, for ancestors, for children, and for lost hope—were crystallized into one very somber but moving place. In a strange way, I felt that I had been rehearsing to be here for most of my life.

. . .

THE MOUNTAIN WOMAN came to pick me up at Mount Doom with my mother and son in the car. As she drove me back to her primordial valley, she asked if I enjoyed my visit. I told her the truth. I said that while I found Mount Doom moving, I was also a little disappointed. I didn't sense the raw energy that so many other people, like the lady from Hokkaido, seemed to feel. I expected to be scolded for my lack of sensitivity, but instead the Mountain Woman seemed pleased. She told me that Osorezan had once been a far more authentic place to visit. "This is not really a power spot anymore," she said, when I told her about the lady from Hokkaido. "Didn't you notice how little the water is burbling? And that hotel," she sniffed dismissively.

Once upon a time when pilgrims came to Osorezan, they did a proper hike up the mountains. In fact, the correct way to do a pilgrimage was to start at the mouth of the river—Sanzu no Kawa—that eventually fed into Osorezan's lake. Back in the old days, that river had been a truly haunted place. People often heard ghosts and spirits. One night, about thirty years ago, for example, people in the town of Mutsu woke up because they heard voices crying and wailing in the streets. "I'm cold! I'm cold." In the morning, they learned of a ferryboat that had sunk during a typhoon. The voices they heard had been the souls of deceased passengers making their way up the river to cross the red bridge at Mount Doom. The spirits then paused at Osorezan before continuing on to the afterlife. Modernity had done away with much of the other world's power, and made Mount Doom too easy to access. There were fewer ghosts now.

I asked if anyone did the old-fashioned pilgrimage anymore, and she gave me an odd look. "Like I said, the true pilgrimage starts at the mouth of the river. The Sanzu no Kawa. Would you by any chance be interested in taking a look?"

I said that I would. She turned the car around and began to drive to the nearby town of Mutsu.

. . .

WE DROVE ALONG the coast, past low houses and modest-looking inns before the Mountain Woman turned and parked the car in the lot of a temple. Six oversized Jizōs sat in a line off to the side, dressed in red capes and presiding over the usual forest of pinwheels. My son was instantly captivated by the motion and the color. I was immediately struck by a strange mark on the gate of the *hondō*, for there, in bright gold, was the unmistakable symbol of the Tokugawa shogunate, the feudal family that had ruled Japan from 1600 to 1868. The temple, however, was new; it must have been built in the past twenty years. I wondered what I was doing at a temple that was clearly brand new. Could such a thing be authentic?

The Mountain Woman strode across the parking lot and into a doorway adjacent to the temple; as was the case at Empukuji, the *hondō* was connected to a house where the priest lived. My son and I followed the Mountain Woman, while my mother stayed in the car.

"Hello! Hello!" the Mountain Woman called out cheerfully. I looked around in the entryway. There was the usual collection of Buddhist temple house paraphernalia: a framed print of the Buddha, numerous umbrellas waiting for a rainy day, slippers for use inside the house. There was a narrow hallway that sloped up at an angle and led into the *hondō*. The window sills of this hallway were decorated with little bamboo toys: dragonflies that balanced on branches.

We heard the sound of metal and then the lumbering of someone pushing a walker. A moment later, an elderly woman rounded the corner. She startled me. She was extremely tall and big. I was reminded of the toy in *Toy Story*, the movie, in which a decapitated doll's head is attached to the metal chassis of a toy car. The woman had that quality of half human and half machine. She scuttled forward like a mechanical crab and eyed us suspiciously.

"Maybe we are disturbing her," I whispered to the Mountain Woman.

"Hello! I am here with a guest who is staying at my inn," the Mountain Woman announced. "She is interested in the true experience of Osorezan, and I have told her a bit about your temple. Would you kindly show it to her, please?"

The Crab Lady looked out at us through her one good eye. She was up high on the landing of her house, and we were down below with the shoes. "He is not here," she finally said.

"Where is he?" the Mountain Woman pressed.

The Crab Lady inhaled and squinted and seemed to think. "Up at the greenhouse." She looked at my son, hiding behind my legs and peering out at her. "Beware of the dog." Then she turned away and retreated to the living quarters of her home.

"Maybe we are disturbing . . . ," I began again.

The Mountain Woman strode off across the parking lot and across the street, while ordering me to keep my son far away from the dog, who was chained to a pole. I did as she said, following her as she made a wide berth around the dog to the door of a large rectangular greenhouse. She yanked open the door, and immediately the greenhouse exhaled, sending out a strong, hot breath of manure and freshly trimmed stems. There was a tangle of orange, red, and white orchids inside; the flowers had been indulged and allowed to grow however they chose, so they clutched each other like incestuous siblings. There were little potted roses and ferns. I stared at the exotic richness. Even the Mountain Woman paused to take in the unexpected site of the disordered, tropical splendor. Then she gathered herself together again.

A man sat in the front corner of the greenhouse. He wore dusty clothing and a pair of long green rubber boots. He hadn't shaved that day, and the hair on his head was about an inch long, a thick carpet of stubble that made him look like a Monchichi, the Japanese toy from the 1980s. This was how I often saw my father when he was alive—tromping around in his beloved flower garden, sweating and dusty and smelling of dirt. But this man—with his unattended head of hair—could not possibly be a Buddhist priest, as no vigilant priest would allow his personal grooming to deteriorate to such a degree.

"Hello!" the Mountain Woman began her spiel again. She explained who I was, and why I was here, while the dog barked outside.

"Okay," the man said gruffly. He pulled off one of his boots and placed his foot inside a sneaker. Then he began to tug on the other boot. "Go back. And I'll meet you there."

The Mountain Woman nodded and turned crisply. "Come on, then."

I followed her back to the temple, making sure that my son and I again skirted the dog. Now the Crab Lady was waiting for us in the entrance. She was not able to hand us any slippers, but she motioned for us to help ourselves. I wondered, fleetingly, just how old she was. She seemed ancient—in her nineties. Most Japanese people who are that old are not particularly tall, and yet even with the walker she had formidable height. I helped my son up onto the landing. By now the priest had returned from his greenhouse and gruffly gestured us to come into his temple.

"You're on your own now!" the Mountain Woman waved to me. She and my mother drove off to go buy some seaweed, for the Mountain Woman knew a place that made it fresh and sold it cheaply. My son and I followed the Fuzzy-Headed Priest into his temple. As we walked up the landing, Ewan paused to admire one of the dragonfly toys, and the Fuzzy-Headed Priest picked it up and put it in my son's hands. "Take it," he said delightedly.

The inside of his temple was quite small, and the gold on the decorations very bright and new. I asked the priest how old his temple was.

Gone was the disgruntled gardener, and in his place now was a man who was delighted to tell his story. He had a bit of mischief on his face, and though I liked this about him, it made me nervous.

"Come here," he said. "Come onto the altar and stand right here." He gestured to a spot just in front of the closed box. "Come on, come on," he said gently, waving us up onto the landing. I held my son's hand.

The priest disappeared, but I could still hear him talking to us. "Are you there? You are facing the box, yes? Please look at the box. Make sure you are looking. Okay. One. Two. Three."

The doors of the box swung open. The figure seated in the box thrust forward. It was the terrifying, skeletal face of the old hag: Shozoku no Baba. My son let go of my hand and immediately ran away.

"Do you see it?" the priest asked gleefully.

"Yes. It's very . . ."

"Isn't she terrifying?"

"Yes," I said, turning around, searching for my son. "I'm sorry but my son . . ."

"I want you to walk to the side and look at Baba from the side."

I could hear my son moving around somewhere within the temple. He'd run off so suddenly, I hadn't seen in which direction he had gone.

"Are you looking?" asked the priest.

I stepped to the right. "Yes," I said.

"Good." He came around the corner, very pleased with himself. "Were you scared?"

"Well, yes . . ."

"Isn't she ugly?"

"Very ugly," I agreed.

"But look at her from the side. Look." His mood had changed now and become somehow gentle. "Isn't her expression different from the side?"

In fact, it was. The old hag was a statue made of wood, and rigged on a platform so she could jump out, like a jack-in-the-box. From the front, the old hag was terrifying—all tongue and teeth and skull. She looked, I thought, like the Crab Lady back in the hallway navigating with her metal walker. But from the side, the hag's expression took on a look of sadness, fatigue, and pity. She looked almost grandmotherly.

The old priest told me that once upon a time, pilgrims crossed the red bridge at Osorezan and then met face-to-face with a statue of the old hag. But then Osorezan became quite commercialized, and the main goal of the priests who ran it was to make money. The true faithful, he said, came here, to his temple, because it was right here that the river started. This was where the souls of the dead began their walk, and true pilgrims knew this and came to pay their respects. The business of death, he explained, was just as shocking as the old hag looked. But from the side, I could see that she was also sad too, and that she had pity for the poor souls over whose fate she ruled.

In all my years of visiting Japanese temples, I'd never seen an old hag enshrined as the main entity, and I told him so. "That's right!" he said happily. "I'm very rare." He went on. Shozoku no Baba was neither Buddhist nor Shintō. She had presided over the underworld for a very long time, long before either religion had been formally established in Japan.

The name of his temple was Ubaji, or "Old Lady Temple." The Fuzzy-Headed Priest was born into a priestly family, but as the second son he wasn't able to take on his father's temple. Ubaji became available when he was a young man, and his mother urged him to take the opportunity. He spent years, he said, begging for money to rebuild Ubaji's structure piece by piece. I had heard this story before—it is the story not only of Empukuji but also of the temple in Nara owned by Maruko, the Zen priest I had met at Eiheiji. The Fuzzy-Headed Priest had only thirty households to support his temple when he got started, and so he had to scrape together the money to build the structure we had in front of us today. Rebuilding the temple cost him roughly one hundred million yen, or around one million dollars.

He was delighted to show me all the details of his accomplishment. His temple, he explained, was part of the Pure Land sect of Buddhism. This was why his head was not closely shaved; Pure Land priests are not fastidious about their hair, as are Zen Buddhists or Shingon Buddhists. His temple was part of a bureaucracy headed by a temple called Jōjōji, to which the Tokugawa shogunate had been a member. As a result, any temple under Jōjōji was allowed to place the Tokugawa crest on its doors, as he had done.

There were many more eccentric touches. He asked me to look up at the ceiling. Did I see three mice scampering across the rafters? I did. After a moment, when the mice did not move, I asked if, perhaps, the mice were sculptures. "In fifty years, my mice will be designated National Treasures," he said confidently, for the mice had been carved by a master carpenter in Kyōtō. One mouse was climbing a rafter; another was hanging on in the middle with a bit of food in its mouth. The third mouse was on its way down a supporting beam. These were, he said, all part of a haiku. At any point in life, man was like one of these mice: on his way up, hanging on for dear life, or on his way down. It was important to remember that even if one were in descent, one would, in all likelihood, also go back up again. He also had two paintings of peacocks, which had been done by another master artist in Kyōtō. They were portraits of his now-deceased peacocks, his pets, and were related to the stuffed peacock in the Mountain Woman's inn. Later, when the Mountain Woman returned to pick me up, she and the Fuzzy-Headed Priest reminisced about their deceased peacock friends.

My son returned to the main hall again, and the old priest thoughtfully closed the door to the old hag's box. He beckoned us to follow him around to the back of the altar. There was an ante-chamber filled with dolls. Each was about a foot high, dressed up as either a bride or a groom, and displayed in a glass box. In some instances, a bride and a groom were in one case together. Scattered around the dolls were photos of young men and women, in the bloom of youth. Very often, the priest explained to me, when young people died, they had not yet married, and this caused their parents tremendous worry. To assuage their worry, family members would come here with a picture of the deceased, and ask that the priest perform a wedding ceremony between the spirit of the dead person and a spirit of the opposite sex. The ceremony cost a fee, and the dolls would then live here in the back room for five years.

Behind this room was yet another chamber, this one filled with little altars, each of which contained the remains of the deceased. In this room, the priest explained to me, no one used candles or burned incense, for fear of fire. He had electronic candles in place, so a person could visit, switch on a candle and pray, and then leave without any fear of fire burning down the temple.

By the time we emerged from the temple, the Mountain Woman and my mother had returned to the temple with a box of seaweed. "How are you doing?" my mother called out to me. The Crab Lady had worked her way up to the temple too. She had a large bag of candy for my son, and she shyly held this out with one hand. It was a very large bag—the size you would buy to feed a neighborhood of children at Halloween—and my son lunged for it. The Crab Lady was not scary after all. The bamboo dragonfly was set aside and forgotten.

. . .

AT DINNER THAT evening, there was a tremendous commotion in the kitchen. The staff at the *ryokan* could not believe that Ewan and I had been to Ubaji, the old hag temple, and that we had lived to tell the tale. Stories were legion about that priest and his old mother, and how difficult and downright rude they were to people who paid them a visit.

"Wait a minute," I said. "That's his mother?"

There followed a heated discussion as to whether or not the Crab Lady was the wife or the mother. The matter undecided, the staff bombarded us with new questions. Had my son and I really stood on the altar? Had the priest really opened the doors to the statue just for us?

I said that all this was true. The Mountain Woman was triumphant. She crowed that it was she who had taken us to the temple. As she proudly recounted her part in our adventure, I could see what a tomboy she must have been, the young girl who had ran away from school to climb mountains to hunt for mushrooms, and who had sided with her father when her parents fought. She was thrilled to be able to tell the local staff the story of the old priest's kindness and, more to the point, of how the Crab Lady had fallen for my son's charms and handed him a bag of candy.

"But they weren't so bad," I said. "I mean, I was a little uncomfortable at first. But he took a lot of time to explain everything to us."

The man serving us dinner shook his head. "I don't know what you did, but you were very lucky to get that tour."

The Fuzzy-Headed Priest was a strange man, they all agreed. Very eccentric. The parishioners hardly knew what to do with him. It was true that he had taken what was once a very small and unimportant temple and turned it into something quite fine. But the locals often worried about what he was doing with their money. Apparently they knew he went to Burma and to other places around the world, helping to build schools and to teach literacy. Such kindness didn't square with his gruffness. Then there was all the work he had done on behalf of the tsunami victims. Everyone knew that he had gone and volunteered, but for some reason he liked to pretend that he had not done anything at all. He was, they said, exactly like Baba, the old hag. He had one face from the front and another from the side.

FOR MONTHS I could not shake the image of terrifying old Baba, the hag who keeps the souls of lost children stuck on the side of a river, and who takes away the clothes and the skin of the newly dead, and the sad and kind Baba whom I had seen when I looked at her from the side. Superimposed on this was the Fuzzy-Headed Priest and his Crab Lady mother. Or wife.

I knew why Baba had such a frightening face. I really hated feeling lost in the abyss of grief, and I often hated the person that I was, this person who was so unhappy all the time, and who had to rein in what she said lest she let other people see how unhappy she was.

Not long after my father died, my husband said to me, "Grief is a form of love, isn't it? And isn't love a form of madness?"

I guessed that the side of Baba's face represented a form of love. But it didn't make sense to me that a being who tortured little children could have anything to do with love.

Many months later, I started to think about her a little differently. She, whose job it was to terrify and to torment, knew exactly how horrible her actions were, and a part of her grieved to have to do this to us. But her job was also necessary and unstoppable. For months I had been looking to return my life to the way it had been before my father and my grandparents died. And when I couldn't do that, when I couldn't bring them out of the underworld, I had felt the touch of madness.

Old Baba had been trying to tell me that it would be impossible to heal my wound by resurrecting anyone who was dead. If I insisted on trying to do this unfeasible thing, then the world would only be reflected back to me as it appeared in old Baba's most obvious expression—with fury and scorn. Indeed, this was how my surroundings had appeared to me for a long time. But if I went about things another way, if I could in fact accept that my world had forever changed, then I could see grief as it was depicted from the side of Baba's face—with sadness, but with compassion for others. Having once seen the face of deep grief, though, I did not think it was possible to go back to a point in life when I didn't know old Baba existed at all.

THE STORY OF the Fuzzy-Headed Priest has a coda. I went back to visit him with my son a few months later, when it was autumn. I didn't phone in advance, but just stopped by with some coffee, for I have found that it is as Furuie told me on Kōyasan: all priests love coffee. Ewan seemed not to remember the statue of the old hag on the temple altar. When we pulled into the temple driveway, he merely looked at me and said with excitement, "Mommy! It's the temple with the mice!"

The Fuzzy-Headed Priest and the Crab Lady were relaxing in the front room; her health had improved greatly since I last saw her, and in the absence of pain, she had grown youthful, and it became clear to me that she was not old enough to be the priest's mother. We sat and had tea, while the wife played a traditional game with my son, which involved whacking a stack of colorful wooden disks with a mallet, specifically trying to knock one disk from the stack while keeping the others in a column. The topmost disk in the stack had been painted with the face of Daruma, one of Zen Buddhism's most enlightened teachers.

We chatted a bit, and at one point in the conversation, I asked the Fuzzy-Headed Priest where he was from. At this, both he and his wife raised their eyebrows. There was a long pause.

Finally, the wife said, "My husband is from a town that has become very famous in the news. It's a town that no longer exists."

"Well, it exists," he said. "But it's having a rough time these days. I am from Rikuzentakata, a town almost completely obliterated by the March 11, 2011, disaster." When news crews arrived, they were unable to find any residents in the town and feared that everyone had died.

The Fuzzy-Headed Priest's older brother had been given the family temple in Rikuzentakata. The older brother had had a son, who had married and had two daughters. The tsunami killed the brother, the brother's son, and one granddaughter. Only the daughter-in-law and one of the granddaughters survived. Once every three months, the Fuzzy-Headed Priest made the four-hour journey to Rikuzentakata to perform memorial services for the many dead *danka* associated with his family. Despite being the second son, he had, in a strange twist of fate, become the head priest after all.

THIRTEEN

SUMMER VISITORS

G RIEF IS NOT A one-way street in Japan, for the dead miss us as much as we miss them. Even if we cannot take the time to go on a pilgrimage, the dead are always longing for us and waiting to return to us.

It is believed that the souls of the dead come home to their loved ones on the autumnal equinox and again on the vernal equinox. Both times of the year are called "Ohigan" in Japanese, a term that roughly means "gathering on the other shore." The curtain separating the mortal and spirit worlds is said to be thin, allowing the spirits to return home. In some parts of Japan, people believe that the ancestors also return home on New Year's Eve. The biggest holiday for the ancestors in Japan, however, is called Obon, and it takes place during the most romantic time of year: summer. It is during Obon that all the dead return home, and the Japanese go all out to welcome them.

IN THE SUMMERTIME in Japan, girls wear colorful *yukata*, sheer kimonos, designed to keep them feeling cool but looking attractive. In the summer, people eat chilled watermelon and shaved ice and carry fans and handkerchiefs. One of the most popular decorating motifs in the summer is the goldfish swimming in a pool of clear, cold water. Japanese people are nostalgic about little children carrying bags of goldfish in the summer, because "goldfish catching" is a traditional game available in the carnival-like environment of the *matsuri*, or Japanese festival. In goldfish catching, participants are given a paper net, which they must use to quickly scoop up goldfish before the paper breaks. Novice scoopers routinely break their nets before getting anywhere near a fish, and experts—usually parents— are often called on to scoop quickly, to staunch a weeping child's tears. At night, surrounded by paper lanterns and the sound of vendors calling out, "Beer!" or "Yakitori chicken!" young people wear traditional Japanese clothing and engage in these games, often with parents and grandparents in tow. The festive, romantic atmosphere of the *matsuri* is a hallmark of Japanese summer.

Historically, *matsuri* were timed around the rice-harvesting cycle and often doubled in meaning as fertility rites. During a *matsuri*, normal social rules are relaxed, as during Carnival in the West. Youths dye their hair, drink, and enthusiastically participate in parades, often pushing and pulling mammoth floats and competing against each other in teams for who can put on the best show. Pretty much every Japanese person I've ever spoken to has agreed that a *matsuri* is the "true face of Japan," and even the most cynical expat will wax nostalgically about *matsuri* past, and how there's no real equivalent in the West.

When I was around five years old, my mother took me to Aomori to see the famous Nebuta *matsuri*. On that particular trip, I became fixated on elaborate, oversized hats for sale in conjunction with the *matsuri*. The hats were made from straw and decorated with enormous paper and plastic flowers, birds, and tinsel. This was to be fastened under the chin with a blue-and-white gauze handkerchief. I begged and begged my mother for one of these magic hats, but she was adamant. There was no reason for us to buy such a thing, and anyway, how would I carry it home?

Still, I pined. Everywhere we went, people were wearing The Hat. I remember seeing two foreigners—two *gaijin*—in these hats. Even *they* had hats, but still my mother said, "No." I continued to beg, and I suspect I was something of a handful on that trip. We were staying with my mother's college friend, who was looking after her nephew. She and my mother hoped that we two children would get along, but I was younger, tremendously shy, and insecure about my language skills. The nephew had never seen a foreigner before and was not sure how to talk to me. I spent a lot of time sulking.

At last it was the evening of the big *matsuri*, and we all lined up on one side of a road. My mother and her friend urged us to be patient, feeding us snacks while they talked nonstop about college and their lives since graduation. From far away, I heard the boom of a drum. Suddenly, a flood of dancers rushed down the street. Men and women dressed in *yukata* danced in unison while wearing smaller versions of the straw hats I had admired all day. "*Ressa sah! Ressa sah!*" they cried. Their costumes were festooned with little bells, and as they danced, a few bells invariably fell off. The nephew brazenly darted into the street to grab a bell. I could not stand the thought of someone else getting a bell while I had nothing.

We started a game—an unspoken competition. We would battle to see who could gather the most bells. As the dancing and the music grew more urgent, we dove in and out of the parade with greater daring, and I stuffed my pockets. It grew darker and darker and then the gods arrived.

They were enormous, as long as thirty-six feet, and each one was a lantern. They were dragons, warriors, and ships gliding through the street. They were demons, samurai speeding on horses, and roaring tigers. Around us, music pulsed, and dancers zigged and zagged across the asphalt. It was dark now, and the lanterns encased us in an orb of yellow light. Then there were new dancers, dressed in even more elaborate *yukata* and headgear. I became drunk on atmosphere, dancing and diving and marveling at the floats. And then, an incredible thing happened.

A man stopped in front of me. His head looked like a tiny sun supporting an enormous galaxy of animals and flowers and metal streamers. On his head was the largest, most elaborate hat yet. He looked at me and asked, in perfect English, "Where are you from?"

"America," I answered instantly.

"Would you like my hat?" Without waiting for a response, he removed the hat from his head and placed it on mine. Then he took my hand and led me into the auburn bubble of the parade and its lights, and we were dancing.

My mother watched me go. It happened quickly. Her five-and-a-half-year-old child, always so obedient at home, simply disappeared, swallowed into the crowd. My mother told me that she watched for a moment, certain I would turn around and come back. But then I drifted out of sight, carried downstream by the superhuman current of the parade. She tried to run after me, but there were too many dancers in the way. She said she tried to cut through the mob to find me, but there were so many people she could not move. In desperation, she finally approached a policeman and explained what had happened.

"Oh, yes," he shrugged. "This happens during Nebuta *matsuri*. The children in particular get so excited."

"But my daughter is a foreigner."

"Well, then. She'll stand out and you'll be able to spot her when she comes back."

On that trip, I learned that time does not always move at the same speed—at least as we perceive it. My mother says that I was gone for a long time—up to an hour.

I remember time moving very quickly. I held hands and danced with the strange man. Some other people joined us, and we all danced down the street together, buoyed by the golden light and the pounding of the drums. After what felt like only a few minutes, I offered the man his hat back, but he told me to keep it. I said goodbye and worked my way back up through the parade, toward my mother, who wisely did not scold me when I finally arrived by her side. The nephew looked at me, stunned. I had won our game.

The next day, Aomori was abruptly struck by one of Japan's intense rainstorms, and the streets were flooded. The shoes in the entry to the house where we were staying bobbed along in a stream of water. My mother—still healthy then—carried me on her back to the train station. Taxis drove along slowly, sending waves of water up to her thighs. With one hand, I gripped her neck, and with the other, I held the hat in a large plastic bag. I had been urged to leave the hat behind, but I considered it a very special gift, perhaps even a sacred one, and nothing would ever part me from this treasure.

The gods, however capable of fun and however appreciative of our parade and our costumes, could still send us a downpour. My mother carried me carefully to the train station. The track was elevated. We departed—slowly—out of the boggy town and headed south, away from Aomori. The rain lifted, and we continued on to Tōkyō, to neon signs, to skyscrapers, to the subway, where a greater power than nature seemed to have the upper hand.

The hat lived in my grandparents' house for years. For a while it was in the front room, on the *tokonoma*, a slightly raised platform where treasures are displayed. Later, my grandmother moved it to a closet in my mother's bedroom. When I was sixteen, I told my parents I wanted to take the hat home. My mother and grandparents protested. The hat was too large, but I insisted that it would fit in the overhead cabin of the plane. And so it did. Now the hat sits in my childhood bedroom in California. The metal streamers are still bright and dance when the heat comes on in my room, as though they carry a trace of the dance in which we met.

DEEP SUMMER IN Japan holds the promise of romance. During the Tanabata *matsuri*, usually celebrated on July 7, a pair of mythical lovers is reunited for one day only. Their names are Orihime, the celestial princess weaver, and Hikoboshi, the celestial cow herder. The princess lived in the sky and wove beautiful garments beside a river called the Amanogawa, otherwise known as the Milky Way. One day she met the cow herder, and the two fell instantly in love and married. Now that she was a wife, the princess stopped weaving, but her father, the Sky King, had loved her beautiful creations, and he angrily separated the lovers, placing them on either side of the river. The princess was distraught. She cried and begged her father to let her see her husband, if only a little. Her father took pity. Once a year, a flock of magpies cluster together, forming a bridge across the Milky Way, and the two lovers cross the bridge and reunite.

The lovers are represented by Altair and Vega, two stars that are particularly bright in the summer sky. On Tanabata, the day the lovers reunite, Japanese children write their wishes down on colorful strips of paper, then hang these on bamboo branches. Cities put on large-scale Tanabata displays, veering away from the traditional decorations to hang up massive chandeliers made of brightly colored plastic. The city of Sendai is notable for its display. When I visited Tōhoku in July, four months after the tsunami, train stations were universally decorated with these branches, and the childish scrawl on each piece of paper asked for "peace."

While Tanabata is magical, as a child, nothing seemed more romantic to me than Obon, a Buddhist celebration. In most parts of Japan, Obon is commemorated over several days, often from August

13 to the 17, with the peak of the festivities taking place on the seventeenth. Some parts of Japan hold Obon in July; the difference depends on whether or not a region follows the old lunar calendar or the Gregorian one for celebrating festivals.

My understanding of Obon as a child was limited. To me, it was an excuse to get to wear a kimono. My mother would dress me and put up my hair. In the afternoon, my grandmother would invite over one of her young students to teach me how to dance.

The culmination of Obon was a large outdoor dance, in which men, women, and children circled around an elevated platform outfitted with speakers, lanterns, and a musical band. The musicians played *taiko* drums and flutes, and a singer wailed songs of longing and heartbreak into a microphone. Many of the dance moves are borrowed from agriculture: hoeing, planting, harvesting. I loved to dance with all the women and the few men who joined in. I loved to see the ferocious older women in their beautiful kimonos dancing with such precise and extroverted confidence as if to say, "I know how this is to be done. Watch me." I wanted to be that way one day.

I did not know that we were dancing for the dead. Obon is not about dressing up, or kimonos, or showing off dance moves. Obon isn't even another permutation of Shintō's many festivals. It is a Buddhist celebration, originating in China, during which the Japanese welcome home the spirits of the dead. It is in August that the ghosts come home, that all lovers and beloveds are reunited. During Obon, much of Japan shuts down to accommodate the flood of travelers going home to visit with their loved ones one more time.

AUGUST OF 2012 would be the second Obon after my grandfather died. We had not managed thus far to bury his bones, but finally Sempō felt comfortable enough about the radiation situation in Iwaki to dig up the ground by the family cemetery plot. My grandfather's bones were finally getting a burial. In preparation for this event, I had decided to take in as many Obon-related activities across Japan as I could, to try to understand the tradition more fully. I started my trip in Japan's old capital, Kyōtō, at Kōdaiji temple, long a personal favorite.

It was once believed that if a chair or a table or any object had been around for one hundred years, it had the right to get a soul. As a result, people in Japan sometimes destroyed things that turned ninety-nine, in order to avoid having to put up with them being alive. Very often, the destroyed ninety-nine-year-old things were resentful to be relegated to the trash heap. Their chance at mortality thwarted, the indignant parasols and notebooks turned into mischievous spirits hell bent on revenge.

I asked my mother how a human could stand to gain in this situation. On the one hand, people wanted to avoid a knife with a soul, but surely it was even worse to have a knife that was now an evil spirit lounging around in a recycling bin. My mother explained that a literal interpretation wasn't the point. The message was to always try to take care of chairs and umbrellas and other things, since even an inanimate object deserves dignity, and how you care for objects says as much about you as how you care for people in your life. This is also why Mount Doom includes a special shrine just for chopsticks and combs.

During Obon, most temples across Japan are preoccupied with welcoming home the dead, but Kōdaiji commemorates the eerie potential that all material objects have to haunt you in your life. The temple grounds are transformed into a haunted house. The already-dark hallways are illuminated with hazy, orange lanterns and populated with half-dilapidated benches and mashed lanterns. Ghostly images are projected onto the exterior of the buildings. There is also an art display, for among Kōdaiji's many treasures are numerous ghostly paintings: octopus ghosts stealing children, a woman in a white kimono with no feet, and hand scrolls depicting the angry ghosts of these discarded items. Furious cherry blossoms march side by side along bamboo shoots, both trailing a broken-down palanquin with a woman's tongue sticking out. There is a parasol hopping on its one foot, an eye open on the crumpled paper skin. You might have seen this parasol before. He is a character in the very modern Japanese anime *Gegege no Kitarō*. The one time I went to see these hand scrolls with all their terrifying, if charming, inanimate objects out to terrorize the living, I thought that it was no wonder the Japanese are such good craftsmen—and so very responsible about disposing of their trash.

OBON CAN ONLY begin when you call home the dead, and there are just so many days that you can do *omukae*, or "the honored receiving." The word *omukae* is similar to the Japanese word used for meeting someone at an airport or coming off a train.

"Today I have to go to Narita for *mukae*."

But there is only one great greeting, the *omukae*. In the great greeting, you bring home the people who left you during *owakare*, the great parting. Generally, *omukae* is supposed to take place between August 7 and the 15. My mother remembers her father lighting a small fire on the corner outside her childhood home. The smoke was a signal to the ancestors that they needed to come back. My grandmother made a horse out of a cucumber and a cow out of an eggplant, and these were placed next to the fire. The spirits flying overhead were supposed to follow the smoke down from the sky to the mortal realm, and then sit on the cucumber horse and eggplant cow, which were moved indoors to the family altar. After about a week, the ancestors were sent home, and the cow and the horse sent floating down a nearby river. In other parts of Japan, people light fires on graves or go to a temple to bring home the dead.

I began Obon at Rokuharamitsuji temple, in Kyōtō. To get there, I had to walk up Gojō Dōri, Kyōtō's Fifth Street, through a throng of porcelain sellers in town for a street fair that has been around for almost one hundred years. Gojō Dōri is on a slight incline. It's the main street that leads up to Kiyomizu temple, the Zen temple supported by hundreds of wooden pillars made out of the zelkova tree.

From a distance, the fair looked manageable—a long line of low, portable stalls filled with pots and cups. But as I climbed the gentle hill, I grew dizzy. I couldn't stop staring at all the dishes for sale. There were *matcha* tea bowls, which I love to collect. I admired one bowl with fireflies, the bodies painted blue and green and the tails bright gold. The mouth of this cup was wide so the tea would cool quickly in the summer. My son had started spending evenings in our co-op garden in New York chasing after the dozens of fireflies that clustered on the lawn. I bought the bowl.

Avant-garde artists with jagged haircuts selling plates and cups with angular edges and spattered glazes proudly arranged their wares on tables constructed out of irregularly shaped slabs of wood. I hoped the wood was grateful to have been salvaged and wouldn't resort to violently shrugging the porcelain wares off onto the sidewalk.

I finally stopped asking if anything had been made in China. "Not here," everyone told me. Never in Kyōtō. I rounded the top of the fair and continued down the other side of the street. A man gave me a discount on a tea bowl with soybeans and demon faces; I would display it in February, to coincide with the lunar New Year. Then I found a *raku* bowl—a kind of earthenware that feels soft in the hands—with *koinobori*, now the symbol for Children's Day, but once exclusively the traditional symbol of boys.

"Once you drink tea from a *raku* bowl," my mother said, "you can't ever drink from any other kind of bowl again."

The shopkeeper agreed with her and, impressed by her connoisseurship, threw in a couple of hand-painted cups with dragonflies. "These are the perfect weight," said the man. "For beer, tea, or water." He was right. Later in the hotel room, I stopped using the cold, white porcelain cups accompanying our complimentary coffee, in favor of the little dragonfly cups.

By the time I arrived at Rokuharamitsuji, my shopping bags were heavy. My mind was scattered. I was thinking about how I would change the decorations on the mantel at home each month. It would still be summer when I got home. The firefly bowl could go next to the watermelon bowl. Soon it would be fall, and I'd put out the chrysanthemum bowl next to the crimson maple-leaf bowl.

It was dark, and Rokuharamitsuji was illuminated by lanterns. While stadium light aims to re-create the freshness and alertness of daylight, lantern light lives symbiotically with the dark. You step into its tent, aware of the night outside, aware that you are sharing a little island of sight with everyone else who is with you. Once upon a time, people walked from island of light to island of light. Once upon a time, people carried light with them. They suspended lanterns on bamboo poles, not unlike the way they carted water from a well. To be in the lamplight always fills me with nostalgia and makes me want to linger where the world feels simpler and therefore safer, though I know this is an illusion.

Rokuharamitsuji was founded in the tenth century and sits in the eastern side of Kyōtō. The long name requires an explanation. *Roku* means "six" in Japanese, and in traditional Buddhism it is believed that there are six realms of existence: hell, hungry ghosts, animals, titans, humans, and gods. Beyond these realms, there is enlightenment, which frees a soul from constantly being reborn; a god, after all, might end up being reborn as a praying mantis if he is not careful. Rokuharamitsuji's long name is intended to remind all beings to practice perfection in whatever realm they inhabit, because that is the best way to become enlightened.

At one point, there was a large cemetery near Rokuharamitsuji that took up much of the eastern hillside of Kyōtō city. People who were too poor to bury their loved ones dumped corpses at the entrance to this cemetery, which was often nicknamed "Rokudo no tsuji," or "the Crossroads of the Six Realms." In the people's imagination, this crossroads became a sacred space between this world and the next. Rokuharamitsuji, and the five other temples situated near this cemetery, thus took on the special role of acting as way stations for the busy traffic traversing the six realms. During Obon, pilgrims walked the road through this cemetery and visited the six temples; the route was considered a symbolic tour through the underworlds of the realms.

Today, there is little trace of the vast old cemetery, and most of Rokuharamitsuji's buildings were restored in 1969 and have a modern feel. Fortunately, old traditions are still remembered and practiced within the temple, and during the period surrounding Obon, crowds of people turn to Rokuharamitsuji to bring home their ancestors and to walk the old pilgrimage route. My *omukae* began when I paid a man sitting in a tent on the Rokuharamitsuji grounds to write down the names of my grandparents and my father on thin strips of paper. I took the strips of paper into the temple and then sat down to pray.

Around me, a few people were already seated on the tatami floor, their heads bent. I copied their poses, and for a while my mind was blank. I have never known what to do when I am supposed to pray. Finally, I asked the people I missed—the people I secretly suspected loved me most in life—to help me. I was exhausted from waking up every morning more sad than happy. I needed their help to right the imbalance.

Rokuharamitsuji is a Shingon temple, and along with an assortment of gold cups, leaves, and gold chandeliers, it houses numerous beautiful statues. My attention was immediately drawn to a growling old Fudō. I thought about how my father would have tried to copy the expression to make me laugh.

It was hot outside, and it had become even hotter inside the temple, now crowded with dozens of people sitting on the floor. At last the priests came out and lit incense and candles, which made the temple absolutely sweltering. The priests chanted sutras, and I furiously fanned my handmade Kyōtō-style fan.

"I want to tell you," said the priest, after the sutras concluded, "that we have a special sutra for you today. For centuries, we were not allowed to reveal its contents. But now that it's been around for a thousand years, we are allowed to open it, and you are the first people to have its benefits. You must now line up, and we will hit you on the head and evil spirits will fall away." I got in line with everyone else and subjected myself to yet another of Shingon's unusual exorcisms.

Once purified, we moved on to another part of the temple to ring a bell. There are a lot of bells during Obon. One temple I had visited earlier in the day had had a bell soundtrack on continuous loop. At Rokuharamitsuji the pilgrims rang the bell—named the *mukaegane*, which is literally "receiving bell"—to get the attention of the dead. While most temple bells hang in a specially designed wooden tower that stands separate from other temple structures, Rokuharamitsuji's bell hangs underground, suspended over a pit, so beings in the underworld can hear it more clearly. In case you are confused about where the dead are supposed to be—underground or in the air—clearly the location of the ancestors isn't a fixed position. If the Japanese don't seem to mind this, it's because they recognize that they are engaging in a ritual activity and not a literal one.

There is a trick to ringing this underground bell, and there was much hand wringing over a failure to produce a good sound. I gave the rope attached to a wooden pole a good tug. I tugged so hard that the bell rang particularly loudly, and I was startled, if also a little pleased. Then we moved over to a statue of Jizō. I poured water over the strips of paper with the names of the dead and left them at that statue's feet.

By now it was dark. A group of neighborhood volunteers was going through the street with flashlights on the lookout for anyone who might be lost. Blocks away, the porcelain festival was breaking down. In the narrow streets of this old part of Kyōto, the modern city felt far away. We walked to Chinkoji, the next stop on the pilgrimage, and it was the same here as it had been at Rokuharamitsuji; we could buy strips of paper in addition to a little pine branch to help bring our ancestors down to us. Here too there was a large bell to ring. The line to ring this bell went all around the bell tower, and as people stood in line—nervous, joking, apprehensive—I kept hearing, "I hope I can ring that bell." And, "That guy did a great job." And, "Oops. Poor woman. Bad sound." It was a curious mix of peer pressure and sympathy and group comfort.

My bell ringing—less successful this time—was one drop in a sea of collective mourning. Here in this country often chastised for its lack of mental health services, for its lack of a language to discuss suffering and depression, we were out in the open, ringing bells, writing down the names of the people we missed, praying for them, and planning on spending several days in their company because we missed them.

There was nothing private about our grief.

Perhaps it was a combination of heat and exhaustion, but I slept better that night than I had in years. I slept without medication. I dreamed of stars in the night sky. I watched them tumble down slowly, like marbles falling down a slope. They cascaded down a hillside onto a valley floor and into my hands.

In the morning, I woke up and told my mother, "It worked. Everyone is here with us."

. . .

IN THE MORNING I returned to Gojō Dōri. The porcelain stalls were gone, and the street was quiet. Almost all the trash had been cleared, and there was little trace of the frenzied carnivalesque energy of the night before. Most of the shops were shuttered, with signs on the doors and windows declaring that business had stopped for now due to the Obon holiday. But at the top of the hill, where Gojō Dōri leads to the entrance to Kiyomizu temple, a few porcelain stores were open. This included the shop where I'd picked up the *raku* bowl and been given the dragonfly cups, and which was now overseen by a woman.

"We have to stay open," the shopkeeper said to me. "Someone will always come by looking for new candle holders or teacups to put on the family grave." I looked at the pile of dishes outside the shop. There, neatly arranged on a table, were rows of incense burners, candle holders, and tiny dishes—the very things a ghost would need for a tea. The porcelain festival's original mission was not to give people like me a reason to buy lots of pretty things, but to give Kyōtōites the chance to replace porcelain teacups and plates used on family altars and cemeteries with something brand new.

The shopkeeper served me cold tea, which I drank gratefully. It was still morning, but it was already hot and my bags had once again grown heavy.

"Where are you going now?" the shopkeeper asked me kindly as I dabbed my wet forehead with a handkerchief.

I told her that I planned to climb to Kiyomizu temple. The altar in the *hondō*, which was usually closed from view, was open to the public, and I wanted to see the main images.

"Oh," she misunderstood. "You are going on a pilgrimage. Why don't I hold your bags for you? I won't be closing any time soon," she said. "Come back when you are ready. Take my card so you have the store number, in case you get lost."

I wanted to tell her that I wasn't actually making a pilgrimage;

I just wanted to see the statues. But this seemed unnecessary in the face of her kindness, so I thanked her, and began the climb.

YOU HAVE TO climb up hundreds of steps to reach Kiyomizu temple. Whether you take a small side path or follow the main road all the way, you will be confronted with numerous shops and restaurants that showcase the sheer delight people in Japan have for making, selling, and buying something new. There are traditional things to eat like chilled cucumbers and bean cakes. Then there are T-shirts for sale with edgy modern designs beside three-hundred-year-old porcelain shops. It can take a long time to get to Kiyomizu temple, and it's perhaps no surprise that one of the first gods inside the temple proper is Daikokuten, the god of money.

One reason why I wanted to go to Kiyomizu was because my guidebook had listed Obon as one of the few times of the year when the temple's treasured Buddha would be on view on the main altar; the rest of the year it was kept shut in a box. I asked a man who looked like he was on the staff of the temple where I could go see the "statues that are normally not on view." He pointed to a staircase that went underground. Gamely, I took off my shoes and descended. Before turning a corner into a darkened corridor, I saw a sign that read, "No light. No photo." Then I was in the dark. Literally. A thick dark. I knew it was the kind of dark that was intended as a test of faith, or perhaps a testament to faith, but I was furious. I was winding around in this underground labyrinth, with no sense of where I was going. The women ahead of me were laughing nervously.

Apparently my question—where can I see the things that are not usually on display—had led me here, to this subterranean chamber, where up ahead a massive stone that was perhaps five feet in diameter was slowly rotating under a very focused light as people reached over to give it a turn. On top was some Buddhist Sanskrit lettering. I touched it, felt its surface, which had been smoothed by countless hands that had come before mine. I made my usual prayer and was soon swept along by the tide of people heading for more darkened corridors, until we all stumbled outside into the light.

Kiyomizu is full of sidetracks like this. There is a Shintō shrine in which one must walk blindfolded from one rock to another in a test of "true love." If you reach the second rock, then you will find your true love—if you haven't already. There's another spot where you can write down angry feelings on a piece of paper shaped like a doll, then drop the paper in water and watch it dissolve. Below the grand Kiyomizu structure is a waterfall, and if you drink the water from these falls (via a community cup, which has been sterilized in a self-serve ultraviolet sterilization unit), you will receive enlightenment. And while all this is entertaining, the skeptic in me can't help but feel that such things are an awfully convenient way to make money, and that Kiyomizu, despite being an impressive architectural wonder, has also become a kind of Disneyland for Buddhism.

The pilgrimage we were on now was said to last for a thousand days, which meant if I could make it into the main part of the temple to pray, I'd be blessed for just over three years, after which I could come back again. Not for the first time, I was reminded of how practical the Japanese can be, even when it comes to providing a manageable expiration and renewal date for good luck.

When we finally arrived to the correct part of Kiyomizu—which looks so different in daylight—a man with a megaphone herded us to a place where we waited patiently beside ropes for the people ahead of us to remove their shoes. Dozens of small bronze bells had been hung over the walkway, and they sang to us in the breeze. Off to the side was a man waiting to collect more money from us and to write down the names of our loved ones on small strips of paper, to call home the souls of the dead in case we hadn't managed to do so yet.

Inside the temple, we were swept up again by the flurry of people on their pilgrimages, and it became impossible to focus solely on the artwork. Before we could even get into the altar area, we were supposed to write down our wishes on a candle, and we had to wait in line to get our own candle. Then there was a line to use the pen to write on the candle, and even when I got to the pen, there was another wait to put the candle on a candle holder. I couldn't help but think that this pilgrimage was about as enjoyable as trying to shop at Whole Foods in Manhattan on a Friday evening. But I dove in. For in all the jockeying, the twisting around, and the slow passage through the corridor to the candle, the pen, and the burner, there was nothing but a patient and persistent kind of focus. Everyone knew what everyone else wanted and needed, and cooperated accordingly, a little like the exercise at Eiheiji in which we had to finish eating at the same time.

When I finally got to the candle and then the pen, I couldn't decide what to write. I looked at the other candles to see what other people had written. They wanted to fall in love. They wanted someone to fall back in love with them. They very much wished to do well on exams. They wanted their father to get better. They wanted a healthy child.

Once I had wanted these things too, but now I had new wants. I wanted to be able to write a good book. I wanted my son to grow up healthy and happy. I wanted Japan to recover from the March 11 disaster. And I wanted what I had asked my grandparents and my father to help me with the night before. I wanted to rebalance the equation of sadness and happiness in my life. I wanted my body to be less bitter.

I wrote this down, set my candle on a spike where a predecessor had burned away, then surrendered to the tide of pilgrims circling the gallery. There were candles all the way through the hallway. And because there was no breeze, all the heat from the people and the candles made everything very hot. At last we tumbled around the corner. And there they were, the pantheon of gods and Buddhas waiting for us to look them in the eye.

A young boy asked his mother, "What do we do? What do we do now? What do we do?"

I heard her hiss: "Do not ask that kind of question in a place like this! You look at what other people are doing, and then you just do it."

All of a sudden, there was an expert pilgrim whose gestures rang with the clarity of authority. She bowed, gave incense, rang a bell, and prayed. The person behind her copied this example. The little family moved forward to take their turn, and I went too, trusting that there would be someone else behind me who knew what to do and order would be restored again for a little while.

I turned my head up toward the Buddhas, then down ahead of me so I could keep pace with the crowd, then up again. I asked for the same things I had been asking for the past twenty-four hours. "I would like to be more happy than sad." Then we all moved on and out onto the landing. I hadn't been successful in getting a good, long art historian's look at the statues, but as had been the case at Eiheiji and Sōjiji, I found myself moved by the experience of sharing an activity with so many anonymous people.

GRAVEYARDS ARE BUSY during Obon, particularly at night, when people are off from work and temperatures drop. Depending on your family's sect or belief, you might need to perform your "great receiving" on the grave of your ancestors. Even if you don't, you will want to make sure the grave is clean and tidy, so everyone—including the dead—knows that you are conscientious. One of the most stunning cemeteries during Obon is the hillside Higashi Ōtani Cemetery. For three days during Obon, ten thousand lanterns are lit above the tombstones in the graveyard, to help signpost the "way home" for returning spirits of the dead. The immediate effect of so many lanterns at once is that they themselves seem to be souls, and you realize how crowded the cemetery is and how many people are beloved but not forgotten.

I went to the Higashi cemetery at night to find the grave of Shinran, the founder of the Pure Land sect, the sect to which the Higashi cemetery belongs. Sometimes I passed a tombstone where someone had lit a candle and incense, a traditional way both to honor an ancestor and to "call him home."

Plenty of tourists were also picking their way through the tombstones and trying to read dates and perhaps a few names. When I finally did find Shinran's grave, it was full of candles and incense—and a bouquet of flowers that included the lotus blossom—a recurring element in the décor for it is from the muddy depths of a lake-bed floor that the lotus flower blooms, a reminder that something beautiful can come up even from the dirt.

IN THE DAYS leading up to Obon, family members often travel home to be together, and airports and train stations are crowded, not unlike the days surrounding Thanksgiving and Christmas in the United States. Trains are full of people leaving the great cities of Ōsaka and Tōkyō for the countryside, and if you don't buy your ticket early enough, you might not get a seat and will be forced to stand or sit in between cars. At home, families have their own traditions—just as every Western family has a slightly different take on Christmas Day—but most center on eating and enjoying the art of being together. Then, usually on August 16, Obon is celebrated and the souls of the ancestors are sent home via Okuribi, or "the great sending-off day."

In Kyōtō's Obon, the great send-off is marked by an event called Daimonji, which literally translates to "Big Characters." The "characters" in question are both Chinese characters, which the Japanese imported into its language starting at the time of Prince Shōtoku, and pictures.

These pictures are large images carved into mountainsides, which are then lit up in the dark via giant bonfires: 大, or "big"; 妙法, or "wondrous dharma"; a picture of a boat; another 大, or "big"; and a picture of a *torii*, or the gate one sees in front of Shintō shrines. At a designated time, volunteers light up these fires, and city lights in Kyōtō are dimmed to allow people to see the flames and to pay their respects; these bonfires are a way of sending back the souls of the dead after their weeklong visit. In Japanese, sending back the dead is called "Okuribi," or "the great fire of sending-off."

Each character has its own distinct location and story. The shape of the boat, for example, is a reference to a "spirit ship" that helps guide the souls of the dead to the Buddhist Western Paradise; the prow of the ship points to the west. The meaning of the "large" characters is less clear, but they seem to have to do with sending off the souls of ancestors with as "big" a fire as possible. Each of the fires is also maintained by a set group of individuals who have inherited their roles. Some of the bonfires have a strict procedure; the *torii* bonfire, for example, is lit all at once. Some of the bonfires involve a procession of men running through the local neighborhood before they reach their destination. Most of the bonfires also have related activities for onlookers; at the "big" bonfire, you can write your wishes on a strip of cedar, called a Gomagi, which you can then present at Ginkakuji, Kyōtō's famous silver pavilion. Your Gomagi will then be burned in the bonfire, the smoke transmitting your particular wish up to the heavens.

While the Kyōtō Daimonji is one of Japan's most famous Oku-ribi—returning the souls via fire—it is by no means the only one. Just as there are numerous ways to call home the spirits of the dead, there are also numerous ways to send them back. It would take a lifetime in Japan to see each ritual; I was going to have to choose just one. Much as I longed to stay in Kyōtō, my heart was calling in another direction.

I had long wanted to see Okuribi in Matsushima, Japan's famous series of pine tree–dotted islands that have inspired so many artists and poets throughout the centuries. There I would send the spirits of my ancestors home.

FOURTEEN

FAREWELL TO OLD SOULS

FOR HUNDREDS OF YEARS, the town of Matsushima has hosted a special Obon in conjunction with the Zen temple Zenkōji. When I arrived at Matsushima for Obon, it was as though I had walked into a scene straight out of my childhood. In the center of a large field by the ocean was an elevated platform with a speaker. The square was ringed by lanterns, and the perimeter lined by vendors selling drinks and traditional festival food: grilled squid, chicken, and *okonomiyaki*, a kind of everything-is-in-it pancake. As the sun was setting, a group of schoolchildren performed *taiko* drumming. Then it became dark, and the lanterns and their soft, magical light took over the square, and the highlight of the evening began: Obon dancing.

Women and children dressed in traditional outfits assembled in a circle, and as a singer's voice began to slide up and down the pentatonic scale, the dancing began. The dance movements were easy for anyone to pick up on the spot or to dredge up out of their memories: Obon movements are slow and often stylized gestures that reference hoeing or fishing. It was not uncommon for men and women to join the procession and continue on in a circle, and then drop out when they felt like it.

.   .   .

In March of 2011, Matsushima was spared the worst of the tsunami. The smaller outer islands buffered the coast so the waves that reached the shore caused only a bit of damage. Because Matsushima, often cited as one of Japan's three most scenic spots, is a major tourist attraction, local tourism officials are eager to spread the word that Matsushima was untouched by the disaster.

"Of course," a tour guide confided to me after we had spoken for a good fifteen minutes, "if your house was on the wrong side of the islands, or in East Matsushima where there are no islands at all . . ." He trailed off.

The neighborhood of Nobiru is just six miles east of Matsushima train station; and it is one part of the larger town of East Matsushima, where over a thousand people perished and where waves reached over a hundred feet in height. Nobiru was the first true tsunami disaster area I visited in 2011, a few days after Sempō had taken me to the beach by the Sai no Kawara in Iwaki. As I rode a bus to Nobiru, I thought everything looked normal: houses were intact, women sat by the road shucking scallops, and a phalanx of cars navigated the narrow streets, which had once served horses and the occasional palanquin. Then the road dipped down into Nobiru, and I disembarked. The bus drove away.

I was left standing on a flat plain. At first, everything seemed quiet. Then I noticed something moving: construction equipment. A police car and an ambulance pulled out from a dusty side road, with lights flashing and the siren off, meaning someone's body had been found. I studied the landscape. It was all a mottled gray. Here and there were the remains of a few houses. I realized that the gray was the pulverized remains of buildings and their contents. For several miles all I could see were sheets and bicycles and glass and teapots mixed in with tree branches and roof tiles and books.

I climbed a slight incline and found a house where the lower floors had been flooded but the upper levels had been spared. The tsunami was cruel this way. Houses just a few feet up a hill gave enough protection to their residents.

Where the road wasn't carved out in the tsunami plain, the ground was a mess of human belongings, of trees, metal, timber, and glass. I saw more than one abandoned Game Boy. Here and there were little corners of order. On a set of concrete steps to a demolished home, I saw a little pot of tea and two cups set up. It was a tidy tea-drinking station prepared for the men driving trucks and bulldozers.

I passed what looked like the remains of a small restaurant or café. At least that's what I thought, because I saw a sign intentionally propped right side up that said, "*Irasshai*." Welcome. A mound by the sign at first seemed like more debris, but when I looked at it carefully, I saw that the debris had a shape. Someone had constructed a tiny pile of order out of flowers, empty drink bottles, beads, and a photo. "Thank you," said a handwritten note that I assumed was intended for the store's proprietor, now dead.

A little farther along I saw another of these tiny piles beside a mound of junk. In the pile was a Snoopy. A plastic doll. A stuffed bear. A rescue worker—perhaps more than one—had found children's toys and placed them there in case someone came looking for them, in case someone needed a favored stuffed animal. I thought of all the tender bonds that were torn by the tsunami, and of how we humans try and try again to knit ourselves together, and how we are at our best and our happiest when we do. I thought that of all the cruel and futile things that can happen to us in life, the very worst is when we are separated.

As NOSTALGIC AS the dancing and the music made me, I had come to Matsushima for something else. I was here to send off my ancestors through *tōrō nagashi*, or "lantern floating." The tradition is quite old, and there are numerous variations of it across Japan. In Matsushima you purchase a floating rectangular lantern, along with a ticket for a boat ride. You then write down the names of those you had called home for Obon—whom you now needed to send back. Just as it was becoming dark, I took my lantern and climbed aboard a boat, which set out into the beautiful Matsushima Bay.

A prerecorded voice welcomed us all aboard and then recounted the events of March 11, 2011. It had been a terrible day for Japan, the voice said, and the citizens of Matsushima and her surrounding towns had also suffered.

Several dozen families stood on the prow of the ship with their lanterns, all laughing and joking as they took turns writing down the names of their family members.

"Look!" one of the children cried.

Off in the distance was a rowboat with a line of floating lanterns trailing behind it. Because it was so dark I could barely make out the shape of the people putting the lanterns in the water. The effect was of little orbs of light launching into the air before coming to rest in the water. Soon there were a dozen lanterns, and then there were hundreds.

Our boat came to a stop, and we were asked to bring our lanterns down to a designated location. I had written my farewells to my father and my grandparents—and the many other people I had realized I was missing over the course of the past few days, and whose names I had added to my prayers. A man took my lanterns and put them in a line with several dozen other lanterns. Someone else helped to move the lanterns through the line, until yet another man, using a wooden implement shaped like a potato masher, gently lowered each lantern into the water, where it took off. I tried to keep track of my lanterns to see where they might go.

By now it was quite dark. Several boats set out from Matsushima to deposit lanterns, and soon the sea was awash with pinpricks of light mirroring the stars overhead. It was humbling to consider that each lantern most likely represented more than one person. The number of deceased people for whom we were collectively grieving was enormous. Far away, back on shore, was an even brighter cluster of lights where people were dancing. This brilliant island of light looked so inviting, and I thought to myself that this was what the dead would see as they left us. I wondered if this final image was as bittersweet for them as it was for me.

After a while, I noticed something odd. The lanterns bunched together. They were riding the currents, of course, but the overall effect was as though the lanterns were traveling in clusters, as though some of the souls out at sea were in fact not alone but traveling home to the horizon with each other.

RESIDENTS OF MORIOKA, a city about 120 miles northeast of Sendai, have their own way of sending off the dead. At dusk, the townspeople carry colorfully decorated ten-foot-long barges to the river's edge; the boats are festooned with paper decorations in the traditional Buddhist colors: red, white, yellow, blue, and green. They are also covered with paper letters and paper banners bearing the names of those who have died that year. When it is dark, the boats are carried into the water one by one and set on fire so that each one explodes as it goes down the stream.

The boats are guided down the river by teams of men who have spent the year meeting up and training for this particular moment. In feudal times, this kind of festival was a testament to the cooperative nature required of farmers and fishermen who had to work together.

The teams color-coordinated, and all the men on each team wear the same T-shirts, shorts, headbands, and, in some instances, *happi* coats; the latter is a special cloak used during festivals. A barge in flames is extremely hot and very often the men end up shirtless in the river. There is always a team leader—there is always a leader in Japan—and once the boat is in the water, there is a lot of yelling about how to keep the boat upright, which the men do by pulling on several ropes that have been attached to the stern and the prow.

This is much more difficult than it sounds, and it is dangerous, as so many of these ancient Japanese traditions seem to be. I can't imagine a festival of this nature passing a fire inspection in the United States—lawsuits would abound—but in Japan, a much less litigious society, tradition rules.

If all goes well, the boat stays upright and burns from the top down until nothing but the skeletal remains are left when the boat reaches the end of its journey, which is when it has crossed under a bridge and is just about to hit the rapids. Then it is hauled off to the side and thoroughly doused by firemen. By this point, however, another burning boat is making its way down the river, while a fore-man frantically shouts orders: "Left! Pull! Pull! Pull!"

While this happens, others take turns reading out letters they have written to their loved ones who died that year. The readers are amplified via a sound system that projects voices on both sides of the river. People have died in car accidents, of cancer, by drowning. Most of the time, the person reading the letter wants to reassure the dead person that things will be okay, and that the soul of the dead should feel free to continue on in the great journey to rebirth. The readers are of both genders and all ages. And contrary to the stereotype of Japanese people, the letters are highly emotional. It is impossible for a listener not to be in a state of tears and at the same time not to be anxious about the burning boats and the men pulling them down the river. The story that most affected me, the year I attended, was from a twelve-year-old boy whose mother had died that spring. "I will take care of my younger brother," he explained.

"I do not want you to worry. I want your soul to be able to keep going. I will study hard, and I will not cause Daddy any problems. Please continue on." Hearing all these stories, I was reminded that on any given day someone is dying and someone is grieving.

It was dark when the letter reading and the burning of the boats came to an end. Once again, volunteers set hundreds of tiny lanterns into the water. These lanterns also bore the names of the souls of the dead and represented the departure of the ancestors from the land of the living. Once again, the little lanterns clustered together, following the movement of the water, bobbing and turning in the currents.

FROM MATSUSHIMA, I traveled to Ugo, a small town in Akita Prefecture located amid fields of buckwheat, from which are made some of the finest, freshest soba noodles I have ever eaten. I came to Ugo because I had read about its famous Nishimonai Obon dance, in which the spirits of the dead danced alongside the living. I was supposed to distinguish the dead because their faces were covered with black masks. Other dancers wore a large straw hat called an *amagasa*, which curved around the face like an enormous sunbonnet, also obscuring their features. These dancers often wore a *yukata*—a summer kimono—which they had made themselves out of old pieces of fabric in a patchwork style called *hanui*.

The Nishimonai Bon Odori dances did not rotate in a circle but instead traveled the length of a city street, moving along the slightly curved road from one end to the other, before the dancers turned and worked their way back in a loop. To my ear the music had the same twangy, pentatonic quality that characterizes most Japanese folk music. But there was a twist. At Nishimonai the songs were sung in Aomori dialect, which can be difficult for outsiders to understand. Nevertheless, a few phrases sounded familiar; the songs were a tribute to farmers and peasants and were often bawdy and earthy, a contrast to the solemn, hypnotic dancing.

The Nishimonai dancers were townspeople who met once a month to practice their moves. They were of all ages and both genders, and despite the masks and the heavy hats, you could occasionally make out a family dancing together. You could also tell in some instances who was aging and perhaps arthritic, and who was less certain of the moves.

As the dancing continued on deep into the night, it became impossible to discern when the looping line of dancers repeated. Some of the dancers occasionally took a break. It was hot—easily still 90 degrees and very humid—and the dancers, in all their fabric and with their hoods and hats, were in danger of overheating. Every now and then a figure—usually a woman—would come by, and she would have such a silky clarity to her dancing, and her robe would be so carefully and beautifully handmade, it was clear that she prided herself on her accomplishments. Most of the time, though, the movements were in synch, the outfits coordinated, and I couldn't tell one dancer from another. Then I had the same feeling that I had had at Eiheiji, when all the monks chanted and moved together and when the little *tōrō nagashi* lanterns had clung to each other as they had been tossed around by the ocean or the river current. People are not actually alone. Whether they are alive or dead, they are not alone.

MY MOTHER AND I had plans to take a train from Kōriyama to Iwaki, but due to one of Tōhoku's late-summer storms, the power was out and a signal on the tracks was malfunctioning. Also, streetlights in most towns were down, if they had been on at all. Trains were delayed, and travelers were being advised to take the bus.

In addition, a major portion of the Jōban Line train was still out of commission due to the earthquake and the meltdown at the Fukushima Daiichi Nuclear Power Reactor; a section of the Jōban train tracks goes right through the exclusion zone. By the time we reached Kōriyama, my mother had been on the phone with Sempō apologizing for our impending late arrival. Today was the day we planned to bury my grandfather's bones. It was August 19, and Obon had ended the day before (even though the peak of Obon is celebrated on the sixteenth, the official dates include a few more days for people to travel home and for stragglers to send off the souls of the departed). I had put off burying my grandfather's bones in order to take in as many other Obon-related activities as possible. I felt a little guilty about this because I assumed the proper thing to do would have been to get my grandfather into the ground before his Niibon, his first Obon after dying.

"You need to get here before sunset," Sempō instructed. "At sunset, the day becomes Tomobiki."

Tomobiki is a "friend pulling day," and it is the wrong day to bury someone's bones. On Tomobiki days, priests at Buddhist temples can perform wakes, or memorial services, but never an actual burial, lest the participants find themselves "friend pulled" into the same condition as the deceased. Tomobiki is a vestige of Japan's old calendar system, and if you buy a calendar in Japan, you'll find that it is clearly marked to indicate which days are Tomobiki and which are *senshō* (good luck before noon but bad luck after), which are *senbu* (the opposite of *senshō*), and which are *taian* (good luck all day and the best day to get married).

SEMPŌ CAME TO greet us with a stern look on his face. "This is not how you are supposed to bury someone. This priest is not happy."

I started apologizing. "I know Obon ended yesterday. I know we should have buried him before Obon ended."

He stopped walking. "That's not a problem." A smile flickered across his face, as though I had said something particularly funny. Then he kept walking and said, in his scholarly and stern voice, "It is true that the official Obon ends on August 18. But then there is another Obon. The Jizōbon."

"What is that?"

"For anyone who got left behind. For people who forgot to do their sending off on time. And for children."

Ah, Japan. Land of exceptions when you least expect them. And there was that nice Jizō again, looking after stragglers like me.

We followed Sempō into the *hondō*, and he asked us to sit while he went and got several bags containing both my grandparents' remains. When he returned, he sat down and started to lecture us. He talked for a long time, which made me nervous because I thought the whole reason we had hurried to get there was to avoid burying the bones during sunset. The sun was already quite low in the sky, and we hadn't even started the actual ceremony. As I understood it, the formal burial would happen only after we had finished offering incense in the *hondō* and Sempō had recited the appropriate sutras. After that, we would have to climb up to the cemetery and open up the grave site. I had no idea how long all of this would take.

But Sempō wanted to talk. He wanted us to know that we hadn't handled matters correctly since my grandmother died six years ago: my grandmother had never been buried, but worse, the bones had been split into three containers and were only just now being reunited.

MY GRANDFATHER'S BURIAL—like anyone's burial—is the end of his story. It is also the end of my grandmother's story, and potentially the end to a long family drama. I say "potentially" because one never knows if there is another chapter to a story.

My grandmother was born to an aristocratic family that slowly lost its fortune during Japan's wrenching transformation to modernity. Her relationship with my grandfather was stormy, though I've read enough of their love letters to know how passionate they were for each other. But the pressure of the postwar years, the poverty, and my grandfather's temper were hard on my grandmother, and before she died, she asked that her remains be returned to her aristocratic, natal plot on the island of Kyūshū. She wanted to be with her servants and her parents.

My mother found this request egotistical and was disgusted with her brothers for indulging it. My mother also hated deceiving her father, who knew nothing of the secret pact. Before my grandfather's actual funeral, I was of the opinion that if an elaborate subterfuge was required to send my grandmother back home, then so be it.

In 2005, my mother and I flew to Japan for my grandmother's funeral. We didn't know it at the time, but this would be the last instance in which my mother, her brothers, and her father would all be together. The night before the ceremony, which would take place at the temple, the family ate dinner together at Empukuji.

As we ate, my mother redirected her frustration about my grandmother's bones to express her dissatisfaction with the post-funeral-lunch-meal seating chart because it placed her sister-in-law in a comparatively senior position. At this, my uncle moaned that beer was in order, and my clean-living grandfather roared that if we did not learn to behave correctly in this world, he would come back as a ghost to torture us all.

The men shifted uncomfortably in their *zabuton*-pillow seats. Then Daisuke wandered down to gobble his dinner in a hasty silence, before parking himself in front of the television to debate Prime Minister Koizumi, who was on the evening news.

The meal ended with no satisfying conclusion. One by one the men drifted off to smoke or, in my uncle's case, to sneak a case of beer out of the refrigerator from the temple's adjoining meeting hall. Eventually, I was alone with Takahagi. In this precious hour of privacy, we talked about his secret girlfriend and my then-secret boyfriend. Finally, I told him that I was interested in seeing the crematorium where my grandmother was cremated. Takahagi asked me why.

"I missed it," I said. "I was in America when she was cremated."

"But you're here for the funeral."

"I guess I'm still curious."

"What does your mother say?"

I shrug. "She's too busy."

"We don't really talk about crematoriums in Japan." Takahagi gave me a tolerant smile.

"I know," I said.

I recounted a conversation I had had a few days before arriving at the temple. I was on the Chita Peninsula, which is south of the city of Nagoya. This is where my mother was born, and like the century-old houses that dot the landscape, where she was able to escape the bombings that decimated so many of Japan's cities during the war. We visited an *onsen*, or hot-spring spa, with one of my mother's childhood friends. They were two of a kind, a pair of sylphlike creatures chattering about grade school memories and the healing properties of vinegar, while I with my pink skin and muscular frame was quite obviously not purely Japanese.

When my mother left the *onsen* for a moment to try the sauna, my mother's friend, who had heard of my desire to visit a crematorium, turned to me and murmured, "There are many things you can't understand about Japan. You aren't going to be able to understand what your mother has gone through, for example. You must let people like me take care of her. You can take care of your mother in America."

I felt side-swiped. It isn't true, what they tell you about Japanese people being habitually vague. Once you speak the language, as I do, a whole world of strong emotion and color will open up to you.

"She was my grandmother too," I finally said.

"Look. Don't be hard on yourself. We don't expect you to understand us." She turned her back to me and paddled out of the water to join my mother.

This was something one heard in Japan from time to time: those of us who weren't fully Japanese couldn't fully understand what it felt like to eat Japanese food, or to relate to other Japanese people during a *matsuri* or Obon. It is a judgment I have resisted. I had always been the bridge between the two worlds my mother occupied. It's a responsibility I have taken seriously, perhaps even more seriously than my father. After all, I'm the one who speaks both languages, who knows how to take off my shoes at the entrance to a house without falling over, how to sense the amount of personal space around me on a crowded train, how to be moved by a *hototo-gisu* singing in the twilight. If there is something new about Japan to grasp, I have the reflexive impulse to try to do so.

And the fact was, because I spoke Japanese but remained something of an outsider, I generally ended up hearing the things that were considered taboo. A family friend confided that he might be bisexual, then broke down and confessed he was actually gay. When I was twelve, my grandmother once showed me a photo of a handsome young man and told me that he was her "true love." It was not a photo of my grandfather. With geographical and not to mention cultural distance, secrets appeared to lose their power.

Here is what Takahagi told me about crematoriums.

Cremation was once reserved for nobles but was now mandatory in most of Japan and is also only one part of the expensive funeral process. In 2003 the average funeral in Japan cost $14,000, a significant portion of which went to the priest; this accounted for the Mercedes-Benz that Takahagi's father drove for a half a year until complaints from his parishioners made him give it up for a Toyota. (Later I learned that in 2002, the average cost for a funeral in the United States was $6,500.)

Cremation generally took about an hour, with an extra thirty minutes or so tacked on to give the remains time to cool down. The ovens reached a peak heat of 500 to 600 degrees Celsius, which was substantially lower than temperatures used in the Western process. This was because in Japan it was important to preserve some bone. There would be no sterile handing off of a small urn, as was the case with my father when he was cremated in the United States.

While the flesh dissolved, unseen attendants kept watch. Some monitored the security of the building via a set of cleverly hidden cameras in case an indecisive family member returned to the oven unaccompanied to try to rescue the body. After about an hour, an attendant would go to a hidden chamber behind the ovens and look through a tiny fireproof window to see just how much remained of the cremated corpse, and to make adjustments as necessary.

"There's a window?" I asked.

"There has to be," Takahagi nodded. "What if there is a mistake when the family goes to pull out the bones?"

"The *family* retrieves the body?"

"You can't let strangers do something so personal."

This had never occurred to me.

"Look. I wouldn't feel comfortable taking you for a visit to the crematorium," said my cousin.

"I understand," I said.

IN THE MORNING, I found my way to the local crematorium on my own. It was a stark, one-story building concealed inside a coil of bamboo and trees in a remote part of town that is only accessible by automobile. A brooding copper brow of a roof hung down low over a dark marble entrance.

Automated doors slid open, and an attendant, wearing what looked like a conductor's uniform, complete with cap and gloves, glided out of the entry. I gave him my spiel. I was here from America, and I wanted to know more about the inner workings of a crematorium, as I had missed my grandmother's cremation. He nodded, as if this were a perfectly reasonable request, then advised me to wait. There was a mourning party scheduled to arrive in five minutes, and he had to prepare.

I watched him wheel a specially designed handcart out to the sloped sidewalk. The cart was a marvel of engineering with hydraulic lifts and an automated conveyor belt. When the hearse, with its gold-and-black headdress, elaborately carved like a temple roof, arrived, the attendant bowed and easily extracted the coffin from the back.

It was quiet inside the marble hallway. Two rows of indoor streetlamps shone a luminous pathway on the floor. A priest and the party of mourners followed as the attendant gravely steered the coffin through this solemn space. The women were wearing black kimonos made of silk so heavy it seemed to ooze like ink in the atmospheric light. I watched as high doors opened up at the far end of the hall and swallowed up the mourning party. It was quiet once they were gone, save for the faint sound of a chanting priest and a ringing bell.

I retired to a small cafeteria with a view of a rock garden, before wandering off for a little bit of exploration. In the distance I could hear the murmur of other guests who had rented out a special waiting room with tatami mats and *zabuton* pillows. They were cloistered together, perhaps eating a specially designed funeral *bentō*, so designated because it would contain nary a speck of meat—only fish, rice, and vegetables. In another wing, someone was cremating a pet dog. At the extreme end of the facility, a funeral service was taking place in a room temporarily dressed up to look like a Buddhist temple of the Sōtō sect. This reminded me of the Japanese weddings I had attended, which were often held in large hotels with generic rooms that could be decorated to look like a Shintō shrine on one day or a Catholic chapel the next.

The only time I actually interacted with anyone other than the attendant was when I met a woman in a black kimono purchasing a can of hot coffee from a vending machine. I commented on this when the glove and cap–clad attendant came to get me from the waiting room. He beamed and proudly declared that the crematorium had been carefully designed to function as a series of systems. There were multiple pathways, he said brightly, which enabled him to direct all parties through the same ritualized experience while avoiding undesirable traffic jams. Then he checked his watch. He had fifteen minutes to give me a tour.

In the second room—a sort of intermediary chamber—was a shrine laden with numerous bouquets of yellow and white chrysanthemums and a portrait of the man who had just been sent to the crematorium. He was perhaps in his sixties, smiling and healthy—a father, husband, and grandfather to everyone who brushed past me in the main hall. He loved cigarettes, baseball, and golf books, all of which had been placed on the altar. It occurred to me that I had crashed a funeral, and I started to feel guilty that my egotistical curiosity had led me to invade what is surely the most intimate and private of spaces.

In a third chamber, the steel jaws of twelve small ovens were clamped shut. Because the crematorium regularly processed more than one body at a time, heat-resistant digital screens above each oven bore the name of the temporary occupant so there would be no confusion. The casket was slid inside under the somber gaze of the mourners, and the head of the family was charged with locking the door and pocketing the key, the only one, he was told, that could open this particular oven. Before the mourners left the stark room, they heard the breath of gas and the snarl of fire as the body, casket, and flowers became consumed. Later, my mother told me that she wished she hadn't heard this sound, that she could have left her mother behind, before the flames during the cremation had ignited.

There was only one thing that modern engineering could not dispense with, and that was the smell. After visiting the crematorium, I wouldn't eat meat for several weeks.

When the staff had determined that the cremation had finished, the attendant went to get the head of the family. After my grandmother's cremation, my grandfather, as the lead representative of our family, was led away from the waiting room to open up the oven with his special key. When my mother and uncle joined him a few minutes later, they found him standing in yet another room, warming his hands over my grandmother's bones, which lay stretched out on a steel table. This, the attendant told me, was not so unusual; there were some who even ate some of the bones of the deceased, or requested a cup of water to make a kind of tea.

My grandfather and my uncle together started the intimate process of picking out bones, each using a pair of unusually long chopsticks. They began with the feet first so my grandmother would not be upside down in her rectangular urn, which was about as large as an ice-cream tub. This is the only time that two people in Japan will hold anything together via chopsticks, hence the reason why Japanese people jump if they both inadvertently reach down to pick up the same morsel of food from a plate.

An attendant in the background identified each bone. "Here is the second joint of the big toe." "Here is a fragment of the femur."

At the top of the skeleton were pieces of my grandmother's skull, jaw, and the all-important hyoid bone from the Adam's apple, which would rest in a separate urn.

In the end, so many of my grandmother's bones survived the cremation that we were given a third urn.

"She must have been someone young," the bone-identifier remarked. "There's so much left over."

"She was ninety-seven," my mother replied.

The bone expert beamed. "Then you've inherited strong bones."

My grandfather, too, was delighted that we had three urns. For him this was an unexpected abundance of riches. "*Three*," he repeatedly bragged to everyone. "We had to have *three* urns." It was the first thing he said that gave me some insight into his feelings for my grandmother.

THE DAY OF my grandmother's funeral, Takahagi wanted to show me the robes he had selected to wear. Most young priests wear relatively bright colors. Daisuke had already donned the standard bright-yellow and cobalt-blue robes that befit a priest under the age of thirty. But the ever-fashionable Takahagi was no ordinary young man. This morning he had chosen a sable-colored robe with a dark-gray overgarment. The sable silk had an iridescent quality to it, sometimes appearing silver, sometimes copper.

"Nice, isn't it?" he held the robes up in the sunlight.

"Did you special order that?" I asked.

"There's a guy in Tōkyō who makes them for me."

After Takahagi got dressed, he showed me all of the things he could do with the overgarment. If you have seen any samurai movies, you know there is always a scene before battle where a kimono-wearing warrior must tie up his sleeves with a rope in order to effectively wield a sword. Takahagi had mastered all of the moves with his priestly robes, which, like a kimono, have billowing and potentially troublesome sleeves. He performed his fashion origami for me, putting the overgarment over his head and tying it behind his back so his arms were free to move unencumbered. Then he unwound the garment and slipped his arm out of a hidden hole, and his arms were free again.

"I'm nervous," he finally confided. "I've never done a funeral for family members before."

"Did Takahagi tell you about the Sony funeral?" Daisuke called out, as he played a round of golf on the PlayStation's video-game rendition of Pebble Beach.

"No," I said.

Takahagi grinned. "It was when I was studying to be a priest in Tōkyō. My teacher got a call that someone had died, and he asked me to go with him to chant sutras. It turned out that we went to the [Sony chairman] Morita house."

"What was it like?" I asked.

Daisuke shook his head in disgust. "He didn't even look around."

"I remember that the windows were very big," Takahagi offered. "But then when we went into the main room, I saw the family members, and so many of them were crying. I had to act like a priest."

In the main temple, my grandfather was carefully placing the three urns of bones in front of the Buddha on the large altar. The floor of the temple was covered with tatami, and once upon a time, we would all have been expected to sit on the floor with our feet neatly tucked beneath our thighs. Because this was a tricky position for many elderly people to assume for long stretches of time, Takahagi and his father had prepared several rows of folding stools.

During the funeral, Takahagi, in his elegant robes, chanted and played a small gong, while his father ecstatically shouted to my grandmother's soul that she was dead and must leave us. I loved the chanting. The priests—Takahagi, his brother Daisuke, and their father Sempō—all listened carefully to each other, making sure to space out each breath so there was never a break in the sound. My mother sang an operatic aria. I recited an original poem. Then it was my grandfather's turn. He pulled a slip of yellow paper out of his pocket and began to address my grandmother's bones.

He thanked her for taking away his heart murmur when she died. He was feeling much better now. He was sorry that he had to leave her body alone in the house when he went out to dinner, but it really wasn't necessary for her ghost to have locked the doors and windows, making it difficult for him to reenter. He knew that she would like to stay and continue to watch over her children, but it was time for her to leave, and anyway, everyone had attended a prestigious university. Then he began to cry. The air grew thick, as though the molecules themselves were stunned by emotion.

The weeping was contagious, and soon I was afloat in grief. My grandfather—that hard, hard man—loved my grandmother deeply. It occurred to me now that some of the frustration he demonstrated all his life must have come from the suspicion, if not the actual knowledge, of the photograph of the other man in her purse.

Late in the afternoon, after the funeral and the meal with the troublesome seating arrangement had ended, and the guests had gone home, the family sat wilted around a table in the kitchen. I noticed that my grandfather was missing. Takahagi, who had changed back into his casual-priest clothing, and I set out to look for him.

"I think I know where he is," Takahagi murmured.

We found my grandfather alone, perched on a rock by the family burial plot, which was etched high up on top of a hill. It was a gorgeous evening. We were ringed by bamboo and pine trees, and above this the sky was turning pink.

"You know you are really poor," my grandfather said, "when you have absolutely no one at home waiting for you."

"I think," I said, "that I hear a *hototogisu* singing." The *hototogisu* is known as the lesser cuckoo in the West. It was a particular favorite of my grandfather's.

My grandfather tilted his head. "Did you know that the *hototogisu* migrates here from Taiwan?"

Lately my grandfather had been telling my mother that his happiest years were in Taiwan. He went to a university there and stayed on for a time teaching English, before marriage and the war brought him back to Japan. He even said to me that my love of Japan was something like his love of Taiwan, which I took to mean that he had finally reconciled my half-breed existence in his very traditional family.

"When I die," he said, "I am going to ride a *hototogisu* back and forth from Japan to Taiwan. When I'm dead, I don't want to ever have to ride an airplane again."

"You won't have to," Takahagi smiled gently.

"Remember that," my grandfather instructed, "when you come here and you hear a *hototogisu* singing. That'll mean I've come back to see you."

That night, as my mother and I lay in our futons, drained from the day, I whispered to her that it would be cruel *not* to let my grandfather have his wife's bones.

"That," she said, "is what I've been trying to tell your uncles all along."

IT WAS MY grandmother's unexpectedly strong bones and her third urn that solved our burial woes.

The largest urn would stay at the temple, where it would sit under Sempō's watchful eye until my grandfather was ready to actually bury it in the temple cemetery.

A second would go home with one of my uncles, who promised

to worship the bones every day in his own family shrine. But I knew that he would quietly take the urn down south to Kyūshū and bury it with the other lords and ladies long since gone.

My grandfather initially wanted my mother to take the Adam's apple back to America, but, thinking quickly, she told him that it was illegal to import human remains. She suggested that he take the Adam's apple back to his house, and he happily packed it in his small travel bag, which he carried on his lap on our trip all the way back to Nagoya.

In the days that followed, he fussed over the small box. He brought it flowers from the garden and sweet bean cakes and fruit from the grocery store. When I lit incense in the morning, I found that the little box, bound up in red and gold silk, had been moved from its position the previous day, as if a mischievous spirit was still struggling to find its place in a new world.

"When he dies," my mother whispered to me late at night, "I'm going to cremate him with that Adam's apple."

Now it was 2012. Both of my grandparents were gone, and my mother and I had finally come to bury their bones. About a month ago, one of my uncles returned to the temple with the other half of my grandmother's bones. He had dropped the container off with Sempō and, after a few pleasantries, headed back down to Tōkyō. He had not been in touch since.

"I thought he was going to take the bones to Kyūshū," I said.

"I don't know anything about that," Sempō said.

"Nagasaki is very far," my mother observed. "It's not that easy for him to get to."

"This just proves my point! This isn't how you treat bones," Sempō huffed. "Furthermore, I left messages for both your brothers

that we would be burying their father today, and yet no one came. I
don't understand this."

There was little that my mother could say to me. She hadn't
been in touch with her brothers for many months. One had stopped
speaking to her completely. But my mother didn't say this. She just
sat stoically and apologized.

Sempō called out for his wife Ryōko to bring him some newspaper. When she returned, he complained that the sheets she had
brought included photographs of meat cuts on sale, making the
sheets inappropriate to use; he was going to pour out all the bones
on to the newspaper and needed something less gory.

"Sempō," I said. "I'm worried about Tomobiki . . ."

"Hmm?" he looked up. "I've been doing this for years, Marie. I
know what time it is."

At last we had fresh sheets of newspaper, this time with harmless
black-and-white printing that conveyed nothing more than world
events. Sempō opened up one bag and dumped the bones on the
newspaper. There it was: all that remained of my grandfather. There
were lots and lots of small pieces of bone that looked like chalk, and
a few that were recognizably bone-shaped. Mixed in with all this
was fine powdered gold.

At my grandfather's cremation, my mother had insisted on
placing the little box containing my grandmother's hyoid bone in
the casket along with an expensive, 18-karat gold-ink painting of
Kokuzosama, the Buddhist deity my grandfather considered to be
his personal protector. My mother's older brother had argued that
the painting was valuable and could be sold for cash. My mother
persisted. Looking at the bones now, in their luminous golden glory,
I had the feeling that I was seeing my grandfather's true interior;
he was a sparkling, rich, and beautiful creature, despite the temper
tantrums to which he had subjected us when he was alive.

Sempō emptied out my grandmother's bag of bones too, before finally putting everything all together in one bag, and then wrapping this up with the newspaper. At last, he said, we were ready for the ceremony. But not quite!

"Do you see the statues?" he asked me, nodding at the ten figures placed along the eaves. They were brand new, commissioned from an artist in Taiwan. "You'll never see another temple like this," he said. "Certainly not a Zen temple."

By now I knew that most Sōtō Zen temples paid tribute to the historical Buddha—Siddharta Gautama—and that it was he who dominated most altars. Sempō's temple had other figures too. There was Dainichi Nyorai, the Cosmic Buddha that the Shingon worshippers love so much. There was Amida Nyorai, the Pure Land Buddha. Jizō was up there, along with several other bodhisattvas I didn't recognize. There was my beloved, ferocious Fudō scowling out at me. There was Senju, bodhisattva of a thousand arms, doing his metaphysical yoga and representing electrons in motion. There was Monjū bodhisattva, who oversees wisdom and to whom people pray for good grades and success in school. In the past, one of Sempō's *danka* might have had to travel to a temple specially dedicated to Monjū, but not anymore; now there was a statue here.

"But Fudō isn't Zen," I heard myself say.

"Nope!" Sempō said cheerfully. "And who cares? I want anyone who comes to my temple to find what they are looking for. Anyone! Maybe they are wandering around in the middle of the night, and they need to see the face of Amida. I don't want them to come here and be disappointed.

"Over the years, as new people have moved to Iwaki, they would come to this temple and ask me if I had a statue of their favorite deity. And most of the time, Marie, I didn't. So I decided, when I rebuilt this temple, that I would include all the statues of the Buddhas and bodhisattvas that people most wanted to see."

All this talking had taken up more time. "Shouldn't we . . ."

"One more thing," Sempō said. "There are two kinds of burials. There is the personal kind, in which you have to come every year for Ohigan and Obon and all the memorials. Then there is the kind where I included your grandfather's name in a list of people I read sutras to every day, and for each memorial. That way you don't have to come from America for every special date."

I started to protest that I wanted to come for my grandfather's memorial services, but Sempō cut me off. "You live very far away," he observed. "It will be harder and harder for you to come. I don't want you to worry."

At last he stood up and put on his special priest's hat. Then he began to light the candles. My cousin Daisuke stepped out from a side room where he had apparently been waiting, and sat down at the drum. The ceremony was about to start.

I was still mulling over Sempō's words. I am often slow to apprehend what people are telling me in Japanese. Sometimes it can take me months to interpret what actually happened in an exchange. Because of this, I'm constantly concerned that I have been rude.

It was only months later that I understood what he had been trying to communicate about the "two types of funerals." After the March 11 disaster, Sempō received call after call from his parishioners, many of whom had evacuated. Some were not even sure they were going to return to Iwaki. Over and over again, they asked him the same thing: "Please take care of my ancestors." And always he promised them that he would.

If you believe—even just the tiniest bit—that your ancestors have the most power to protect you from hungry ghosts, from the demons of winter, from the great catfish Ōnamazu, then you will want to do your best to protect them back. This was Sempō's most important job; he had to look after the ancestors so they could look out for the living.

And he would do this no matter what happened. Sempō, as I wrote earlier, was adopted by my Great-Aunt Shizuko at the age of twenty-seven. To become a priest, he gave up his career in the law and agreed to cut off ties with his former life—including his mother. Such an act may sound harsh to modern ears, but tradition demands this kind of complete commitment. For years I couldn't understand why or how he could have done this. But one afternoon, when I was visiting, he told me quite casually that his biological father was Jitsuo, my grandfather's brother, who had opposed corporal punishment at school in Taiwan. Sempō hadn't really been "adopted"; he had come to the temple to claim his birthright.

Much later, I asked him how he could have spent so many years away from his mother, and why he had become a priest. He thought about this for a minute, and then gave me this answer: "I thought that if I worked hard, I could make Empukuji a success. And that I could ensure it would survive for another hundred years or so. I thought I could do a good job for everyone."

WE CARRIED THE bones up the hill to the cemetery, climbing almost to the very top to the family plot. There are actually two plots—on the right side of the path are the graves of past priests, reaching back five hundred years, their status made clear by the exclamation-shaped tombstones that mark their graves. In most cases, we have no idea what their names are, but we try to pay our respects when we can since they are the many links in a long chain that has kept the temple and these grounds intact for so long.

To the left are the burial spots of the people I do know—my great-aunt, my great-uncles, and very soon my grandparents. Some day Sempō will be buried there too, and if he ever figures out which of his sons will inherit the temple, that son will be here also, along with his children and their children. At one point my mother whispered that she planned to make arrangements for her ashes to be buried at the site, so I would have a reason to come to the temple every year. "That way," she said, "they cannot stop you from visiting." This observation sounded clever on her part, but also ominous. Would someone stop me from visiting?

Sempō's moodiness had disappeared, and he was now in his element. He and Daisuke moved aside the metal vases on top of the cemetery plot and then dislodged the heavy marble slab covering the interior of the tomb. Inside was red earth. I didn't notice until that moment that there were also bags of red dirt sitting nearby. Sempō explained that he used a special kind of dirt for his tombs. He placed the bones inside and sprinkled some dirt on top. And then, he put in two white flowers.

"I always use flowers," he said to me. "When you go to sleep tonight, and you remember the funeral, you are going to see two white flowers."

"Does everyone do this?" I asked.

"No," he said cheerfully. "My own idea. The last thing I want anyone to remember is the sight of bones. Or the bags. I want you to see white flowers." He didn't close the tomb then. He left it open, explaining that he would take time later to make sure that the tomb was put back together properly. It wasn't something that I needed to see.

We lit candles and incense, and then Daisuke and Sempō chanted sutras again, and my mother and I bowed our heads.

When I remember that day, it is as Sempō said. I can still see the golden ashes belonging to my grandfather. But the impression that remains in my mind is that of a white flower against red earth.

MY MOTHER AND I spent the night at Sekinoyu, the spa that faces the ocean and whose fate had so worried me after the tsunami.

At breakfast the following morning, we were greeted by Rumi, a woman who'd taken care of us many times over the years. I thought she looked a little bit drawn and even thinner than usual, but I didn't want to comment on her health. I simply said, "Hello. It's nice to see you again."

"Welcome back," she bowed.

At one point, I went over to the self-serve station to get myself a cup of coffee. Rumi came over to me.

"Excuse me, but are you by any chance related to Mita Sempō?" I said that I was.

At this, she became excited, and her eyes brightened. "I thought so," she said. "*En desu ne.*" It's fate, isn't it? "Sempō is a very fine person," she said to me earnestly. She explained that her son and his young wife had been living with her since their marriage. The wife had become pregnant. Then came the March 11 catastrophe and the subsequent problem with the nuclear power plant.

Rumi's daughter-in-law began to fret that she could not properly raise her son in Iwaki. How could any of them know if the water, the milk, or the air was safe? What if something happened to the baby? In despair, the young woman hanged herself not long after the baby was born. Suddenly, Rumi found herself with a small child and a grown son to take care of.

An immediate complication was that the young woman was not from Iwaki and did not have a funeral plot, or a temple to which she belonged. Rumi confided her troubles to the owner of the spa, who turned to Sempō for help. Now, said Rumi, her daughter-in-law's remains were at Empukuji. Rumi and her son could not afford a funeral plot, but Sempō made everything easy and cheap and placed the bones in a small cubbyhole behind the shrine. They had an altar in the house too, she explained. And every day, they took the baby to the shrine and explained that this was where his mother was now and where he could visit her. And on the special memorial days, they had a place to go—to Empukuji. "I'm grateful to your cousin," she said to me. And then she repeated, "What a fine man."

I have seen Rumi several times since then, and we always greet each other now with small gifts. She brings things for me to give to my son, and I bring her chocolate from New York, or a small present for her grandchild. One time I went to Japan with my husband and my son, and in the morning Rumi was waiting to serve our breakfast.

"I helped prepare your room the night before," she said happily. "And I thought—I wonder if they are coming! And here you are!"

FIFTEEN

Autumn Colors

By the start of September in Japan, shopping alleys in cities hang plastic colored leaves to add a bit of seasonal décor. Mixed in with these branches you'll see other symbols of Japanese fall: chestnuts, chrysanthemums, rice cakes, and the moon.

The latter two require some explanation. The Japanese inherited from the Chinese the practice of viewing the autumn moon. Because of the earth's position relative to the sun and the moon during this time of the year, the full moon is said to glow with exceptional intensity. A beloved folktale involves a rabbit who lives on the moon, and who pounds rice cakes, which can bestow immortality if eaten. During September, it's not uncommon to see decorations of rabbits along with the moon and rice cakes. Even McDonald's gets into the action with a special "moon-viewing hamburger."

One September I went to visit my friend Isao, who was then still living in his hometown, Kyōtō. He had researched seasonal activities for us and discovered that Kōdaiji temple held a special moon-viewing event for a limited period of time during these early fall days.

We arrived at dusk and waited in a Zen garden full of angular rocks and roundly sculpted shrubbery sitting on a bed of white gravel. The sun set, and we were invited into the temple. After we took off our shoes, we wended our way through a series of wooden hallways and suddenly found ourselves in a moon-viewing room.

The rectangular room was perhaps fifteen tatami mats in all, comfortable enough for a group of twenty, and smelled of wood and straw. The light was a heavy amber. The outside wall, made up of sliding doors, had been completely removed to afford us a view of the interior garden. The air outside was warm, and the autumn insects sang in an orchestrated chorus.

The old priest of the temple had been waiting for us, and as two kimono-clad women slowly and silently passed around a tray of rice cakes, the priest told us how during the Momoyama period—the medieval period during which this temple was built—aristocrats had sat here, as we did now, luxuriating in the last remainders of summer and contemplating the sadness and fullness of the moon.

He held three lacquer objects, each of which dated from the sixteenth century, and passed them around to all of us. They would have been used by the widow of Hideyoshi, the great general and unifier of Japan who had also been an aesthete. We were all sitting on low chairs, which formed an L shape along the perimeter of the room. One by one we reverentially passed around a spoon, a tea caddy, and a bowl. I have always loved Japanese lacquer. One of my early connections to my father's love of art history was medieval lacquer, with its sprinkling of gold and its many layers of lacquer painted on wood, giving the effect that the object is in fact a mirror of an infinite sea.

The priest held up a simple painting in black ink on paper. It was a circle. An "O." "I'm very fond of this painting," he said. "On a day like today, when we are gathered to look at the moon, I think to myself that this painting is the moon. But then, on other days, I think it is a symbol of emptiness, of nothingness, which you know is at the heart of Zen." Unfortunately, he continued, it was cloudy tonight, making it difficult for us to see the moon. As a group, we leaned our bodies toward the open wall, craning our necks, and the floor beneath us creaked. There were only clouds, and we all swayed back into our seats and the floor sighed.

One of the kimono-clad women passed out bean cakes. She stood before each of us and bowed, and in turn we bowed back. Then we each used a long pair of chopsticks to select one cake for ourselves. The skin of each sweet was made of rice, pounded until it had become glutinous and translucent so the gold bean paste in the middle glowed through; it was a miniature moon. I ate my cake slowly, then accepted a round bowl of frothy green *matcha* tea. The sugar and the caffeine together gave me a jolt, and I felt awake and refreshed.

Later, we went for a walk through the grounds of the temple, crossing the old Dragon Bridge, so called because its back was arched and its roof shingled, and in the near dark it looked like the scaly back of a dragon. We followed a stone path up to Spirit Hall, where Hideyoshi's wife is entombed. The hexagonal building is famous for its liberal use of gold dust on black lacquer depicting flowers and musical instruments. There was a breeze up there, and the air was much cooler. It felt as if we were floating on a gleaming, golden island of light above a sea of darkness.

We went through the dark again, down the other side of the hill, then plunged into a thicket of fat old bamboo, lit up so the grove glowed, as though it contained the source of some otherworldly, emerald power. The wind was singing in the tops of the bamboo branches, and Isao and I stopped and stared at the leaves rustling overhead. The clouds parted, and then the moon popped into view, looking down on us like an eye. The effect was like flying, as though for a time I could feel that we were standing on a planet that was hastily rotating through the heavens.

"Look!" someone shouted. "Finally! The moon!"

"The moon! The moon!" voices shouted all around me.

I thought about the story of Kaguyahime, the Moon Princess, one of Japan's most beloved folktales. In this story, an old and poor bamboo cutter came upon a glowing stalk of bamboo. He cut it open and found a baby girl inside. Because he and his wife were childless, he took the baby home, and they rejoiced in their good fortune at becoming parents at such an advanced age. Thereafter, whenever the old man cut down a stalk of bamboo, he found a nugget of gold inside, and soon he and his family became wealthy.

Years passed, and the little baby became a beautiful and accomplished young woman. Her fame spread, and before long she had a bevy of important suitors who asked for her hand in marriage. She gave each man a task to perform to win the right to marry her, but each man failed. One died while climbing a ladder to try to reach a cowrie shell born from a pair of swallows. One man sailed out to recover a jewel from a dragon's neck, but he gave up after encountering severe storms. The Moon Princess had also sent three other men to retrieve the following: the Buddha's own begging bowl, a jeweled branch from the floating island of Horai, and a robe made from the fur of the legendary Fire Rat. Each man tried to present the princess with fakes, though, and was harshly rebuffed.

Years passed, and the old bamboo cutter and his wife began to age and to weaken. Their beautiful daughter continued to care for them, but the old couple became alarmed by a change in her behavior. When the Moon Princess looked out the window at the full moon, she sobbed uncontrollably and could not be consoled. Nor did she explain her sadness. Finally, at the end of summer, she told her adoptive parents the truth of her origins. She was descended from the Moon People and had come down to the earth only to care for this elderly couple. During the next full moon, she would be called back to her people.

The bamboo cutter went to great lengths to keep his daughter from leaving. He enlisted the help of the emperor and his army; by now the emperor was in love with the Moon Princess too. But it was to no avail, for during the next full moon, a retinue of celestial beings came down from the sky and placed a cloak of feathers around the Moon Princess's neck. Instantly, she forgot her sorrow and ascended up to the moon. Soon after, the old bamboo cutter and his wife died. The emperor wrote a note to tell the princess of his own sadness, and burned it from the top of Mount Fuji, hoping that the smoke might reach the moon and carry his message of grief. For many years, Mount Fuji continued to burble and emit fumes, and it was said that this smoke was a remainder of the broken-hearted emperor's futile efforts to reach his lost princess.

IT WAS OCTOBER of 2013, and my mother, my son, and I were driving out to a temple called Kaizōji at the invitation of Kaneta, the priest who runs Café du Monk. I knew very little about the ceremony that was going to take place at this temple, except that it involved his son, who had been at Eiheiji for two years, and that it would commemorate the deaths of fifty people who died in the tsunami.

The temple belonged to Kaneta's second cousin, who was stepping into the role of *jūshoku*, or the new head priest; his father, wheelchair-bound, was retiring. Next year, my own family members would be enacting the same ceremony when Sempō, now settled on a successor, handed over Empukuji to Daisuke. Because such ceremonies were conducted only once a generation, they were like a coronation in which a king hands his kingdom to a young prince.

The drive out to Kaizōji was spectacular. The rice paddies were ready for harvest: they were not gold, but a greenish yellow, a powerful neon color that stood out in strong contrast to the surrounding environment, whose greenery was fading day by day. The landscape was dotted with *higanbana*, an eerie red lily that blooms around the autumn equinox, or Ohigan.

My friend Isao once told me a story about collecting a bouquet of *higanbana* to take home to his grandmother. She was upset at the gift, explaining that because the *higanbana* bloomed during Ohigan, the flowers were associated with the earth opening up to let the dead pass through. The flowers, while beautiful, were unfit for decoration. He never again collected a single red lily.

When the low sun bore down on the vegetation, though, the scarlet blossoms and the ripe, bright rice fields made the landscape glow, as though everything was covered in stained glass. Along our way, farmers harvested the rice with small industrial combines. After the rice is cut, in some parts of Tōhoku, the farmers will then hang the rice in a row on a wooden fence. In other places, they stack the rice into sheafs that look much like the drying bales of wheat in Van Gogh's paintings. In yet other parts of Tōhoku, farmers make spiral stacks.

When we stepped out of the car onto the parking lot at Kaizōji, I smelled an intensely sweet odor. It was so strong, I looked around for the source of an artificial deodorant.

"It's just *kinnmokusei*." My mother pointed to a tree covered with little orange blossoms. "This is the smell of autumn."

On the edge of a rice paddy, a chestnut tree dropped a few nuts on the ground, and my son ran to pick them up.

AT 8:00 A.M. a group of children walked up to the temple's main gate. They were dressed in white, purple, and red silk outfits, and wore golden headdresses. They are called Chigosan in Japanese, and are the children who take part in a Buddhist or Shintō ceremony. Children in Japan are believed to occupy a state in between adult life and death, and they were once considered able to communicate with the gods. Their participation now is a nod to a very old tradition in Japan, but it is still seen as bringing good luck to any important festival.

While I admired the children and took a few photos, someone called out, "Hey! I know you!"

It was the mother of the little boy my son had played with at the Minamisanriku temporary shelter a few months earlier. We exchanged pleasantries, and I asked about Hina's family. "Everyone is doing much better," she said. Then we entered the temple for the formal ceremony.

The rest of the morning unfolded over several hours and involved much chanting and drum pounding and at least two hundred people. Kaneta's oldest son, Taikō, participated in one part of the morning, the *hossenshiki*, which in English is often translated to "combat dharma ceremony." It is a ritual that all Zen Buddhist priests must undergo.

The "combat" isn't physical, though the person undergoing the ceremony holds a bow. The true conflict comes in the form of questions and answers, which are pre-scripted, but nevertheless give the young priest a chance to show off his command of the Zen canon. The questions and answers are shouted, and to the untrained ear, you might think you were listening to soldiers at a military boot camp and the equivalent of "Sir! Yes, Sir!"

The questions cover the basic territory of Zen: What is zazen? Who was Dōgen? How might one become enlightened? Most dharma combat ceremonies use a script, and the initial "combat" between Taikō and the other young priests who had volunteered to take part in the ritual involved questions usually used in such situations. But then a curious thing happened.

A key role in the *hossenshiki* is played by a young child who will

one day be a priest. That day, a ten-year-old boy on the premises
shouted questions to Taikō. Among them was this: "How do you
propose to help the victims of the tsunami?"

Taikō, an extremely handsome young man who was seated in his
black robes, with his posture perfect and his hands sturdily holding
a bow, replied, "I will do everything I can to help them with their
tears! I will listen, and I will help them until they are no longer
crying!"

"And what will you tell the people who lost someone in the tsunami about their loved ones? Where do the dead go?"

Taikō broke from his posture and touched his chest. "The dead
remain in our hearts. That is the only place we will find them and
the only place to look."

Around me, the women dressed in black who had helped to
grease the gears of the ceremony—giving tea and ripe persimmons
to priests—were crying. I was crying too. I was deeply moved to see
a young person like this, so committed, and so intent on taking care
of all of us—especially the older people—who had been touched
by grief. Taikō's attitude had been honed by his father, and by his
grandfather, whom I also met that day. Kaneta's father was in his
eighties, but he spoke to me about his desire to help the world to
understand Buddhism, and how he gladly brought foreigners and
scholars into his home to share with them whatever he could.

Taikō's conviction was sincere, and all his own. His forceful declaration was a moving reminder of my own age and place in the
succession of generations.

I SPENT SOME time with Kaneta and his family after the dharma
combat ritual. Their temple, Tsūdaiji, or "Temple of the Great Way,"
is located in Kurihara. Before the tsunami, Kurihara had the unfor-

tunate distinction of having the highest suicide rate in all of Japan, and Kaneta devoted his energy to suicide prevention. After the earthquake, he turned his attention to the victims of the tsunami.

When I met Kaneta's wife, I at last understood how he was able to devote so much time outside of his own temple, for she was beautiful, extremely smart, and very kind. She was dressed in a kimono the day that I met her and had the slim, perfect grace that I envy in women who embody the very perfection of the Japanese female ideal.

Later when I visited their home, she showed me how she had hung up Taikō's black-and-white robe from a rafter separating the living quarters from the living room. As it swayed in the breeze, the robe seemed slightly alive. "I'm trying to pretend he is still here," she said to me wistfully.

She worried about her oldest son. He had lost a lot of weight at Eiheiji, and she said she will be relieved when he comes home in six months and starts graduate school at the University of Tōhoku. Because he was in his second year at Eiheiji, he was granted special privileges: He had his own room. He had also been allowed to keep a cell phone, provided, in the Japanese way of making exceptions, no one saw it. He and his father had worked together to write out the questions and answers used during the dharma combat cere-mony. It had been their joint idea for Taikō to address the issue of the tsunami head-on, and to declare in front of all the *danka* there that he intended to make it part of his work to continue reliev-ing their suffering. The final script they had come up with together had been sent out to the young boy who participated in the dharma combat ceremony, and to the other young priests.

One night, exhausted from a late-night cram session, Taikō fell asleep with the phone in his hand. He was discovered by his *rōshi*, his master, and duly punished. The phone was removed. From here on out, Taikō would have to communicate with his parents only by letter.

Over noodles, we—my mother, Kaneta, his wife, and I—talked about the changes Kaneta had seen in the past two years. He told us about Okawa, a small community in Ishinomaki that had suffered the single highest loss of children's lives due to the tsunami. At the Okawa school, a disagreement between teachers over what to do with the children who had not yet been picked up by their parents had led to a delay in evacuating, which meant that the students and all but one teacher were not on higher ground when the first wave hit.

In the beginning, Kaneta had gone around to visit the parents and the families and listened to their grievances. Two years ago, they had all been shocked and paralyzed by grief. But, said Kaneta, things changed this year when a group of parents traveled all the way to Eiheiji to stay overnight. Then, as I had also done, they woke up early in the morning to watch the *hōyō*, the early-morning ceremony.

"Taikō said it was extraordinary," Kaneta grinned. "He said everyone was shaken by the power of that *hōyō*, when they read out the names of all seventy of these lost children. But it goes to show," he nodded, "how far we have come that the parents felt well enough to come to Eiheiji, instead of waiting for us to go to them."

He took me on a tour of his temple, and my son followed along, banging all the drums and ringing all the bells. As I had expected, Kaneta's temple was a neat, sharp, confident structure with airy rooms and a tidy, immaculate garden. Everything about the place suggested that it was good at taking care of people's needs.

I asked Kaneta about Hina's family.

"Everyone is much better," Kaneta said. "The grandmother has stopped crying every day, and she doesn't watch the videos all the time." It helped that Hina's little brother was now a sturdy fellow who was walking and saying a few words.

Lately Hina's grandmother started to talk about how late at

night, the little girl had asked her grandmother to take her out to look at the stars. In the weeks leading up to her death, she had asked to be taken out every night. She rode on her grandmother's back and craned her head up to look at the night sky.

"Do you know the story of the Moon Princess?" Kaneta asked me.

Hina's grandmother thought that perhaps her granddaughter had been like the Moon Princess, that she had known somehow that she was nearly out of time, and that she had wanted to look up at the night sky to which she would soon return. The Japanese liked such stories, Kaneta said. It helped to be able to find just the right ending to such a sad tale.

JAPANESE STORIES OFTEN end with a beautiful image. The Japanese psychoanalyst Kawai Hayao has proposed that in many Japanese fairy tales, the conflict in a story is resolved by what he calls "the aesthetic solution." In his book *Dreams, Myths and Fairy Tales in Japan*, which has been translated into English, Kawai writes, "In the West, the hero's virtue is rewarded by a happy ending. But in Japan, beautiful endings are much preferred to happy endings." Beauty is the ultimate democracy, because a beautiful thing, particularly if it exists in nature, belongs to everyone.

Kawai argues that in Japan, the highest form of beauty is imperfect. In *Dreams, Myths and Fairy Tales in Japan*, Kawai further elaborates:

There is a famous story about a Zen master who shows what beauty is for him. A young monk is sweeping a garden. He tries to do his best at the job. He cleans the garden perfectly so that no dust is left in it. Contrary to his expectation the old master is not happy about his work. The young monk thinks for a while and shakes a tree so that several dead leaves fall down here and there in the garden. The master smiles when he sees this.

Anyone with even a passing knowledge of the terms *wabi* and *sabi* will recognize the monk and the master's attitudes. The simplest definition of *wabi sabi* is that it is a kind of beauty whose highest form is expressed through imperfection. The venerable art historian Miyeko Murase instructed her students to consider that a full moon glowing brightly in the sky is undeniably beautiful. But how much more beautiful is the moon when it is partially obscured by a bit of cloud? A geometrically symmetrical tea bowl is a lovely thing to drink from, but how cold and precise it looks beside an earthen tea bowl whose surface is slightly marred.

The Japanese love the beauty of cherry blossoms in the spring. However, say the aesthetes, how much more beautiful are the cherry trees when they are just past their peak, and petals begin to drip-drop onto the ground.

Kawai writes in his book, "The Japanese fairy tales tell us that the world is beautiful and that beauty is completed only if we accept the existence of death." Beauty heals us. But we shouldn't make the mistake of thinking that perfected beauty is any kind of true antidote to suffering, for everything is always changing, never holding fast to its shape. Everything must one day die, and we are all always only just passing through. So it is that we might heal a bit by experiencing the passing beauty of a dance gesture, a fading ghost, or a flower.

I THOUGHT A lot about Kawai's theory of the "aesthetic solution" when I heard the following modern-day equivalent of a ghost story. Sutō Ayane is a young woman in her twenties whose life has been completely transformed by the earthquake and tsunami of March 11, 2011. Sutō grew up in Kesennuma, the seaside town in which a large blue boat washed up onto city streets, and where the port caught fire while the water raged.

Before the tsunami, Sutō was a budding writer who worked in Sendai as a caretaker for the elderly. She lived with her fiancé, who is also from Kesennuma. Sutō's father worked in the Kesennuma harbor as a radio technician on a fishing boat. The Sutō family home is up in the hills, far away from the shore, and after the earthquake, Sutō was able to very quickly get through to her mother, who assured her that all was fine at home, and that her father would most likely be back soon.

By evening, Sutō's father had still not made it home, nor did he return the next day. Across Tōhoku, the earthquake had disrupted power lines and the water supply; Sutō and her fiancé stayed in their apartment for several days, in the dark, unable to bathe. Finally, a family friend offered to pick up Sutō and take her out of Sendai to the friend's home farther inland, which did have electricity and running water. Nearby there was even a large *sento*, or public bath, offering discounted admission. Sutō took the offer of hospitality.

The public bath was traditional: one left one's shoes in a locker by the entrance, then went into the women's changing room to disrobe and to bathe. It was the first bath Sutō had had for a week. When she was done, she dressed and then went back out to the entrance of the spa to exchange her slippers for the shoes she had put in the locker. It was still winter, and Sutō had been wearing a pair of stylish black booties. As she slipped her foot into the shoe, she felt something strange: something was inside the shoe. She pulled out her foot and then inspected the boot. Inside was a round, white flower.

Sutō took the flower and held it in her hand. It was in perfect condition and had not been squashed, which ruled out the possibility that she had spent the day walking around with a flower in her shoe and hadn't noticed. The locker door had been shut tight with a key—only Sutō had had the key. How, then, did a flower get into her shoe? It was a puzzle, and though certainly strange, it was not at all the most pressing matter on her mind. After showing the flower to her friend, Sutō eventually threw it away in a garbage bin and went on her way.

About a week later, Sutō received the call she had been dreading. Her father's body had been found. No one knew why he had been swallowed by the tsunami; all of his coworkers had made it to dry land. Perhaps, someone postulated, he had tried to help someone stranded in their home? Whatever the reason, Sutō returned to Kesennuma for her father's funeral.

The body was returned to the family in a casket. Sutō and her mother and sister spent a fitful night of sleep, with both Sutō's mother and sister claiming to have received visitations from their father. Hearing this, Sutō felt a little bit left out; she alone had not been visited by her father's ghost.

Family members arrived at the house. Soon Sutō's father would be transported to the crematorium, the ash collected and the bones picked off of the metal gurney, and then the remains would be buried. Before all this, everyone was to see his face one more time. Sutō's grandfather offered to go first. He lifted the upper lid of the casket, so just the face of the body was visible. Then it was Sutō's turn.

A great effort had been made to clean her father's body and to cover the scratches, but she could still see how he had been injured during his time in the great waves. He had been carefully wrapped in white cloth, as was the custom. And on his chest, there was a single white flower. It was the same flower that Sutō had seen in her shoe at the bath. The experience was overwhelming, and she cried.

Much later, she would realize that the incident with the flower at the bath had happened exactly a week after the earthquake. According to Buddhist tradition, it takes exactly seven days for the soul to travel from its body to its next destination. That day was also March 18, the start of the spring equinox Ohigan, when the curtain separating the mortal and spirit realms is said to thin, making it an ideal time to see the spirits of beloved ancestors.

It was impossible to miss the meaning in the strange incident of the white flower, and Sutō wrote of her experiences in a prize-winning short story that was published by a prestigious Japanese literary journal.

When I met with Sutō nearly two years after the tsunami, she was moving on with her life; she and her fiancé planned to be married and she hoped that they would return to Kesennuma to raise a family. Her fiancé, too, had lost family members: a two-and-a-half-year-old niece and a grandmother.

Sutō had an aura of elegance and graciousness that is unusual in one so young. She was the kind of person for whom you wanted to put on your best behavior. At the same time, she emanated tremendous sadness. As someone nearly twice her age, I found myself yearning to help her. Now that I am middle-aged and a mother, I want people who are younger than I am to be happy, to be living their lives to the fullest, and to be unassailed by grief or circumstance.

We spoke about what the white flower might mean. She remained mystified by the experience, as though she could not quite believe what had happened. Even now she continues to search for an explanation for how the flower ended up in her shoe. But even if she were to learn where it came from, she said, that would not explain how it had been the exact same species as the flower on her father's body in the casket, a type of flower she had never seen before or since.

We both spoke of how love is an invisible thing, impossible to see even if someone is still alive. I wanted very much to believe that the flower was a final act of love and hope. The love we have for people, after all, never truly goes away, even if they leave us in *owakare*, the great parting.

SIXTEEN

The Blind Medium

B UT WHAT IF, DESPITE the lanterns, the yearly return of the spirits, and all the incense and temples and equinoxes, you are still heartbroken? What if you remain in the grip of grief's madness? Who can help you if the one thing you really want is to talk to the person you have lost, just one more time?

As I traveled throughout Tōhoku and spoke with people about the tsunami and their losses, I kept running into stories about the *itako*, the blind mediums who gather on Mount Doom twice a year, and who for a small fee can channel the souls of the dead. Often the stories went like this: There was a man who had lost his wife in the tsunami and whose body had not been found. He missed her so much, he finally turned to an *itako* to help him communicate with her spirit, and though the itako had been unable to locate the remains, she had helped him feel more at peace.

Endo Shigeru, the director of the documentary in which I participated, kept running into stories about the *itako* too, during his location scouting and prefilming research. But the *itako* were elusive. Endo had wanted to arrange for me to meet one. The *itako* were said to be very busy in Tōhoku, due to the number of people who died, and were moving around, like itinerant priests. Endo followed the stories, going from town to town, asking where the *itako* had been and where they were heading. He reached Kesennuma, where someone told him that the most recent *itako* to visit had been in her eighties, and had died.

Yet another person told him that the *itako* were not really dying out, but that they now "hid" their profession. In Tōhoku towns, where residents were traditional and old-fashioned, the owner of the corner grocery store might well be an *itako*. But you would not know this if you weren't from her town, and even if you asked her to conjure up the spirit of someone whom you missed, she would deny being able to do such a thing.

I had long been fascinated by the *itako*, ever since I had first learned about them in a college religion class. And as I traveled around Tōhoku, it became clear to me that no real examination of grief in Japan would be complete without trying to meet an *itako* in person. Since I wasn't able to find an *itako* on my own, I decided to go to Mount Doom in October, where I knew the last remaining *itako* would convene during the Mount Doom Autumn Festival.

IN 1975, WHEN historian Carmen Blacker wrote *The Catalpa Bow*, a look at Japan's shamanistic heritage, there were twenty *itako* at the yearly festivals on Mount Doom. Even then, Dr. Blacker was fairly certain that the tradition would die out, another casualty to progress.

But modernity isn't the only force at work hastening an end to the *itako*. When I called Mount Doom to ask about meeting one, I was patiently told that the blind mediums did not have an official relationship with the temple, and that I was welcome to come during the Autumn Festival and to hire a priest to read a sutra to commemorate anyone I might be grieving. "You know, there are only two *itako* left, and one is very old and might die at any time."

It is often said—by the Japanese themselves—that Japan is the country of nuance. There is a great deal of nuance contained in the conversation I had with the priests at Mount Doom. Even though the place is most famous for its *itako*, visitors are discouraged from coming for the sole purpose of meeting with the mediums, all of whom are female and the final inheritors of Japan's old matriarchal, shamanistic tradition. Instead, visitors are encouraged to visit with Buddhist priests, who are male.

Before going to Mount Doom in the fall, I exchanged a series of emails with a young Buddhist priest with whom I had become friendly, and who lives in Tōhoku but isn't officially connected to the Mount Doom bureaucracy. I asked him if the *itako* would most likely show up on Mount Doom for the Autumn Festival. His answer was carefully worded. Yes, he said. There would be *itako*. But I had to understand that it was not the policy of the temple bureaucracy to support the work of the *itako*, and there was no guarantee that the *itako* would show up. Further, if what I wanted was to truly understand the meaning of Mount Doom, then I ought to meet with its vice president, a mercurial man named Minami Jikisai who was considered a great Buddhist thinker and teacher, and whose writings on grief and modern spirituality had made him quite famous in Japan.

This young priest in Tōhoku was not the first person to bring up Minami Jikisai with me. Kaneta, of Café de Monk, had also once laughingly suggested I try to meet with Mount Doom's vice president. "A very interesting man, I hear. Most unusual." I had had dinner with the folklore scholar Hijikata Kisashi, who had also told me once that I ought to read Minami Jikisai's book on Mount Doom, if not try to meet the great man himself. At that time, I had not read Minami's book, though I would later when I was not traveling so much.

Arrangements were made for me to meet this vice president during the Autumn Festival. But there were conditions: I was not allowed to photograph the vice president, and I could not record our conversation. Further, if I wanted to meet with him, I was requested *not* to meet with an *itako*.

So there was the choice: I could meet with the vice president of Mount Doom, but not the blind medium. Or I could go to Mount Doom hoping that the *itako* would be there, but I would not be able to speak with Minami Jikisai.

I have said that Japan is the land of exceptions. And in reading the emails from my contact in Japan, I sensed a hesitancy in the way he worded the instructions. "It was requested . . ." "You are requested . . ." I asked my contact how it would be if I went to see an *itako* the *day before* my scheduled appointment with the head priest. I had lost my grandfather and my father, and I wanted to be able to consult with a blind medium if at all possible.

Oh well, my contact wrote back to me. If I were coming the *day before*, and I was not going to be mixing my meeting with an important leader of Mount Doom and a private consultation with an *itako* whose services I would be procuring due to a very real and recent loss, that seemed like a situation with which one could not argue.

IT WAS JUST after eight in the morning when I arrived at Mount Doom, but already the parking lot was full of cars and there were two tour buses parked off to the side. I paid my admission fee and crossed the first gate. To the left were two very low tents made out of blue tarp. Each had a line of about fifteen people in front of it. I chose the farther of the two stalls and took my place, bracing against the cold wind.

In front of me, there was a man dressed in down pantaloons and a down vest. It was so windy, he had fashioned a kind of helmet out of a white towel, and that covered his head and mouth. I had seen farmers wearing towels like this as they drove around in their cars; presumably it was a local method of dealing with the unpredictable weather. The man stood just off to the side, and as I approached, I could hear him lecturing the people waiting ahead of me on the correct protocol for visiting an *itako*. He spoke partly in dialect, so it was somewhat difficult for me to understand, but I gathered that he was chastising the people ahead of me for failing to do a complete circuit of Mount Doom's grounds before coming to see the medium.

"The proper thing is for you to go to all the main temples! Visit the lake! Then come around there," he gestured toward a pathway.

Two of the women in the line nodded apologetically. The man kept up his tirade, and I couldn't figure out if he was there to vet all the guests, or if he was in line waiting for a medium himself. He was so insistent on the rightness of the procedure that eventually a few women left the line and began the long walk through the temple grounds. Then the man's gaze settled on me.

I was wearing a hat and a scarf, items I hoped would keep some of the wind at bay, but which I also hoped might disguise my obvious foreign features. The man with the white towel on his head now barked at me. "What about you? Have you done a complete circuit?"

"Many times," I said. Then I tipped my hat so he could see my Caucasian features. He stared at me for a while, trying to take in the conflicting pieces of information, nodded, and drifted off toward a shed behind the tents. Around me, people in line exhaled with relief.

"Is that man here with you?" I asked what remained of the little party in front of me.

"Oh no!" they said. "He was setting up some flags and fighting with the wind. And then he came over to talk to us. He wouldn't stop."

"I think," offered a woman behind me, "that he is a yearly volunteer. He seemed to know a lot."

After a few minutes, the women who had scattered off to do a "complete pilgrimage" drifted back into line, and so our queue recongealed.

I waited nearly three hours for my medium, a very short time according to some of the "experts" I met that day. Behind me stood a little group of ladies who said they came every year, but usually in the summer when the line snaked all the way around the temple grounds, and then one had to wait for seven hours. Things had only grown worse now that there were only two *itako* alive.

In front of me, a family of four—mother, grandmother, daughter, and father—explained that they had come from the Tōkyō area. The grandmother had been before, but this was the first time for the rest of the family. Every now and then, the grandmother went to the front of the line to eavesdrop on the session under way. Then she would return and triumphantly declare, "She's just repeating herself!" And we would all laugh nervously.

Up ahead of this family was a young woman whom I guessed was in her late twenties; she would later emerge from the tent in tears. Another man was there by himself; when it was his turn to consult the medium, I would hear the *itako* repeatedly examine the issue of marriage. "I guess he wants to get married," I said to no one in particular.

The grandmother—the one who liked to go and eavesdrop—immediately turned around and said to me, "Oh, he had someone he wanted to marry, but she died in the tsunami."

After about an hour, I couldn't help but notice that the line to our particular medium had grown quite long while the other one was short. The ladies behind me noted this too, and again the grandmother ahead of me had the answer: "That *itako* in the other line is old. Ours is young. And she has a book. And she can see."

We all stood on tiptoe to try to look into the tent. There sat the *itako* in her white robes, her hair pulled back with a piece of elastic.

She had on not one shred of makeup. Above her hung a wooden board with her name: Matsuda Hiroko. It was a name I recognized as the author of a book, *The Last Itako*, that had been recommended to me. I had purchased the book and read about half of it before coming to Mount Doom.

Over the course of the following three hours, it stormed, it rained, and it brightened. When it rained, those of us with umbrellas joined forces, creating a kind of roof so that those without umbrellas could try to stay dry. We held places in line so people could go to the bathroom. At one point, the women behind us handed out rice crackers. Most of the people in line were women who were coming for the first time. A few had tried to come in the summer but had given up due to the heat and the length of the line. Many had stories about friends, or friends of friends, who had come to see an *itako*. One woman had lost her best friend in the tsunami and had asked for the deceased spirit to locate itself because the body was never recovered. A man who had lost his wife wanted her to forgive him for his temper. There were families who wanted to say good-bye one more time to the patriarch of their family.

Because the medium tents were located at the end of the pilgrimage route, we also attracted the attention of those exiting the temple complex, just after they passed the last of the Jizō statues and the field where tufts of grass were tied together. Sometimes they stopped to ask us how long we had been waiting. Sometimes they tried to eavesdrop for a moment before walking away. Many took photos; they knew who the *itako* were and knew that a consultation was a rare privilege. But most did not join the line; they were on schedules and had places to go, or did not have enough warm clothing on for the long wait.

The person I was most interested in happened to be standing behind me. He seemed to be about my age, or perhaps a few years younger; it can often be difficult to guess ages in Japan. He wore

jeans and a sweatshirt with a hood, and all the women worried that
he might catch a chill. He had a beard, and his hair was unkempt,
but he had an easygoing manner. He reminded me of a Dr Pepper–
guzzling computer engineer I might meet standing patiently in the
checkout line at Fry's Electronics in Silicon Valley.

"So what do you think?" I asked. "Three hours total?"

"I've been timing her. She gives each person an average of twenty
minutes. And judging by the people in line . . . some people are
here together . . . some are alone . . ." I could see him recalculating.
"I think we will be done before lunch."

"Twenty minutes!" I said. "I was thinking that standing in line
like this is sort of like waiting for a ride at Disneyland. Except there
the ride is only five minutes. Twenty minutes is definitely better
than five."

"Oh. Oh." He nodded earnestly. "Well. I guess perhaps there's . . .
well this is cheaper than Disneyland too, if you factor in the cost of
the tickets." I could see him calculating the cost differential and
then deciding against sharing this information. Then he looked at
me, and I could see that he didn't seem quite sure how to proceed.

"I'm sorry," I said. "Typical American. When we are nervous,
we try to say something funny. I ought to know better, but I still
do this."

He laughed with relief. "Typical Japanese. When we are nervous, we take things too seriously." From then on, we conversed
easily.

He was originally from Kyūshū, Japan's largest southern island,
and he was an engineer. He had been hired by the Japanese government to help plan the new roads in Tōhoku, and had been living in
the northeast for the past year or so, working three weeks straight,
then taking one day off. Most days, he argued with the locals. He
wanted the new roads to be high to keep cars safe from future tsunami waves, but the locals wanted easy access to the ocean. The

locals often thought that since a major tsunami struck only once every six hundred years, Japan, and certainly Tōhoku, would be safe for centuries. But he, as an engineer, knew that "once every six hundred years" did not mean "in six hundred years." "It could very well mean tomorrow!" he said passionately.

The Engineer had long wanted to come to Mount Doom. He had finally been given three days off to coincide with the national holiday. He had immediately hired a car and headed for the Shimokita Peninsula.

I couldn't help but wonder why an engineer, which is to say, a man of science, wanted to stand in line to see a medium.

"Have you always wanted to see an *itako*?" I asked.

"Yes. Since I first heard about them. And then when I got transferred to Tōhoku, I was hoping for this chance."

"Do you think they are accurate?"

"Hahaha!" he laughed. "Oh, I don't know. We Japanese. We believe. And we don't believe. Half and half."

"But you still wanted to come," I said.

"Very much!" he replied cheerfully.

Around eleven o'clock, a group of priests started chanting from inside one of Mount Doom's temple halls. They were hitting a drum and reading sutras. About fifteen minutes later, we could hear their wooden shoes clicking on the pavement, and a group of priests in mustard and purple robes walked down the walkway and into the warmth of the information center. I thought to myself that there were so many more men at Mount Doom than there were women. And one day the place would be completely in the possession of male priests because the female shamans would finally be gone.

As the line grew shorter, and my turn was imminent, I became nervous. I told the Engineer that I was worried I wouldn't understand the medium. The research I had done indicated that the women spoke in Aomori dialect, and not standard Japanese. I suddenly realized I had forgotten my Japanese grandfather's date of death; I would need to provide it to the medium. I pulled out my cell phone to call my mother, before I remembered that there was neither Internet access nor cell phone reception on Mount Doom. I thought about making up a date but then decided that I would always wonder forever after if I might have had a different reading had I provided accurate information. My father's date of death is ingrained on my memory. I wondered how it would work for a Japanese medium trained in Aomori Prefecture to summon up the spirit of my American father. I knew that *he* would not have minded. I asked the Engineer what he thought.

"Well, I would assume that dead people all go to the same place," he said. "Although maybe the way we can communicate with them depends on culture. I say go with your father's date." That settled it.

I listened to the tail end of the session in front of me. The *itako*, now channeling the spirit of a deceased person, advised that next year the father in the family needed to be careful of a possible traffic accident. It would not be fatal if it happened, but it was best that it did not happen. Then she sang the spirit away and the family departed from the tent.

I took off my shoes and knelt down inside the tent, keeping my hat on until I was completely seated, in an effort to conceal for as long as possible that I was not Japanese.

The medium was magnificent sitting on her pillows. With her white pantaloons splashed all around her, she looked like an archaic figure from the medieval period. In her hands, she held a long rosary made up of wooden beads. Now that I was in her tent, I could see other objects on the rosary: polished bone and a bird's foot. And then, in front of her, I saw a rectangular basket with a few objects. I later read that these objects were considered to be her most important tools, and that she would put her rosary there when she was not using it. Among the other items in the basket were a rolled-up scroll, something wrapped in embroidered cloth, and a box of cookies labeled "Marie."

The *itako* cleared her throat. "What is the relationship between you and the person who has died?"

"My father."

"When did he die?"

"June 8."

"What did he die of?"

This was complicated. There was the actual cause of death listed on his death certificate, then there were all the factors that had led up to a very bad emergency-room visit and actual death, which should not have happened in the way that it did. But I said, "Illness. Unexpected."

She nodded and began to sing.

I couldn't make out all of what she was saying at this point. I thought I heard her asking for the spirit of the person who had been turned into a Buddha on June 8 to please descend. She rubbed her long rosary loudly as she did this. I hadn't paid her any money yet, and I kept wondering what would happen if she decided that my father's spirit wasn't willing to descend. But then she started to talk.

"Well, you've come a long way. I can't believe you've come all this way to find me. I'm rather humbled by that. I'm so sorry I went the way that I did. I really wanted to stick around longer and to spend more time with you. There have been so many occasions when I wanted to give you some more advice. It does make me feel good to see you getting along so well with the rest of the family, though. And you know, I try to come and see you in your dreams, but lately that's become much harder. You'll notice I don't show up in your dreams so much."

Hadn't he, though? And then just as quickly, I told myself to be reasonable. It was true that after my father died, I had seen him repeatedly in my dreams. It was almost always the same dream or variations on the same dream. I went into the room where he had slept toward the end of his life and found him sitting in the red armchair we had bought together at Macy's. Sometimes he was reading a book. I would explain to him that he was dead, and he would look disappointed and sheepishly apologize. I always woke up gasping for air because I didn't really want him to be dead.

But after about a year of this, the dreams started to fade, and I didn't have to tell him he was dead quite as often. A part of me wondered if there was any truth to the superstition that the dead who don't mean to die are shocked to find themselves in this condition. This is what Kaneta was always telling everyone in his cafés: "You have to let them go! They have to move on!"

Although, there was the time when I had pneumonia, two years after he died. I was in Japan and had plans to go to the blind-medium festival on Mount Doom. I woke up in my hotel room in Sendai, shaking because of yet another of the nightly earthquakes that rattled the area for at least a year after the disaster. I discovered that I had a fever and a cough. I remembered I'd seen my father in a dream that night, and that he'd told me I needed to see a doctor. I ignored the advice, figuring that a day of medication and rest was all I needed. But the cough would not go away, so I flew back home, where I was told I had pneumonia and was put on strong antibiotics.

"Do you have any questions for me?" the medium asked.

I was unprepared for this. Unlike everyone else in line, I hadn't really come to Mount Doom with a specific question for my father. I racked my brain for something to say, then sputtered out two questions. I told the *itako* I was worried about writing this book. The *itako*'s response was guarded. She thought I should not be in a hurry to get my work done. When I asked her about a possible move to the West Coast, she answered my question with a question: wasn't where I lived now a good location?

Then the *itako* opened her eyes and looked at me. Her face was expressionless, but it was clear now that our session was about to end. "I don't foresee any major illnesses. Nothing seems to be terribly wrong, though you need to make sure you take care of yourself. You worry too much." She began to sing the spirit of my father away. "I will try to come and see you in your dreams, but it is getting harder and harder for me to do so. Just do me a favor and talk about me every now and then. I like it when you remember me." This last line made me tear up. I rarely talk about my father. I miss him too much.

Then the session was over, and I paid the medium my three thousand yen, or about thirty dollars; this is the fixed rate for all *itako* readings.

As soon as I got out of the tent, a small group of women came running up to me. "Did she get it? Was she accurate?"

"I don't know," I said. Then, honestly, "I think I don't have sufficient Japanese to explain what just happened."

Immediately after the reading, my logical, scientific brain insisted that I had simply received one of six possible variations for all possible *itako* readings. I knew from Dr. Carmen Blacker's book that the *itako* had different messages for their subjects depending on how the deceased had passed away. The Mountain Woman had told me this too. She had said that while there were mediums who could "see," it was not logical that an *itako* could service over one hundred people in a day and allow that many dead spirits to inhabit her body. Of course, most of the people who went to see an *itako* were simply hearing a script.

A second part of me was chastising myself for not having been better prepared. What was I doing asking the dead spirit of my father about my job and about my living situation? Why didn't I explain how difficult it had been since my father had died, and that

I wished I had been at the hospital that night, in the place of my mother, to converse in fluent English with the doctors who provided him with substandard care?

Yet a third part of me, perhaps the most important part, was quickly silencing these other voices. This part of me didn't have a voice yet; it just had a feeling. And the feeling was this: I felt very much like I was eight years old, and I had woken up my father from a nap to tell him something that seemed very important—the sprinkler system appeared to be out of rotation, for example—that ultimately was *not* important and certainly not worth waking someone up for.

That was the feeling I had now, striding across the stone walkway to get away from the women asking me, "Was the medium right?" Why on earth had I taken the time to wake my father up from the dead?

I DAWDLED AROUND the temple information booth. It was warm in there, and I wanted to give my body a chance to relax after standing in the cold for three hours. After a little bit, I saw the Engineer outside, walking slowly toward the second great gate. I rushed out to meet him.

"Hello!" I said.

"Hello!"

We walked along the stone path together. The wind was still very strong, and the pinwheels were screaming, though in their chattering I thought they sounded a bit like manic laughter.

"How did it go?" I asked.

"Well," he said, and then immediately launched into a blow-by-blow account. "She successfully conjured up my father, and I was able to ask him something that has bothered me for years." Here he paused. "My parents divorced when I was very young, and I barely knew my father. When I applied for college, I had to get my *koseki*, the family registry." This is the standard practice in Japan, and in dramas and novels it is often the pivotal moment in which the hero discovers some long-suppressed truth about his or her family. In the case of Sempō, for example, he had no idea that his mother was his mother and not his sister until he applied to college and took a look at his *koseki*. It was also from his *koseki* that Sempō learned the name of his biological father. As for the Engineer, he looked at his family's *koseki* and discovered that his father had been dead a long time.

The Engineer continued. "No matter what we did—and my younger brother researched it—we couldn't find out where he died or how he died or if anyone was with him. And this bothered me."

As we talked, I was moved by the Engineer's simple desire to know if his father had died peacefully or not. There was no angry talk about how "he wasn't there for me," as I might hear from my Western friends who wrestled with their fathers' abandonment. The Engineer hadn't seen his mother or his other siblings in nearly twenty years, but he had worried very much about his father's spirit. Once he had been transferred to Tōhoku to work on the restoration of the northeast of Japan, he had been waiting for the day when he might finally put his questions to rest via a personal consultation with an *itako*.

"And he said that it was like going to sleep. It was an abrupt illness—nothing really foreseen. He went to sleep, and then he died."

"How do you feel?"

"Oh, I feel incredibly relieved. Although, she did say that I ought to lose some weight. And she sort of laughed when she said this."

"The medium laughed?"

"Well, presumably it was my father in the medium's body. But since she was laughing . . . I also." Here he began to apologize that he had not meant to overhear my own session, but that he could not help but notice that I had asked about my work. This had prompted him to ask about his work too, which he would not have done otherwise.

"Oh, you listened!"

"I'm very sorry," he bowed.

I told him I didn't mind because I had been very worried about understanding the medium in the first place, and he admitted that part of his reason for eavesdropping was to help me later in the event that I needed his assistance.

He asked if I felt better for having had a chance to hear that my father did not mean to die so early, that his intended fate was to stick around longer. The kind gesture touched me. I said that I did feel some relief. As we talked about the session, the Engineer and I came across inconsistencies in the *itako*'s words. For example, "the *itako* told you not to hurry while writing, but surely she knows that all writers have deadlines." But then the Engineer suggested that such words of comfort might have been the kind of thing that my father *would* have said to me were he alive.

When we parted, I asked the Engineer to keep in touch with me. I could see getting a beer with him some day and talking about our "wild experience at Mount Doom." He promised to write to me. Then I hurried back home to the Mountain Woman and the inn because I knew my son was waiting for me there. I checked my watch before getting in the car. It was just before noon, just as the Engineer had predicted.

All the way down the mountain, that slightly mollified feeling I had—the impression of having disturbed my father from a nap—continued to grow. I felt the childish regret of having displeased an elder.

Then a voice inside my head said, You don't really need your father anymore. You miss him, but you are actually okay now.

The voice said this a few times. And in my entire body, I realized it was true. I remembered learning to ride a bike. When I glanced back to see that my father was not actually behind me holding me steady as I did a loop around the driveway, he laughed gleefully. "See? You don't need me!"

Back down in the valley, I found my son sitting beside an enormous dustpan-shaped basket filled with chestnuts. There had been a big storm the night before, he explained to me, which meant that many new chestnuts had fallen off the trees. He and the Mountain Woman had gone chestnut hunting as soon as I left because otherwise other villagers would show up and gather all the nuts, and there would not be any left. He sat like a king in front of his big pile, while the Mountain Woman chuckled that she had no idea what to do with so many nuts. Perhaps, she said, she would give some away.

THAT EVENING I slept very soundly. When I woke up, I knew that I had seen my father in a dream, but I couldn't remember any of the specifics. I remembered that he had seemed slightly annoyed, but lovingly so. I had tried to hold on to him, to recall where he had been and what he had been doing, but the details of the dream left me immediately when I opened my eyes.

SEVENTEEN

DARTH VADER

O**N THE LAST DAY** of the Autumn Festival on Mount Doom, I drove my rental car one more time up the winding road that connected the Mountain Woman's spa to the underworld. The ferocious wind from the day before had unleashed a torrent of yellow leaves to the road. I drove carefully; the leaves were slick. There was little traffic. That morning at breakfast when I had spoken to the other guests, most said they were going home. The long weekend was coming to a close, and everyone needed to head back to the major cities.

The staff at Bōdaiji—Mount Doom's temple—had been expecting me. They urged me on to the main hall, where I could participate in a memorial service. I took off my shoes and walked the long wooden hallway connecting the visitors' entrance to the *hondō*. I relished the familiar feeling of stepping into a temple that I had already encountered, and which I loved for its hidden treasures and solemn purpose.

After a few minutes, I could hear the brisk footsteps of priests crossing the wooden hallway outside, and not long after, the unmistakable swish of silk sleeves brushing against silk robes. The priests were entering. One was familiar: the man who had sung the sutras so beautifully early in the morning when I visited in May. And then there was a figure dressed in purple, with a high black hat on his head. This would be Minami, the vice president of Mount Doom.

He struck me as unusually tall, and he had a long, pointy face and a mouth that naturally descended into a tight, pouty frown. In his body he carried years of Eiheiji training; he was precise and graceful. But his movements had a shadow, a hint of a lack of coordination. He bowed his head slightly as he crossed the threshold, as though he had long ago learned to expect low doorways. He was also extremely thin, and his fingers and thumbs were very long. He did not use his hands to speak in the wired, taut manner that so many of the priests I had met at Sōjiji and Eiheiji used. His hands were often relaxed, the long fingers curled. When he unfurled his hands, I thought of a sea anemone and the way its tentacles reach out to grab at absent-minded prey. Something about his hampered physicality hinted at a pure cerebral power. He looked like a scholar who had learned to move like a monk and not the other way around. I couldn't help but think that Minami was some form of human being I had never met before, a hint of what was to come after years of evolution.

I had heard a lot about this head priest of Mount Doom, whose family name, Minami, means "South." His given name, Jikisai, is made up of the characters for "Direct" and "How!" or "Alas!" or, as one dictionary put it, "An archaic exclamation!" Minami trained at Eiheiji, and like all priests, he changed his name when he pursued his education. I took the name as a sign. Mr. "How Direct!" priest had a point to make and would make it directly. But he was also a scholar and perhaps even an elitist who delighted shocking people with the truth. He was not like Kaneta, whose given name, Taiō, meant "great sunshine."

In fact, when Kaneta learned that I would be meeting Minami in person, he was immediately delighted and—intrigued.

"You know," Kaneta gushed, "Minami chose to be a priest. He was only twenty-five years old. He graduated from Waseda, got a job in Tōkyō, and then renounced the world and went to stay at Eiheiji for twenty years, before he finally left to head up his own temple. People rarely choose to go to Eiheiji and then stay there for twenty years." Kaneta smiled. "He's quite famous. But complicated. I wonder how you will get along."

When I was at the Mountain Woman's inn, I had mentioned to some of the girls in the newly opened café just outside the spa that I would be heading up to Mount Doom for a private audience with Minami. They, too, had squealed, "He's very famous!" before adding, "He's also very smart."

One of the girls was in her forties, and she divided her time between Spain, where she danced flamenco, and Japan, where she came home to the Shimokita Peninsula to work during the summer months. Soon the tourist season would be over, and she would return to Spain. "I would love to meet Minami," she enthused. "You know, he married my classmate."

From here, the conversation in the café around me descended— or ascended, depending on your point of view—into gossip. Bōdaiji, the temple that oversees Mount Doom, is connected to a larger temple called Entsūji, which is located on the Shimokita Peninsula in the town of Mutsu. The priest at Entsūji had had only one daughter. "There really was nothing very distinctive about her," the girls in the café recalled. "But she was the daughter of the head priest of Entsūji, and that gave her a certain standing in our community."

Entsūji's only daughter repeatedly visited Eiheiji with the intention of finding a spouse. "She met Minami and that was it," one of the women declared. The couple got married when the woman was forty-two. "It would have been *girigiri* for having a child," said another of the women, using the onomatopoeia for "barely and just in the nick of time."

"They have a little boy," someone else exclaimed. "Of course, he's brilliant like his father. Everyone says he's the best in the class."

Here I tuned out of the conversation, which had now gone full throttle into gossip. I knew all about the pressure and the relief a temple family feels to find an heir, and empathized with Entsūji's predicament. But I was now very intrigued by this man who had graduated from one of Japan's finest universities, gone on to have a career, and then abandoned the secular world for twenty years of Eiheiji, before leaving that haven behind to become the vice president of Japan's Mount Doom.

AFTER THE MEMORIAL service ended, I went to the visitors' center to wait for Minami. About five minutes later, he came out to greet me, his head slightly stooped and his face a taut mask of caution and wariness.

"Hello," he said. He had a low, very masculine voice, but he also spoke briskly, as though constantly plagued by impatience. "Please follow me."

We made our way to the hotel where I had spent the night that spring. Here again a white, granite Jizō greeted me cheerfully, framed against a somber wall of polished black marble. I was feeling intimidated by our impending conversation, but the sight of the happy Jizō cheered me up a little. I exchanged my slippers and followed Minami to the lounge area, where we sat down opposite each other in two enormous armchairs. He arranged his robes around him with fastidious little hand twitches and then settled down, like a cat finally come to rest on a favored pillow. In his left hand, Minami clutched a Buddhist wooden scepter called a *kotsu* or a *nyoi*. The scepter was about a foot long and had been carved in an S-shape, meant to replicate the curve of the human spine. The head of the scepter blossomed in the shape of a bulbous, cerebral fungus, a symbol of wisdom and intelligence in the Far East. Only high-ranking Buddhist priests can carry these scepters, which are usually used as a tool for emphasizing some teaching point. Minami's long fingers curled over the top of the *kotsu*, absent-mindedly toying with the coiled, curling head or sliding along the spine. It was a strange and unsettling object, but in its human-form-meets-mushroom appearance, it also conveyed a sense of otherworldly knowing.

By now I had learned that the best way to introduce myself to priests in Japan was to explain that I had family in Tōhoku who ran a Sōtō Zen temple, and that I had done a pilgrimage to Eiheiji. Indeed Minami's face brightened, and some of the caution slipped from his eyes.

"Ah, yes. You stayed overnight and did the basic training."

"When I told my family members, they said to me, Now, imagine doing that every day for years."

"I was there for twenty years." As he said this—very dramatically and with deliberate articulation—Minami did not bask in the rosy, beatific glow emanating from so many of the older graduates of Eiheiji I had met. Nor did he project the beleaguered-but-relieved-to-have-come-out-on-the-other-side pride exhibited by some of the younger priests with whom I'd spoken during my travels. There was instead a hint of bitterness mixed with self-confidence in his voice, and I was alerted immediately that I was talking to someone who fell outside the usual parameters of opinion and experience. I was at once intensely curious, but nervous. I did not want to do or say anything stupid.

I said, "I've been thinking that Dōgen was right. There is really something to training the body, and then letting the brain catch up."

Here Minami laughed—a short, knowing chortle. He had a habit when he talked of turning his head slightly to the side and keeping his eyes cast down, only every now and then looking up.

The impression this conveyed was of shyness. But such passive mannerisms were at odds with his way of speaking, which was laden with impatient intelligence. "Yes," he purred, still keeping his head to the side and his eyes cast down. "You Westerners like to know why you are doing things before you do them. Only then will you do what you are asked to do. We train our Japanese differently. We make them do things, and then they learn why later." He glanced up and looked at me, holding my gaze sharply for an instant, before he looked back down again and stroked the head of his scepter, nodding slightly.

It was an opening that caught me off guard. I was, by now, very familiar with the caution that Japanese people have when coming face-to-face with Westerners. But it is uncommon for someone in Japan to make it so directly clear that he has had his own experiences with Westerners, and that he has observed us and thought about us perhaps even more than we have thought about them.

Minami had known two Italian monks at Eiheiji. Over time, they had come to understand Zen as deeply as anyone else. He also told me that he had been at Eiheiji for three years before he had gone off to Minneapolis to see how Zen training was done in America. "My first thought was that American training is superior because you only bring in people who truly want to understand Zen. But then, over time, I've come to see what it is about Eiheiji that has made it so successful for twenty years. We can train *anyone.*"

There was a weird, hidden combativeness to the way Minami was speaking to me. I felt it partly from his voice, a deep, masculine voice that lingered over certain words and at times spit out others. I tried not to take this method of conversation too personally. Hadn't I just a few days earlier witnessed a dharma combat ceremony in which young priests virtually shouted at each other in question-and-answer format? Perhaps, I thought, this was what it was actually like to speak with another Buddhist priest. If I thought back, there was something slightly martial about many of my encounters with Japanese priests: the monks on Kōyasan, Kaneta's method of disarming those lost in grief, and even Sempō's warning that I could not understand Japan.

Before I could say anything else, Minami offered up the following jewel: "My master told me when I entered Eiheiji that I would understand *everything* in three months." He turned his head coquettishly to the side, eyes downcast. "That was all it would take for *me* to understand the *essence* of the training. But he told me to be quiet and just to observe. And so I *was*. And then, after three years, I began to voice my *opinions*." The corners of his mouth were still turned down as he smiled slightly. He was the sort of person who frowned even when he smiled. His eyes grew distant, as though looking at a photo of a cherished memory. The purr in his voice became silky. "I was an *outsider*. They called me *Darth Vader*." He glanced up to see how I had taken this admission.

In my application to speak with Minami, I had stressed that I was curious to learn the venerable priest's thoughts on how Japan had been coping since the disaster. Minami was in the unusual position as the head of Mount Doom to know many who had suffered as a result of the tsunami. But here he was presenting himself as an outsider, with knowledge of the West and with his own distinct understanding of Buddhism, which didn't necessarily have anything to do with Eiheiji's official party line.

He said, "You know our system of temples is dying in Japan."

"It is?"

He scoffed and shot me an irritated, admonishing look. "Don't be silly. It's *fated*. This system of passing on temples from father to son can't go on. Everyone is leaving the countryside. The situation is going to collapse. But there will be some who remain. Some of us who truly believe in Zen."

"What is the point of zazen?" I asked.

This question seemed to delight him. He looked down to the side, his head at an angle and his mouth in a tight ball. Now his face glowed with animation, and little of the false modesty that he had employed earlier. "We live," he began, "in a world created by language." He ran off the names of French philosophers, whom he assumed I had read. He spoke about the world of commerce, and how so much of our lives were shaped by language, and by talk and how we could in fact convince ourselves of reality just by speech alone. Here I stopped him and asked for a concrete example.

"How does a child learn what a table is? We tell him: This here is a table. You may not climb on a table. You may not go under the table. You may eat off a table or put things on a table. Of course, you should only eat off of certain tables." To sit zazen, he said, was to sit outside this world in which everything was formed by talk. Zazen meditation forced us into self-consciousness.

"That's Buddhism."

"Well, that's what *I* think. As an outsider."

"As Darth Vader."

"Yes!" He laughed for the first time, his lips rising up into a full-fledged gummy smile, and I caught a glimpse of what he might have been like as a child, or perhaps what he was like when he was home and unguarded. But just as quickly, he pulled his expression back into a solemn and watchful resting position.

Since the tsunami, Minami had met with countless survivors, each of whom had a story to tell. For these people, mourning the dead—the loss of a beloved—was a pain so acute, it had the power to create an alternate reality. Because so many people had died at once in Japan, the disaster had created tremendous anxiety, a sense of "I might be next," which was not easy to quell. But for Minami, Buddhism offered a true balm.

"How?" I asked.

"The point of Buddhism," he said, "is that it is natural to live with wounds. Everyone has wounds and will be wounded. This can be shocking at first, but in fact it is completely normal. That's basically it." And so it was with grieving, he said. Intense grieving was recognition of this wound, and it always took a person some time to grow accustomed to it.

Minami had suffered from intense asthma as a child, and the attacks had made him ponder illness and death from an early age. Only Buddhism, he said, had offered any kind of answer to suffering. He repeatedly insisted to me that if he ever found another philosophy that could address the troubles of human existence, he would happily embrace it. But up until now, only Buddhism seemed to come close to truly being what he thought people needed.

He made it very clear that Buddhism was different from Christianity, which stressed the idea of original sin. That it was natural to live with suffering was, he said, an entirely different concept than original sin, which implied that there was something not quite right with human beings. On the contrary, he said. Things were right and things were wrong, but this dichotomy didn't get at the heart of the human experience. To live with pain was entirely normal. Once a person accepted this, he or she could get on with life. "But just so you know, Buddhism is *not* humanism. They are not the same thing."

Our conversation went on for about an hour. Speaking with Minami stretched the limits of my Japanese, but like all kind teachers, when Minami sensed I could not understand a vocabulary word, he provided it for me in English. Our conversation ranged across many subjects: how he saw young people in Japan now refer to themselves as "characters" and not as "personalities," and how they were obsessed with raising the monetary value of their "characters."

I'd heard echoes of this concern from other people, and there were stories in the news about young people taking pictures of themselves in humorous positions and then posting the photos online to try to impress and amuse their friends and strangers. In an incident that is hard for a Westerner to understand, but which makes sense in Japan, a young man had arranged to have a picture taken of him lying inside of the ice-cream freezer in his father's convenience store after hours. He had meant just to amuse his friends by posting it on Facebook, but the photo went viral, and there was outrage. It was inappropriate for the young man to put his body inside of a freezer containing food. It was dirty. People panicked; the store practiced poor hygiene. Remember in Eiheiji and Sōjiji I was told never to touch the wooden platform that monks used as a table. Japanese are, in general, fastidious about being clean. The outrage against the freezer boy was so strong that the franchise from whom his father operated the store revoked its permit. The family had been forced to close down the business. "And for what?" my Japanese friends had said to me. "He was trying to perform. He was trying to appear like an interesting *character*." And this, I assumed, was what Minami meant: people in Japan were less and less interested in the essential truths about their natures, but instead were concerned too much with their external appearance and the worth of their personas.

Language was not the only thing that worried Minami. Money bothered him too. He did not like the iniquity that money had created, and he was not a fan of capitalism. He was very dubious about the efficacy of counselors and therapists to console the grieving; this was a monetary transaction, and any time anyone took money in exchange for "help," one ought to be suspicious. Better to come to Mount Doom, where a person could grieve the dead. "Mind you," he said, "I believe in the dead. They are very different from ghosts. This is not a place for ghost watching. This is a place for grief."

Our talk came to an end. Minami walked me outside to the

grounds of Mount Doom. The banners and special flags, which had been erected for the fall festival, had come down, and one of the *itako* had also abandoned her tent. Only a few people remained in line to speak with the remaining blind medium. The sun was setting, its round orb positioned perfectly on the very center of the peak of a distant mountain. The Japanese refer to this phenomenon as a "diamond," because it looks as though a mountain is holding the jewel. All around us, the pinwheels continued to chatter in the wind, and the numerous statues of the Jizō maintained their stances of stoic vigilance.

I asked Minami what he thought of Mount Doom on his first visit.

"It is a strange place," he said. "But it is an important place. I think its power lies in the fact that there is nothing here. Nothing lives. And that means people can bring anything they want or need into Mount Doom. And we can accept it."

We parted company shortly afterward, and I stopped to look inside the gift shop just outside the temple grounds. There I found Minami's book written in Japanese, and whose title roughly translated to "Osorezan: Where the Dead Exist." I ran back to the temple one more time to ask the priest to sign the book for me, and then I truly left Mount Doom and went back down to the valley.

MY SON HAD been out with the Mountain Woman all day picking mushrooms. She was going to cook them for dinner for us. I hugged him and asked if he wanted to come to the café for a bite of cake while I warmed up my feet in a wooden tub filled with water from the valley's hot spring. He readily agreed. The café was abuzz with activity. The young girls wanted to know about my meeting with Minami and what we had talked about. Then, as with my encounter with the blind medium, I balked, because I was not sure how to sum up our conversation.

Later that evening, one of the girls from the café and the Mountain Woman came to our room at the inn, where my mother, my son, and I were eating dinner, which was largely composed of foraged mushrooms and chestnuts. The two guests regaled us with ghost stories of Mount Doom. In the old days, they said, before the hotel had been erected, it was possible to stay on Mount Doom and wake up in the middle of the night and find that a ghost was in your bed with you. The new hotel had completely ruined the other-worldly quality of Mount Doom, though people who had *reikan*, or "spirit vision," could still see ghosts.

The Mountain Woman told us the story of her brother, who had been a sickly baby, not expected to live. "We have a saying," she said. "When someone dies, the family makes *mochi*, or rice cakes. So, when someone is very sick, we say they are so sick the family is already preparing rice cakes. That's how it was with my brother." He survived, but as an adult he had been plagued by ghosts. A biologist, he had a job researching the waters of Lake Usori, where a rare species of fish lived because they were able to tolerate the high levels of sulfur. He frequently came home with stories of how he encountered a little old lady who was lost on the shores of the lake.

"Where is the *hondō*?" the lady would ask, and he would point the direction in which she ought to walk. "I'm so tired. Would you take me?"

Exasperated, the biologist would take the lady's hand, but she would stumble and ask to be carried. And so he would help her onto his back, and she would grow heavier and heavier until he was no longer able to stand. Then he tried to release her, only to find that she had completely disappeared and that he had been conversing with a ghost. His problems improved recently, after his father died and took away the curse of sight with him.

"That is how Osorezan used to be," the Mountain Woman said confidently. "Full of ghosts. But not anymore."

From here, the women went on to tell more and more ghost stories, each one more creepy than the last, until our room was filled with shrieking laughter.

SUCH STORIES WOULD have filled Minami with disapproval. In his conversation with me, he had made a distinction between the dead and ghosts. Very late at night, after everyone else had gone to sleep, I cracked open Minami's book and began to read. There was a familiar retreading of many of the subjects we had talked about that afternoon when I had been granted my audience. Then he began to write about the grounds of Osorezan itself.

He made note of the small rocks on which the grieving write to the dead. On one was a note from a mother to her son: "I want to hear your voice again." On another, a mother wrote to her child, "I will come and see you again." This, Minami wrote, was the essence of Osorezan. It was not a place to come in search of ghosts and ghouls, but to connect with the dead at the deepest level. In another section, he wrote of the phenomenon of grown men coming to the shores of Lake Usori and crying out to the mountains on the opposite side: "Mother! Mother!" By crying out like this, the men hoped to summon their mothers' spirits. Grown men in general do not cry like this, Minami noted. And yet, on Mount Doom, when one man saw another crying out like this, he would join in, and the faces of both strangers would be covered in tears.

IN OUR CONVERSATION, Minami stressed the importance of time, and how a person must adjust to a loss—or the wound, as he put it. I found this to be true. It was now five years since my father passed away, and I found that I had adjusted to his death. I was not the same person I was even a year ago, visiting so many Obon services and asking for help to feel less sad.

When I traveled around Japan on the tour of Obon ceremonies, I repeatedly asked my ancestors to "make me feel more happy than sad." In a way, that was what had happened, but with one very important difference. It was not that my sadness had shrunk so much, or that my happiness had grown; instead, I now saw my own sadness in the context of everyone else's grief. I am, after all, just one person on a planet of millions, all of whom, if they have not already, will also suffer the same intense feelings of shock and loss that I have, and many of whom will do so in far more traumatic settings. My little lantern of grief was but one in a sea of other lanterns.

I couldn't help but think about Minami's observation that as a Westerner, I would always want to know why I was doing something. I would never be willing to just go through an experience and then learn the lesson at the end. That would feel too passive. Grieving, I thought, was a perfect example of just such an experience. I had been angry to be so sad so much of the time, unable to trust that in time I would recover and adapt to the lessons of grief.

EIGHTEEN

MESSAGE FROM
THE OTHER WORLD

WINTER COMES, AND MOUNT Doom closes. It snows, and the residents of Yokote make igloos for the water god, hoping he will return in the spring, which he does; the ice thaws, the cherry blossoms bloom, and then it is spring again.

Spring is my favorite season, and I'm sure this is partly because of my parents. In California, where I grew up, spring comes early. My parents were expert gardeners and took advantage of its early arrival, planning flower beds and the vegetable garden months in advance so something would nearly always be blooming. According to my mother, the backyard had once been nothing but a mess of tall weeds, because the former owner had liked to sunbathe privately in the nude. Beyond the fortress of poison oak and acacia, my father envisioned a miniature paradise. There would be a vegetable garden to the west. Daddy lined this garden with white walls on two sides to generate even more heat, so we could have sweet corn in the summer, strawberries in the spring, and carrots and lettuce year-round. Before breakfast, I picked whatever fruit was ripe that day, and before dinner, the season's vegetables.

To the east, we had an orchard, a never-ending laboratory where my parents experimented with pears, apples, plums, and peaches. When storms broke the branches of the trees, my father tenderly bandaged the severed limbs together with duct tape. It was a yearly joy for me to look out of my bedroom window and watch and wait for the first plum to ripen. For years after I left home, my mother selected plums from the garden, placed them in egg cartons, and shipped them to me via second-day air.

Daddy was forever creating a better way to do everything, and his inventions absorbed his time and interest. He pruned pine and maple trees into bonsai for the front garden. He reshaped all the birdfeeders to keep out aggressive jays and opportunistic pigeons so my mother could enjoy songbirds in the morning during breakfast. He strung a low-level shock wire around the fishpond and waterfall (also his design) and attached it to a timer. Every so often, we'd wake up in the middle of the night and hear a raccoon scream. But in the morning, all the fish were safe.

Our days were filled with worries over which plants were coming up and whether the fuchsias and roses would survive the winter. If the weatherman forecasted a deep freeze, my father and I wrapped his old, wool army blanket around the Meyer lemon tree. In the spring, my mother made miraculous, heady meringue pies. We ate soba on the patio while the hummingbirds fought angrily over the sugar-water feeders. We fed our leftover noodles to the fish in the pond.

A cynical mind—an adult mind—would look at this arrangement and realize it required spare time and enough money. Since my father did not have a conventional job, and since our income came mostly from the family wheat farm in Nebraska, keeping the garden and the grounds depended on frugality. When my mother fell ill and we became her caretakers, we drew inward, guarding our paradise with increased thrift and caution. Our lifestyle bred in us a certain disagreeable pride. We did not admire people who hired gardeners and called plumbers at the first sign of a blocked sewage pipe. We drove our cars until they died, and did not think much of people who needed a BMW or Mercedes-Benz. We were irritated when neighbors could not appreciate the gift of a paper bag filled with zucchini from our overly generous garden. If there was something I wanted—a prom dress, pizza for dinner, a dollhouse—we always tried to make it ourselves.

PEOPLE OFTEN MAKE the mistake of assuming that my American family must have been unhappy that my father married a Japanese woman. Actually, it was the other way around. My American grandmother, usually so equitable, was absolutely and prejudicially for my parents' union, and thrilled that she had a half-Japanese granddaughter. Grammy believed in the beauty of the world and cultures different from her own. In the letters that she wrote during the early years of my parents' marriage, when they lived with her, my grandmother gushed to my Japanese grandparents about how accomplished my mother is, how quickly she learned to bake pies and sew aprons and make pot roast. The gushing continued after I was born, with my grandmother ecstatic that I was being raised with two languages. Years later, I learned that Grammy had paid for my trips to Japan, which couldn't have happened any other way. I also learned that my grandmother had played favorites: she hadn't paid for her other grandchildren to take trips anywhere. "Teach Marie about Japan," she instructed my mother, in no small part because learning about Japan in childhood was something my grandmother would have liked to have done. "Teach Marie what is beautiful about Japan. Teach her as much as possible while she's young."

My mother took this instruction seriously. I was two and a half when we took off for the first of our adventures together. As soon as we were on the plane, my mother firmly held me to a "Japanese-only" rule that she wouldn't relinquish until we were back home. As a child, the language rule felt akin to a magic spell; now we were going to go through the tortuous hazing of flying for hours, switching planes in Alaska, watching the motionless sun—all things that felt against nature's intentions. At the end of the voyage, I'd have to be a slightly different version of myself, one who didn't swing her legs when sitting on a chair, and who ate with her elbows tucked in. She continued the trips, even when she was in poor health and in constant pain, as she was after she recovered from viral meningitis, and then later, after she developed stage-four rheumatoid arthritis.

But her determination—the magic spell cast over me from the travel—had a reward. My grandmother wanted to make sure that I would grow up understanding the things that "make Japan beautiful." My mother shared this idealism and always timed our trips to coincide with Japan's most brilliant and festive *matsuri*, when women dressed up in gauzy *yukata*, and playful music teased the streets. The country felt open, magical, and beguiling. Family members welcomed us with an intense and sincere warmth; Japanese hospitality at its best knows no rival. On each trip, I'd wait for the special night when I would go to sleep and wake up knowing that I had dreamed in Japanese.

"You talked in your sleep last night," my mother would say.

"And?"

"You said something in Japanese."

Then I would know that the spell was complete and that my insides now matched the outside world. I could see like a Japanese person. My grandmother's simple request—to see another kind of beauty—had an unintended consequence.

My stormy Japanese grandfather was very hard on my mother. He was afraid of what would happen to his only daughter—and to me, a child of mixed race. At one point, my grandfather had disowned my mother. One of my mother's brothers had done the same, and my mother had been deeply hurt.

I only found out about these things later in life; the adults tried to hide the tensions from me when I was a child. But if I paid attention to the background, then I could feel something lingering, the way you can see ripples in the water long after a large vessel has churned past.

One night when we were visiting my grandparents in Japan, I woke up. It was summer and very hot, but the room was reasonably cool because we'd left the window open and it was raining outside.

My mother's breaths were deep and even; she was asleep. Most of the time when I woke up in the middle of the night, she would wake up too; I think it is this way for mothers and children everywhere, as I have discovered since having my son. But that night, my mother did not wake up, and I felt painfully alone.

Summer storms in Japan are often tempestuous, and old houses, such as my grandparents' house, rattle terribly in the wind. As I lay awake, every shingle and every nail struggled in the storm. The house seemed to tense and push back against the wind. The tension made me feel increasingly afraid.

There was just enough space in my mother's childhood room for the two of us: she was on the floor in a futon, and I was on a cot, which had been presented to me as a positive. When we traveled, I was always desperate for anything familiar, and the bed, everyone thought, would make me more comfortable because it would seem American. I would have preferred a futon. Then my mother and I would have been side by side.

I could see out the open window just beyond the foot of my bed. Bamboo lurched in the wind. The leaves looked like hands tapping the screen. I wanted the noises and the wind to stop. I tried to go back to sleep. This is what my mother would tell me to do if I woke her up. But I couldn't sleep. Then just for a moment, the storm breathed more quietly and the leaves stopped tapping the window, as though the volume outside had been turned down. I heard a crack. Over the years, my grandmother had discarded empty clamshells on the ground outside after we'd eaten the meat in our miso soup; she said the shells made great fertilizer. Something was now crossing the shells, and I could hear the shells breaking. A man stepped into view.

He was dirty and was smiling unkindly. I had never seen him before but felt sure he was not Japanese. I did not know where he had come from. I felt that he could read my thoughts and knew my fears and found them amusing. He was here to have fun. We were to be his playmates. This was something about cruelty that I learned early. Mean people often think they are being funny.

"Mom," I said.

Her voice, when she spoke to him, was tired and irritated. "What are you doing?"

He said, "I want to come in."

"Well, we're sleeping." Matter of fact.

My heart began to beat very fast and very loud. I wanted to escape, but I had the sense that if I got up, the man would not hesitate to come into our room. We were only separated by a thin wire screen. I was also confused. My mother continued to talk to the man, as though he were someone with whom we could reason. I did not think we should be doing this. I thought we should probably scream and run away. But I also did not want to disappoint her by questioning her authority.

"Does this change anything?" He pulled out a gun.

"Now that," said my mother, "is ridiculous. And where did you get that anyway? We are trying to sleep. It is raining outside, and you should not be outside and you should go away."

He waved the gun around. This, again, would be a good time to leave, but I was too terrified to move.

At last, he said, "Okay. I'll go away. But I want you to know that I will be back."

While he was speaking, he was looking at my mother. But now he smiled at me, as though he wanted me to know that I was a part of this drama whether I wanted to be or not. It was an awful feeling to make contact with him and to know that he saw me. His eyes really saw me—into me—and he smiled and pointed the gun. He pretended to pull the trigger, and the gun barrel glowed. Then he pointed the gun at my mother and pretended to pull the trigger. And then he was gone. Once again the leaves were battering the window, and the sound of rain rose up all around the house.

It took some time for my body to warm up, and for me to work out of my near catatonic state. I heard my mother breathing deeply again and knew she was asleep.

"Mommy?"

She was doubly irritated this time. "What is it?"

"Mommy, what about that man?"

"He's gone."

"Shouldn't we tell someone?"

"You'll be tired if you don't sleep. You need to sleep." My parents were always telling me to get enough sleep.

"Mommy . . ."

"Go back to sleep. We will talk about it in the morning." As afraid as I was of the man, I did not want her to scold me further. Gradually, my body relaxed, and that thing I was afraid of—giving in to the helplessness of sleep—took over.

In the morning, I wasted no time asking all the adults to call the police. My mother refused, and my grandmother looked confused. She wanted to help, but my mother cut me off when I tried to bring up the subject of the man at the window.

"We are not calling the police," my mother said firmly.

"But there was a man . . ."

"Stop it."

"If there was a man . . . ," began my grandmother.

"We are not calling anyone." My mother was growing more and more irritated. So was my grandfather. He wondered what I was going on and on about and why my mother could not control me. Now my mother and grandfather were irritated with each other, and my mother, reader of her father's shifting moods, was trying to steer us all in a direction where her father's temper would not explode. We never did call the police. I told my mother I would sleep with my grandmother. The next time we went to Japan, my grandparents arranged two futons so my mother and I could sleep in the main part of the house and avoid the "haunted" room completely. From then on, we slept side by side in futons, Japanese family style, which made me feel safe. And for many years, I did not go into her childhood bedroom at all.

They have always insisted it was a dream. All of it. At no point, my mother insists to this day, did she ever wake up. I had imagined everything. But even now as an adult, I know the difference between a bad dream and reality, and the power of the man in the window has never left me. I realize how improbable and strange this sounds, and here I have to assure you that I'm a rational person, with a deep and abiding respect for science.

The impact of these strange experiences from childhood has never left me, and I have always wondered what I should make of them, and if they contain some hidden meaning. In time, I have been able to work out part of an explanation, for fear of what we do not know and cannot understand is highly potent, and can be far more compelling than any scholarly treatise on the exact chemical components of fear, grief, or guilt. And fear speaks to us most strongly when it arrives in the form of inexplicable but personal visions.

The old Japanese believed it was important to take care of chopsticks, lest they come back to haunt you. As my mother explained to me, this did not mean that a chopstick literally had any power. But a careless person who routinely did not take care of his possessions did have the ability to harm his environment and others who depended on him. If I indulged the man at the window I saw in childhood, I would be afraid of Japan and what I perceived as its weirdness and the strangeness of the people to whom I was related. And we would all remain afraid of each other unless I made an effort to understand them, and give them a chance to understand me. Like old Shozoku no Baba the old hag, the man at the window might very well have two faces too, and it was up to me to find a view of his face other than the one he had offered to me through the open window.

When my son was born, the man at the window was never very far from my mind. I wondered what my son would see in Japan that I might miss, and if he too would find it to be a strange place, or if he would naturally flit between countries and cultures. I hoped it would be the latter.

ONE MAY, I took my husband and my son, now three and a half, to visit Tōno, land of the fabled *Tōno Monogatari*, or *The Legends of Tōno*, a collection of folktales. The town, though friendly, also had a subdued quality to it, like almost all of Tōhoku; it isn't just the tsunami zones that have struggled since the disaster. Though the recovery crews and NGOs had left Tōno, tourists still hadn't returned in their place. My family and I were thus an oddity— authentic tourists, and *gaijin* at that.

The second night at dinner, a young Japanese man sat next to us in the dining room of the inn where we were staying. More a boy than a man, he was tall, if slight, with long thin arms and fingers that danced as he talked. While he ate, he watched my son running from one end of the facility to the other, chattering in Japanese. The young man's eyes widened when my son insisted on three helpings of miso soup from an iron pot, which was suspended from the ceiling by a giant hook over a low-burning fire in a sand pit in the middle of the floor. Then my son disappeared into a hallway again, and we could hear him engaging the staff in a conversation.

"I wonder," the young man said in Japanese, his deep baritone voice at odds with his still immature appearance, "if your son has seen the *zashiki warashi*?"

"The what?"

"The *yōsei*." When it was clear I didn't understand either of these Japanese words, he said in English, "Fairy."

Well, here was something new. "Fairy? Like Tinkerbell?"

"Yes," the young man continued excitedly. "This inn is very famous for its *zashiki warashi*." He looked at my son, now back in the dining room, with an eager, almost envious intensity. "The *zashiki warashi* likes young children."

"How do you know?"

"Searching for fairies is a hobby of mine," the man continued blithely in the happy, trusting way of the youthful. And then again, with great intensity, "Your son is so active, I thought he might have seen something."

The conversation left me puzzled. The inn felt old, but not *that* old, and I associated anything supernatural with age. The family members running the facility were pleasant, though slightly distant; I didn't think they were the type to harbor secrets. Still, before going to sleep that night, I read my son a children's picture-book version of the *Tōno Monogatari*, translating for my husband so he could follow along too. I skipped the sad story about the dead horse hanging from a tree, and went on to read about a magical house for the gods. And then I read about the *zashiki warashi*.

"Have you seen the *zashiki warashi*?" I asked my son.

His expression was blank.

"The *yōsei*," I explained. Then, in English: "The fairy."

"Oh, yes," he replied easily in Japanese.

"Where was it?"

"*Onēsan* was working," he said. Older sister is working.

From what I had read, the *zashiki warashi* liked to appear to children and play with them. Perhaps my son did not understand my question, so I put *The Legends of Tōno* aside, and went on to read another book.

AMONG THE PLACES I wanted to visit in Tōno was the site of the five hundred *rakan*. A *rakan* is best understood as a disciple of Buddha, and throughout history it's been a popular if challenging undertaking for a temple to commission and display large "fields" of *rakan* sculptures, which are usually carved out of stone. Other temples forgo displays of hundreds of *rakan* in favor of hundreds of Jizōs. But in either case, the effect and the point of the installations are the same: the enlightened beings are there to honor the dead.

Just a few days earlier we had all gone to the Adashino Nembutsu temple in Kyōtō, which is famous for the Jizōbon in August. There the small, worn faces of over eight thousand Jizōs were neatly lined up in rows, many wearing red bibs. My son found the gridlike arrangement fun, as though all the rocks comprised a kind of maze. Now we were in Tōnō, and the taxi driver who took us to the foothills of the site asked us to please stay together and to speak loudly at all times. The day before, a bear had been spotted roaming the mountains.

It was only eleven in the morning, but already somewhat dark in the forest; the canopy of leaves overhead was thick. The taxi driver banged a metal can with a stick to fend off any nearby bears, and peered beseechingly up at us as we climbed. I mistook his nervousness for neurosis. It had been the driver's idea to visit the *rakan* first thing in the morning; he didn't want to drive later in the day. I started to wonder what the big deal was—Where were all the statues? Was there really a bear? All I saw was a rocky, mossy hillside.

Then, as though suddenly animated, a face peered out at me through the moss. Below this, someone had left a tiny amulet made out of a toothpick and blue origami paper. Then I saw another face, and another. It was as though the rocks were coming to life, triggered by our presence. Faces creaked and pushed through the soggy greenery to have a look at the humans. The higher we climbed, the more faces emerged. These were the *rakan*, carved in 1782 by a priest who hoped to pacify the spirits of hundreds who died in a famine; throughout history, Tōhoku struggled to raise rice and other crops, which grew so easily in areas closer to the capital, and famine had always been a problem. To me, the rocks represented Tōhoku's pain—the fear of famine, of not keeping up with the west of Japan— those areas closer to the capitals of Kyōtō, and later, Tōkyō.

A few days later I would learn that a man foraging for wild vegetables in the mountains of Aizu had been killed by a bear. The family searching for him had also been attacked.

MY HUSBAND HAD not seen any of the devastation from the tsunami and the earthquake, so while my son napped in my lap, our new taxi driver drove to Ōtsuchi and Kamaishi, past rows and rows of temporary housing, where stooped men and women were slowly taking down their laundry as the sun was fading. The driver stopped to purchase four bouquets—one for each of us—which we placed on the foundation of a home that had been washed away. "It takes thirty years," the taxi driver explained, "for ghosts to subside. It's important to treat them with dignity." In the days immediately following March 11, the taxi driver ferried more than sixty journalists out to disaster sites. He brought flowers each time. It disappointed him, he said, to meet writers from Ōsaka and Tōkyō who refused to take flowers themselves. They were Japanese, he said, and should have known better.

Back at the inn, the taxi driver came out of the car with us. He knew the owners and wanted to say hello. I also chatted with the staff, and my son immediately began to run through the hallways. Meanwhile, my husband went for a run through Tōno's town center and out into the rice fields. He wanted to loosen himself up to shake free the image of the half-digested coastline. When he returned, he took a bath.

That night at dinner, there was a new face among the staff—a woman wearing an allergy mask. She was speaking to a group of men at the table next to us, and they, half drunk, were offering up bits of philosophy concerning illness and the importance of taking care during the weeks when winter slowly morphed into spring. Transition times were tricky, they said. From the way the woman lingered over the guests while politely but authoritatively issuing orders to the staff, I decided she must be the current Okamisan, or the mistress of the house. When Okamisan made her way over to us, and we exchanged pleasantries, I told her how much we had loved eating the freshly picked *sansai* and fish from the *irori*, the open hearth in the middle of the floor.

There was kindness in her eyes. And yet I again felt the presence of a quiet, unasked-for burden on her shoulders—just as I had all over Tōhoku. She and her family had much, much more than did the evacuees living in those tiny houses all across Japan. But still she, like everyone else, had suffered.

My son ran by, carrying two toy cars. And then, somewhat abruptly, Okamisan said to me, "You know, we have a *zashiki warashi*."

I smiled. "A guest told me yesterday at dinner. He said that children are good at seeing the *zashiki warashi*, so I asked my son about it."

"And?"

"Well," I stopped. My son's answer had been so nonsensical. "Honestly, I think he didn't really understand my question. He said: *onēsan* is working."

I was still laughing apologetically when I saw Okamisan's face turn white. She turned to look at another woman, now also quite pale. For a brief moment, I was afraid I had done something offensive.

Okamisan turned back to me. "You know," she said slowly, "this is exactly what we said about the *zashiki warashi* in the old days. We said that she was working."

Silence.

Okamisan continued. "When I was very young—when I was still a young wife—sometimes I had to take tea up to the room for one of our guests. I would start up the stairs, and realize I hadn't turned on the stairway light. And then the light would go on."

"All by itself?"

"Yes. And sometimes a guest would call from a room and say that they needed an extra set of sheets. And I would go up with the sheets, only to find that they had been delivered, but no one could remember the face of the girl who had brought them. It's been a long time since we had a child as a guest. Especially a foreigner. I would assume she's happy to have him to play with."

"The *zashiki warashi* is a girl?"

"That's what guests say. I've never seen her. I am not supposed to. If I or any of the household see her, it means she is getting ready to leave, and our business is going to fall apart. Also, if you came here expecting to see her, then you wouldn't have. She only comes out when people don't know she exists."

One room over, I could hear my son shrieking with laughter as he corralled one of the male staff into playing with him yet again.

. . .

LATER, I RELAYED this conversation to my husband, thinking that in his logical, European way, he might find it intriguing or amusing. To be honest, after the events of the day, the whole story about the *zashiki warashi* had spooked me, but midway through my eager retelling, it was my husband's turn to pale.

"The hair just stood up on the back of my neck!" he declared, using a common British expression of surprise. "Today, after I came back from my run, I had a bath. And you know, there are two rooms in the bathroom—the actual bath and the changing room."

I nodded.

"I was in the bath, when I suddenly realized I hadn't turned on the light in the changing room. This meant that another guest might not realize that the bath was occupied. So I started to get out of the bath to turn on the light, when it suddenly turned on. I thought that maybe I had forgotten to lock the door, and that someone else had entered the changing room, not realizing that the bath was already occupied. I assumed that person had turned on the light. So I stuck my head out of the bathing room, and said, '*Sumimasen.*' But no one was there."

Our rational minds immediately began to tackle this new mystery. "Was the door locked?" I asked.

"Yes. I checked. Maybe there is a motion-sensitive sensor that turned on the light?"

"Or a switch outside. Maybe someone saw you were in the bath, and turned the light on for you."

We went downstairs. There was no sensor. There was no light switch outside the bath.

TIME IS A confounding thing. When we are in misery, we want it to end immediately. But this is not always possible. I thought about

Tōno's five hundred *rakan*, still up on the hillside, still appeasing the spirits of the dead hundreds of years later. Even today, during Obon, townspeople take offerings of food for these spirits. I thought about the Tōno taxi driver and his gifts of flowers. *It takes thirty years for the spirits of the dead to be put to rest.* But one should also assume that good spirits—like the *zashiki warashi*—are acting on our behalf, even if they are invisible.

I spoke to Okamisan one more time before we left, and thanked her for her hospitality. I told her we would return. I told her that even though the inn—not to mention all of Tōhoku—had undergone tremendous hardship, and would no doubt continue to do so in the future, the fact that the *zashiki warashi* was doing her job meant that brighter days were still ahead. Otherwise, I said, she would be preparing to leave, and would not have appeared to my son or helped my husband. When we left the *ryokan*, I pictured an invisible, beautiful young girl in her kimono, standing under the cherry tree and watching us leave, before turning her attention to see who else might need her help.

THE END

Acknowledgments

A book is a journey, and I am grateful to the many people who helped me along the way. Thank you to Irene Skolnick, my agent, who said to me, "I think you are going to write a memoir one day." You were right. Thank you to my editor, Alane Salierno Mason, for her early belief in this project and keen eye and intelligence. Anna Mageras kept us all on track. Additional thanks to Remy Cawley and Megha Majumdar, and to Mary Babcock for superb copyediting. Thank you everyone at Norton for bringing this book to life.

I am grateful to the Japan–United States Friendship Commission and the National Endowment for the Arts, both of which made it possible for me to live in Japan in 2013. In particular, to Margaret Mihori, Christopher Blesdel, and Minami Imamura. Thank you to Endo Shigeru for his patience and kindness. A special thank you to Kaneta Taiō and to the staff at Tōhoku University. Akasaka Norio and Hijikata Kisashi deepened my knowledge of Tōhoku and folklore. Tokita Nobuhiko opened his beautiful temples and home to my family. Thank you to the many priests I met in Japan, including Minami Jikisai, Kōho Maruko, Nagaoka Shunjo, and Asano Masami. I greatly appreciate Hara Sanaeko's wonderful hospitality.

Thank you to family and friends in Japan: Ogawa Ryūnosuke

and Momoe, Mita Sempō, Nobata Katsunari and Akemi, Nomoto Hideo, Sakurai Isao, and Morino Sakiko.

Special thanks to friends who knew just what to say when I needed to hear it: Maud Newton, Kaytie Lee, Hasanthika Sirisena, Tomas Morin, Ellis Avery, Jeffrey Lependorf, Michael Taeckens, and Laurence Hobgood. I am grateful to Marine Noguchi, Amanda Tranmer, Amelia Mockett, Lori Fromowitz, and the staff at Baachanchi. Saori Nishikawa and family and Sekiya, Hoon, and Ryko kept my spirits up with brunch, coffee, and friendship.

Thank you to Yuji Miyoshi for the use of his beautiful photograph of Mt. Osore, and to Ian Drummond for his creative input at an important moment.

Finally, a special thank you to my mother, who made everything possible. To my grandparents and my father—I will always miss you. Thank you to my husband, Gordon Drummond, for reading drafts and putting up with all the travel, and to Ewan Drummond for following me on so many adventures. May we all have many more adventures together.